A History of THE PORT of DUBLIN

Contents

Preface

IN 1852, the British Admiralty announced its intention of publishing a history of all the ports in the United Kingdom and each port was asked to supply the necessary information. The Dublin port authority of the day asked one of its members, Charles Haliday, to 'favour the Board with a history of this port and harbour', and he readily agreed.

Haliday was a prosperous businessman of considerable commercial acumen and was a director of the Bank of Ireland and a member of the Chamber of Commerce. He had a deep interest in history and literature and was a member of the Royal Irish Academy; he was, therefore, an obvious choice. His research led him into an intensive study of ancient Irish records, particularly those relating to Dublin in the Viking era. As a consequence, his researches in port history became submerged in a study of the origins of the early settlement and its development, and his work culminated in the posthumuous publication of his well-known *Scandinavian Kingdom of Dublin*. Although that book contains references to the history of the port, the proposed history for the Admiralty project was never written and, indeed, it does not appear that the Admiralty project ever materialised.

There are many other books dealing with the history of Dublin, almost all of which make some references to the port. There have been many papers on specific aspects of the port presented from time to time to professional institutes and historical societies, and also articles in newspapers and magazines, but I have been unable to trace any detailed work dealing solely with the history of the port. The present work is an attempt to fill that gap, even if the end product is on a much more modest scale than that which, I believe, Haliday would have proposed.

I have been encouraged by having had an opportunity to examine the extensive collection of Haliday's books and papers in the Royal Irish Academy and, of course, the advantage of access to the records of the port authority, including those covering the 120 years since Haliday's death. My objective has been to describe the stages of port development carried out by the port authority under its various titles and constitutions and to outline the background to the authority's other functions and activities; since the growth of the city and of the port are closely interwoven it seemed desirable to preface that description with a short historical sketch which would place the port in perspective in relation to the development of the city. Although political and economic influences are touched on, a comprehensive analysis and evaluation thereof must await the attention of a modern Haliday. In that connection, the scope of this work did not admit of an account of the various communities, both within the city area and around the bay, which over the years have provided much of the work force not only for the port authority itself but also for the shipping companies, stevedores and other organisations engaged in port activities. The history of the fishing communities of Ringsend, Clontarf, Kingstown/Dun Laoghaire and Howth also remains to be written. I believe that a rich vein of local and social history here awaits research, and I am sure that it will prove as enjoyable a task as mine has been.

In a sense, this book marks a final farewell to the port of Dublin after my forty-six years in the service of the port board and another three writing the book. I made many friends both in the port of Dublin and elsewhere, and my farewell concludes with my wishes for the continued success of the port of Dublin and the welfare of all those who work in it.

H.A.G.
Dublin
June 1988

Acknowledgments

IT appears to me that research for historical works relating to Ireland owes much to the courteous assistance of the staff of institutions such as the National Library, Public Record Office, State Paper Office, Royal Irish Academy and the Dublin Corporation public libraries: in my own case I am indebted to all the personnel concerned for the help they gave me in the course of my enquiries.

Specialists in a number of fields co-operated freely and I am happy to acknowledge the assistance given by Dr Patrick Wallace of the National Museum; Dr Edward McParland of Trinity College; Dr Maurice Craig; Ms Mary Clarke, City Archivist; Mr Peter Fields of the Ordnance Survey; Commandant Peter Young of the Military History Section of the Department of Defence; Mr A. O'Hagan, Secretary to the Commissioners of Irish Lights and Mr Michael Costello of the same authority; Captain Peter Mason of Trinity House, London; Mr David Burrell, formerly of Lloyds of London; Mr Philip Booth of the Maritime Institute of Ireland; Mr S.M. Riley of the National Maritime Museum, Greenwich; Capt. Frank Forde and Mr Matt Coleman, B & I Line; Mr P.P. Hannigan, formerly Canals Engineer, CIE; Mr John Lambe, Secretary/Manager of the Royal Dublin Golf Club; and Ms Sheila Burns of Guinness Ireland Ltd.

Turning to the port Board, I am grateful to the Chairman of the Board at the time of my retirement, Mr John Donovan, and the Board's General Manager, Mr Bob Hayes, for inviting me to undertake the book. The encouragement given to me and the facilities placed at my disposal by the present Secretary and Deputy General Manager, Noel Shanley, have been invaluable as has been the help extended by the staff of his department and indeed by the staffs of all the Board's departments. It would be remiss of me not to mention in particular Desmond O'Sullivan who was patient and indefatigable in searching out old records from the Board's archives; Arthur O'Connor, Rory O'Connor and Niall Dardis, all of the Engineering Drawing Office, for producing old maps and drawings; the Board's Hydrographic Surveyor, Eamonn

McAteer, who provided me with details of the Board's Hydrographic Survey service; Bill Taylor, Assistant Warehousing and Commercial Manager, and John O'Dwyer, Public Relations Officer, both of whom supplied me with photographs from the Board's collection; and the Board's Planning Officer, Patrick Power, who provided the statistical data.

I am happy to acknowledge the co-operation of the Board's Chief Engineer, Mr Michael Ennis, his predecessor Mr M.C. Smyth and the present and former Harbour Masters, Captains Colum Lawless and Hubert Walsh, who kindly vetted the technical matters mentioned in Chapters 19, 20 and 23; my appreciation extends also to Mr J.F. Furlong, Warehouse and Commercial Manager, for material relating to the Board's warehousing service.

From the Board's former Paymaster, W.J. Murphy, I received personal recollections of the Ballast Office during the 1922 'Troubles' and from another former member of the staff, Jim McNeice, I acquired data on the Dublin Dockyard Company.

It is very pleasant to be able to record and acknowledge a family contribution in the form of the maps on pp xvi, 20, 52, 138, 146, 165, 176 and 200 which were drawn by my son David.

I am particularly glad to have this opportunity of expressing thanks for the patience and efficiency with which the task of typing the draft and revisions of the manuscript was carried out by the three ladies who shared the work — Delia Fairclough, Miriam Flynn and Mary Finneran.

Finally, but far from least in the value of his assistance to me, I wish to thank an old friend and former colleague, Gerald Daly, who like myself has retired from the Board's service, for his whole-hearted assistance not only in historical enquiries but in assembling the illustrations, including some photographs which he took for the purpose.

H.A. Gilligan

List of Illustrations and Maps

Unless otherwise stated, all illustrations are reproduced by kind permission of the Dublin Port and Docks Board. The publishers have employed their best efforts to trace the copyright holders of all illustrations reproduced. Any errors or omissions brought to their attention will be corrected in future editions.

Jacket: James Malton's view of the Custom House.

National Gallery of Ireland

End Papers: Captain Greville Collins's map of Dublin Bay made in 1686.

Frontispiece: A section of John Rocque's map of Dublin (1756) showing the double wall—now Pidgeon House Road—from Ringsend to the 'Green Patch' and the line of piles running eastwards from that point.

(pp. 153–160) *Colour Illustrations*

A replica of the Viking longship discovered at Gokstad in Norway, built as part of the Dublin Millennium celebrations. Named the *Dyflin*, the building of the craft was conceived by the East Wall Watersports Group and carried into effect with the co-operation of the port board and other sponsors.

William Sadler's painting of Pidgeon House Harbour and fort, c.1820.

National Gallery of Ireland

Edwin Hayes's painting, The Emigrant Ship, painted in the mid nineteenth century. The ship is moored to a buoy in Halpin's Pond.

National Gallery of Ireland

An aerial view of the Custom House Docks complex, prior to its transfer to the Custom House Docks development authority in 1987.

A view of Clontarf Sheds made in 1785 by Francis Wheatley. It shows the shoreline at the junction of the present-day Vernon Avenue and Clontarf Road.

Prior to the construction of the present Baily lighthouse, completed in 1813, the Howth lighthouse, shown in this 1799 painting by F. Jukes, was situated further up the hill near the present carpark.

The City of Dublin mailsteamer *Connaught* in rough seas off Kingstown. The painting, by Richard Brydges Beechey, is dated 1868.

National Gallery of Ireland

A view of the old Custom House near Essex Bridge in 1782 by John James Barralet. The old Custom House is shown in the extreme left background.

A model of the sheer float designed by the port engineer Bindon Blood Stoney for lifting 350-ton concrete blocks for use in the construction of North Wall Extension.

Trinity College, Dublin

A model of the bell float also designed by Stoney for the preparation of the river bed to receive the concrete blocks.   *Trinity College, Dublin*

A late nineteenth-century watercolour entitled *A View of the Custom House, Dublin.*

An aerial view of the modern port viewed from the north.

The Bull Island, with the Bull Wall in the foreground and Ireland's Eye and Lambay Island in the background.   *P.J. Carroll & Co. Ltd*

The new headquarters of the Dublin Port and Docks Board at Alexandra Road by night.

Two views of shipping at the North Quays and the North Wall extension, 1929.

Bindon Blood Stoney, chief engineer to the port board from 1862 to 1898. The illustration (*below left, opposite*) shows the title page of his textbook on the theory of stresses.

Alderman Alfred (Alfie) Byrne, Lord Mayor of Dublin, at the opening of the reconstructed Butt Bridge in 1932.

The present Poolbeg Lighthouse.

The Eucharistic Congress 1932 created an unprecedented challenge for Dublin port. Among the eight liners which berthed at the quays were the *Sierra Cordoba* and the *Dresden* (*above*) which were moored in Alexandra Basin and the Dutch liner *Marnix Van St Aldegonde* (*below*) at Sir John Rogerson's Quay.

The four lighthouses on the north side of the river channel. These four photographs show the lighthouses at the North Wall extension (*above left*), the Eastern Breakwater (*above right*), the North Bank (*below left*) and the North Bull (*below right*).

Sir Richard Martin, one of Dublin's leading commerical figures in the nineteenth century and a member of the port authority for over 36 years.

Mr Patrick Martin

(pp. 189–196)

Sir John Purser Griffith, chief engineer to the port board from 1898 to 1913.

The Clarecastle, one of the colliers purchased by Guinness from Kelly of Belfast in 1915 and converted for the transportation of stout in barrels.

The foreground shows the final completed section of the North Wall extension in 1937. The background shows dredgers working on the proposed reclamation for the abortive oil refinery project.

The view from the big gasometer at Sir John Rogerson's Quay shows an Isle of Man passenger steamer in mid stream and an LMS cargo ship and a Burns & Laird passenger/cargo ship berthed at North Wall, c.1938.

Nicholas Proud, secretary to the port board from 1867 to 1921.

The port board's steam tugs, *Ben Eadar* and *Coliemore* towing the disabled collier *Kylecastle* into Dublin port.

The *Melida*, one of the Liberty ships which brought American coal to Dublin in1947.

Pat Sweeney

The hulk *Shelfoil*, which was used as a temporary oil storage ship pending the completion in 1954 of the new oil jetties.

Pat Sweeney

The four gas company colliers, *Glenbride*, *Glencree*, *Glenageary* and *Glencullen* in Ringsend dock.

Maurice Craig

A general view of shipping at Alexandra Quay showing Liberty ships and a Texaco oil tanker, 1947.

An aerial view of Alexandra Basin, 1949.

One of the Blue Funnel Line ships engaged in the Far East trade in Number 2 graving dock.

(pp. 227–234)

The US aircraft carrier *Saipan* arriving at the port of Dublin in July 1952.

The launching of the B & I's cargo livestock ship *Meath* from the Liffey Dockyard in 1960.

The car carrier *Hoegh Trader* discharging cars at the south quays.

The Bull Wall, a favourite promenade for Dubliners.

The *Memmon* discharging cargo from West African ports at Ocean Pier.

The *Miranda Guinness*, the world's first specially commissioned bulk liquid carrier, arriving at the port of Dublin.   *Guinness Ireland Ltd*

The early Dublin pilot cutters were similar to this Bristol Channel pilot cutter (*right*), photographed around 1890. The photograph (*below*)shows the *Dodder*, one of the modern diesel engine pilot cutters operating from the pilot shore station at the Eastern Breakwater.

National Maritime Museum, Greenwich (right)

The method of discharging coal cargo remained unchanged for many years. The photograph shows dockers filling tubs in the hold of the collier and a filled tub being tipped into a railway wagon for CIE.

The modern method of discharging coal by grab at the South Bulk Terminal.

Coal Distributors Ltd

Aerial view of the port in the mid 1960s. In the left foreground, the quay serving the ESB Ringsend station is visible; on the right, the Eastern Breakwater is in the foreground, and immediately behind it lie the two oil jetties, Ocean Pier and Alexandra Quay East.

Past and present in the modern port. The photograph (*above*) shows the Argentinian sail training vessel *Libertad* and the Norwegian liner *Royal Viking Sea*. The photograph (*below*) shows the Italian sail training ship *Amerigo Vespucci*.

Shipping at Alexandra Quay and Ocean Pier.

The Chairman, Mr E. W. Beck, addressing the last meeting of the Dublin Port and Docks Board to be held in the Ballast Office, Westmoreland Street, February 1976.

Maps

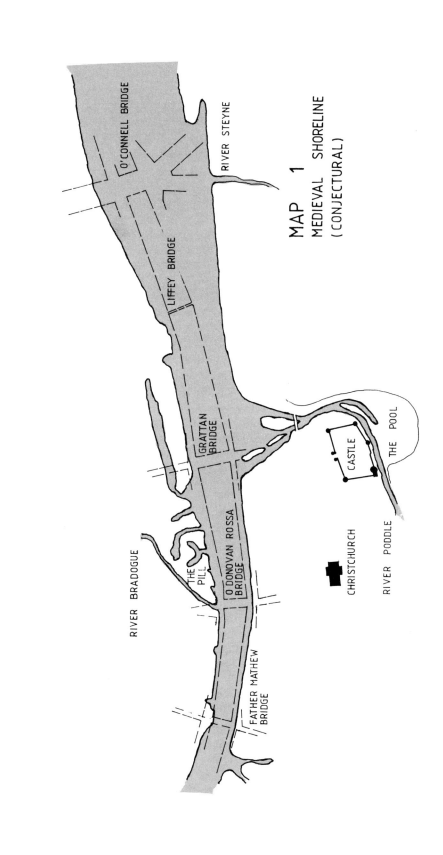

MAP 1
MEDIEVAL SHORELINE
(CONJECTURAL)

RIVER BRADOGUE

FATHER MATHEW BRIDGE

THE PILL

O'DONOVAN ROSSA BRIDGE

GRATTAN BRIDGE

LIFFEY BRIDGE

O'CONNELL BRIDGE

RIVER STEYNE

CHRISTCHURCH

CASTLE

THE POOL

RIVER PODDLE

The Early Settlement

THE origins of the earliest settlement at Dublin are to be found in the existence of the river we know as the Liffey, its estuary and bay. The growth of the settlement in the later Middle Ages was assisted by the development of facilities, however primitive, for ships engaged in the settlement's trade with Britain, the near Continent and with Mediterranean ports.

It is difficult to visualise the panorama which the early settlers beheld in pre-historic times when they ventured to take their primitive craft up the shallow waters of the estuary. Even for those citizens of Dublin whose business or pleasure takes them across O'Connell Bridge in the 1980s, it may come as a surprise to learn that as late as the 1870s sea-going sailing ships berthed and discharged or loaded their cargoes at Eden Quay and Burgh Quay; indeed until recent years these thoroughfares continued to be the location of the offices of many shipping companies and shipping agents.

The archaeological excavations at High Street and Wood Quay in recent years have aroused considerable public interest in the Norse settlements in that vicinity in the ninth and later centuries. The origins of Dublin as a place of commerce, a fortified town and a port have, however, been the subject of a controversy among historians which is as yet unresolved. While the balance of opinion seems to support the view that Dublin was little more than a monastic settlement prior to the Norse invasions in the eighth and ninth centuries, Dr George Little in his book *Dublin before the Vikings* has adduced substantial evidence in support of his contention that long before the arrival of the Norsemen there was a settlement at Dublin with a large and stable population and with a substantial maritime trade with Britain and elsewhere. According to the Manx historian, C.W. Airne, the artistry of Irish craftsmen in metals was well known at least a thousand years before Christ. Their wares and also their raw materials were exported to Scotland, Wales, the Isle of Man and elsewhere; there is ample evidence extant of artifacts made from gold mined in the Wicklow mountains, and it is reasonable to assume that the early traders were aware of the advantages of the Liffey estuary for their purposes.

Whatever view one takes of the origins of the settlement, it is clear that the geographical location of Dublin Bay provided relatively easier access to the central plain for the early settlers than was available from most other landing places on the east coast. Although primitive Mesolithic shore dwellers lived on the coast of Dublin Bay over 5,000 years ago, the later and more adventurous Neolithic settlers were attracted by the plain of the Liffey and they had stone implements capable of clearing the dense forests which covered much of the country and impeded their progress. This gateway to the central plain (constituting the line of least resistance) together with the existence of a natural ford near where Father Mathew Bridge (Church Street Bridge) now stands, were factors contributing to the development of a road system radiating from an early settlement on the estuary of the Liffey. Unfavourable weather and tidal conditions could of course render such a ford impassable. According to Dr Little, the later artificial ford from which the settlement took its name (Ford of the Hurdles or Atha Cliath) was in effect a pair of causeways projecting from the North and South banks of the river and consisting of stones reinforced and decked with timber; the causeway was not continuous but contained a gap or gaps to accommodate the river in spate. The gaps were crossed by primitive wooden bridges.

Although wooden ships were used around Irish coasts from a very early period, hide covered vessels predominated not only on river and coastal voyages but to British and Continental ports. Indeed, in our own day Tim Severin's voyage in the *St Brendan* clearly demonstrated the ability of such craft to cross the great oceans. With relatively shallow draught and flat bottoms, these vessels could not only be beached on the strands of Dublin Bay but could probably have navigated the Liffey for a considerable distance in suitable tidal and weather conditions; in unfavourable conditions they could anchor at the mouth of the river and transfer their burden to smaller craft, a practice continued by larger ships in later centuries. The map on page xvi shows the shoreline of the medieval city; the shoreline is conjectural only and is based partly on geological data established early in this century, and partly on the earliest map of the city by Speed in 1610. Perhaps the most notable feature is the tidal indentation where the waters of the Liffey were joined by those of its tributary, the Poddle, resulting in a large pool roughly on the present site of Dublin Castle garden, between Ship Street and South Great George's Street; from this pool, the shoreline of the Poddle ran northwards to the site of the present Olympia Theatre. Here the Poddle joined the Liffey the south bank of which ran eastwards along a line somewhat south of present day Temple Bar and

Fleet Street. At Fownes Street the shoreline turned south-east until interrupted by the outflow of another small tributary known as the Steyne at the junction of present-day Westmoreland Street and Fleet Street. On the north bank, another small river, the Bradogue, joined the Liffey roughly where O'Donovan Rossa (Winetavern Street) Bridge now stands.

The earliest settlement appears to have been located around the site of present day Cornmarket and High Street. A natural gravel ridge, known as the Esker Riada, has its eastern spur on the present site of High Street and this elevated location clearly had advantages later for the construction of defensive fortifications. In addition, it was near the original (natural) ford. As the settlement developed eastwards it acquired the name Dubh Linn from the dark waters of the pool on the River Poddle which has already been mentioned.

It would appear that the earliest form of facility for vessels discharging cargo at the settlement consisted merely of wooden poles erected on the banks of the river, to which vessels could be moored and their cargoes transferred from ship to shore or vice versa; the use of such a facility was probably subjected to a charge levied by the owner or occupier of the adjoining land over which the cargo had to pass. In the Viking era more efficient and secure means of mooring ships and landing or loading their cargoes evolved, in the form of earthen banks and wooden wharves or jetties. Eventually the timber wharves were replaced by masonry quays. But before considering these structures in more detail, it is necessary to sketch the historical background.

The appearance of Scandinavian raiders off the coasts of Britain, Ireland and France in the eighth century was due to some extent to the campaigns of Charlemagne who, in his rôle of champion of Christianity, subdued pagan peoples of northern Europe. These Scandinavian raiders, otherwise known as Norsemen or Vikings, were frequently Danes although not exclusively so and while there were socio-economic reasons for quitting their homelands, a major objective of the raids was to exact retribution for the oppression they had suffered under Charlemagne by sacking Christian settlements in Northumbria, the Isle of Man, Wales, Ireland and part of the French coastline near the Seine estuary. The later waves of Vikings in the ninth century were more concerned with finding new homes and establishing their own kingdoms, and their conquests included the Orkney and Shetland Islands, part of the mainland of Scotland, the outer Hebrides, the Western Isles and the Isle of Man. According to Airne, the Isle of Man became a popular rendezvous as a base from which attacks were launched on neighbouring coasts, and also as a staging post en route to Spain and the Mediterranean. Following the Viking settlement at Dublin, it became a more convenient base than the Isle of Man.

The first appearance of Norse raiders near Dublin is recorded as having taken place in the year A.D. 795 at Lambay Island and raids continued in intensity on the Irish coast until the following century. In 837 a large raiding party with sixty-five ships reached Dublin Bay. Their first landing was marked by the erection of a stone slab called the Steyne at a spot which is now the junction of Townsend Street and Hawkins Street. The Steyne gave its name to a whole district as well as to a tributary of the Liffey. Later the invaders built a fortification near the confluence of the Poddle and the Liffey, roughly on the site of Lord Edward Street. Since one of the objectives of these early raids was plunder, Irish monastic settlements were obvious and vulnerable targets. Christian settlements in the Dublin region at the time included Howth, Ireland's Eye, Dalkey Island, Finglas and Tallaght and there is evidence of a number of churches on the banks of the Poddle. Raids on such settlements were by no means a new experience for their inhabitants who had been victims of many previous raids by native tribes. Later in the ninth century, the Viking raiders became less aggressive, mainly because of internal disputes, and in 902 they were expelled by the natives. In 918 Viking raiders re-appeared and in the following year one of the decisive battles of Irish history was fought, resulting in a Viking victory and the establishment of a permanent presence of Norsemen in eastern Ireland. The newcomers were concerned not so much with the use of the settlement as a base from which to mount raids but with the creation of a larger town which, with its relatively easy access to the rest of the country on the one hand and its established maritime trade on the other, could and did flourish as a major Danish trading colony. Within a few generations, conformity to Gaelic customs was a natural consequence of inter-marriage with the native population and an acceptance, at least nominally, of Christianity followed.

The development of the colony in the tenth century was by no means free from conflict. The King of Leinster, Mael Seachlainn, captured it in 981 but later entered into an alliance with the Danes. The alliance was a disaster, suffering defeat by Brian Boru in the year 999 and again at Clontarf in 1014. In his book *Dublin*, Peter Somerville-Large says ' . . . Clontarf was less a contest between Irish and Norse than the conclusion of a revolt of the Leinster men against Brian Boru in which the Vikings . . . only played a secondary role.' Although Dublin was sacked on a number of occasions subsequently, gradually a more peaceful period ensued. The Vikings were absorbed into the native population, embracing Christianity and eventually losing their language and Norse identity.

Peter Somerville-Large states that by the twelfth century Dublin's true importance lay in its position as a prosperous trading port, possessing a fleet of over 200 ships which traded not only with English ports, particularly Chester and Bristol, but with distant Continental seaports. Indeed it was through trading contacts with Bristol that Dermot McMorrough succeeded in getting an introduction to Henry II for the purpose of enlisting assistance in his attempt to regain the Irish high kingship.

Following the grant of the City of Dublin to the men of Bristol by Henry II in 1172 Dublin was flooded with settlers from South-West England and South Wales, notwithstanding that the Charter specified that the newcomers should only be men from Bristol. These settlers were mainly tradesmen and artisans and no doubt many found employment in the expansive building programme which continued throughout the thirteenth century. Many churches and public buildings were built or rebuilt in stone, involving the transport of large quantities of this material from quarries in Ireland, Wales and England. This stone had to be unloaded at the timber jetties already referred to. The recent excavations indicate that the earliest jetties were situated substantially to the south of the modern Wood Quay and Merchant's Quay. The requirements of larger vessels with deeper draught involved the construction of successive structures (embankments, timber revetments, timber jetties and masonry walls) at different stages further into the river, culminating in a stone quay wall built in the early fourteenth century. It would appear that the line of this stone wall coincides substantially with the line of the quay wall at present day Wood Quay.

The excavations on the site of the early settlement at Dublin conducted by the National Museum between 1962 and 1979, under the supervision of Dr Patrick Wallace, produced a great deal of new information on the old town and the lifestyle of its inhabitants; in particular, the successive stages of waterfront development at what came to be known as Wood Quay were revealed for the first time.

Geological data established in the early years of this century indicated that prior to the ninth and tenth centuries, the upper reaches of the estuary of the river Liffey were much broader than a casual glance at the walls now bounding the river on both sides would indicate. While the river was wide opposite the site of Wood Quay in the Viking and Anglo-Norman periods, it was relatively shallow. In order to accommodate ships by providing landing places where they could berth and still lie afloat at low tide, successive banks and walls were built further out into the river, as described in detail by Dr Patrick Wallace in a lecture delivered in 1979. For the purposes of his paper, Dr Wallace prepared a schematic cross-section plan of the medieval waterfront showing the successive positions of these works as they were built further out into the river. A drawing of a revetment appears on page 30.

The earliest waterfront appears to have been an earthen bank identified in Dr Wallace's paper as Bank 1 and dated *c.* 900. It is described as a low flood-bank, not more than one metre high, scarped out of boulder clay above high water line, and was possibly one of several whose primary purpose appears to have been intended to keep property on the foreshore dry at high water or during flash floods.

A later work, described by Dr Wallace as Bank 2, appears to have been built *c.* 950 on top of dumped organic refuse and stabilised at its core by a post and wattle boundary fence. A ditch was cut in the natural limestone bedrock immediately outside this bank at its central section; the ditch measured 1.6 metres deep and 2 metres wide, and its purpose appears to have been the retention of water at low tide to enable ships to lie afloat. What appears to have been a boarded slipway was set on the outer part of the bank to facilitate the beaching and launching of boats. This bank appears to have followed the high ground at the west end of the site and then turned south-westwards, thus suggesting that it may also have filled a defensive rôle by encircling the early town.

Bank 3 was probably built *c.* 1000 and is a more substantial embankment and built further out into the river than its predecessor. This bank was revetted on the river side by boards driven into the ground and in another place by a post-and-wattle revetment. A wattle revetment was bedded in a channel cut into bedrock, the stones of which had been backfilled and tamped around the upright posts. In its final phase, this bank was covered over with estuarine mud brought from the bed of the river; this mud dried out and formed a hard and firm surface. This bank also appears to have encircled the town.

Although there is a general similarity between the Viking fortifications at Dublin and the more massive structures at the great Scandinavian trading centres, a closer parallel appears in Anglo-Danish ramparts which were excavated at York, where the erection of a bank to complement the natural defences seems to mirror the experience at Dublin. An English rather than a Scandinavian inspiration for these banks is more acceptable since it coincides with the later waves of Viking colonisation in the early tenth century which are believed to have come from Britain and not Scandinavia.

The next advance into the Liffey is represented by a stone wall about 1.5 metres wide and possibly originally about 3.5 metres in height, although the surviving height averages only 2 metres. This wall runs roughly parallel to and about 5-10 metres north of Bank 3. In its course it diverges somewhat from a straight line due probably to any one or a combination of circumstances, e.g., change in the nature of the bedrock from limestone to gravel, the existence of a pool in the river or the desire to follow the line of the previous banks. The wall comprised a rubble fill within mortared stone facings and was partly built on a dry stone plinth to the south of which have been found mortar platforms where the mortar for the upper courses was mixed. There is evidence that the outer face was completed first and the wall completed on the inside, and that it was repaired in the thirteenth century. It appears that the ground surface behind the wall was much higher than that on the north or river side and, if it was not free-standing, that it was a revetment or quay wall. However, the surviving maximum height of the wall at the west end of the site suggests that it was a defensive structure and extended right around the town.

In the early thirteenth century the need for deeper berthage for ships became urgent due to the flourishing European trade which followed on the Anglo-Norman settlement, and which was accompanied by an increase in the size and draught of ships. Close approach to the existing berthage was made difficult by the gradual accumulation of silt and the absence of dredging facilities.

The next stage in the development of the waterfront seems to have been about 1200 when a line of post-and-wattle about one metre high and thirty-five metres long was erected on the river gravel, roughly parallel to and twenty-five metres north of the wall already described. This line was intended to provide a stabilising core or retaining fence for an embankment (Bank 4) but it appears to have collapsed soon after erection; it may have been intended as a temporary measure since it was replaced by a wooden revetment. Six similar lines divided the area between the wall and Bank 4 into a series of rectangles which may have indicated property boundaries but may also have facilitated reclamation. These north-south fences were overlain by later thirteenth-century sill beams of a warehouse complex, showing a continuity of these property lines.

About 1210, a strong wooden revetment (i.e. retaining wall) was built on a line about two to three metres on the river side of Bank 4. The structure consisted of six distinct units, implying a division of ownership or responsibility or, less likely, of the building contract. The fact of their being built together on a line indicates a degree of civic or municipal control which was not so evident in the case of the earlier banks and wall. Each unit of the revetment measured about twelve to fifteen metres long and comprised squared oak posts about 1.8 metres tall tenoned into baseplates; behind the posts planks were set on edge horizontally and held in place by the pressure of the town refuse heaped behind them. The vertical posts were supported from the front (i.e., river side) by braces consisting of squared oak beams tenoned into subsidiary baseplates which were set at right angles to the principal baseplates.

A subsidiary structure consisting of vertical posts and baseplates but without horizontal plank cladding was erected on the riverside of the main revetment but not secured to it. This outer work was probably intended to act as a buffer to prevent ships colliding with the front braces of the main revetment. The vertical posts were taller than those in the principal structure, being about 2.2 metres high.

Although the original revetment extended east and west beyond the bounds of the Wood Quay site, it cannot have extended very far to the west in the area now known as Merchant's Quay but described as the 'Strand' in the thirteenth century. However, it appears that the revetment was later extended westwards along the 'Strand'.

One section of the six units of Revetment 1 appears not to have been completed or possibly had been dismantled as only the principal base-plates and buffer structure survived. This may have been due to a change of mind on the part of the builder or owner of the particular section of the quay front, as another revetment was built about twenty metres further out into the river from the incomplete section, and linked to the main quayside by means of a rough fence which may have served as a boundary demarcation rather than to facilitate berthing of ships on its east side. This side was also protected by a post-and-wattle breakwater infilled with estuarine mud.

Later in the thirteenth century a long wooden revetment was built still further out in the bed of the Liffey. In contrast to Revetment 1 and its extension, this second revetment was back-braced. This revetment made a sharp right-angled turn at Fishamble Street and appears to have presented a boarded quay corner at Fishamble Street east-west and north-south fronts. The turn at Fishamble Street may have been intended to protect the revetment from tidal action as in the case of the earlier breakwater; alternatively, it may have been associated with a slip used for landing fish which is well documented, being described as a 'fysshe slypp' at Fishamble Street. The street takes its name from the shambles or market which was situated there.

A final wooden quay front was erected just north (i.e., on the river side) of Revetment 2, and was similarly back-braced.

The wooden revetments which have been described above may have been primarily intended to act as the facing for an expanding vertical dock-side outside the city wall, and to protect the reclaimed land from tidal erosion. The associated encroachment into the Liffey was probably intended to increase the depth of water available for ships, but whether the builders seriously believed in the possibility of such achievement remains open to doubt; the accomplishment of such a task in a broad, shallow estuary seems to have been doomed to fail and it would appear that the contemporary practice was to allow ships to rest on the river bed or, as it is known, 'take the ground' at low water.

About 1300, a stone quay wall was erected just north of Revetment 3.

This marked the final medieval extension to the waterfront and brought the line of the quays almost to that of the modern quayfront. This wall appears to have been no more successful than the earlier banks and revetments in providing deeper berthage and as late as 1358, the merchants of Dublin complained to Edward III that 'from want of deep water in the harbour . . . there never has been anchorage for large ships from abroad'. Dalkey Sound remained the main anchorage for large ships for many years, their cargoes being partly discharged into lighters, thus reducing the draught of the vessels to enable them to get up the river at Dublin.

2

The First Port Authority

UNDER Anglo-Norman law, jurisdiction over tidal waters was vested in the Crown, irrespective of the claims of those whose properties bordered on such tidal waters. Unless the Crown granted the franchise of a port no one had the right to create one or to demand payment for the use of tidal waters. The rights of the monarch were protected and exercised on his behalf by the Lord High Admiral. Although the early charters granted to the city by Henry II and John contained no reference to the port, a later charter of John gave liberty to the city to build on the banks of the Liffey and the first quays (or 'keys' as they were described in the medieval records) of the Anglo-Norman period were built in exercise of the powers granted under that charter. The powers claimed by the Lord High Admiral were to become a contentious issue with the city fathers in later centuries.

While local sources provided the citizens of medieval Dublin with ordinary foodstuffs, luxuries such as wine (of which there was a good deal), dried fruits, nuts, spices and jewellery were imported as indeed was wool since local wool was too coarse for fine weaving. Fish, particularly oysters and other shell fish, was a popular and cheap foodstuff, and fishing boats were unloaded at a slip at Wood Quay opposite Fishamble Street. Exports included hides, livestock and surplus foodstuffs. Apart from the imported wine, there was a large home industry in brewing ale and beer and in distilling whiskey. In the absence of other social amenities or distractions, city taverns appear to have been one of the main attractions for the citizens of medieval Dublin. Indeed a contemporary commentator stated that the whole profit of the town was derived from taverns; bearing in mind the recurring cycle of war, siege, fire, disease and civil unrest generally, it is small wonder.

The sixteenth century saw a resurgence of trade between Dublin and English and foreign ports and an interesting consequence of this increased trade to the port was the transfer to individual citizens of responsibility for the maintenance of the quays and slips. In 1560

Thomas Fitz Symon was granted all the 'slyps of the Merchaunt Key' for a term of sixty-one years, the grantee to keep the slips and walls 'stiff and strong' and to be granted stones for the work. In return he was entitled to levy a charge on vessels using the slips. In the same year Walter Clynton was permitted to build a slip upon the 'key' on the same terms as those granted to Thomas Fitz Symon. In that year also Gyles Clyncher was appointed overseer of the river to see that no refuse or ballast was dumped in it and in particular to see that the bank at the south side of the 'Polebegge' was preserved from taking of ballast 'and also at the Rings Ende'. These would appear to be the earliest records of the city taking steps to control and protect the facilities (such as they were) for shipping arriving at Dublin.

In 1566 Gerald Plunkett was authorised to set buoys or marks at the bar as a guide to shipping and in return for his labours he was empowered to levy a toll on every ship arriving in the harbour. The task of maintaining and replacing the buoys seems to have been too much for Plunkett and indeed for a host of successors appointed over the next twenty years. However, a buoy and a perch are shown on a map of Dublin Bay dated 1685, made by Thomas Phillips, an engineer in the service of the Crown who had been sent to Ireland to make maps of the country together with designs for defences. In the following year Captain Greville Collins, a naval officer, was commissioned by Charles II to make a survey of the coasts of the kingdom and his map of Dublin Bay also shows the buoy and the perch.

In 1583 the City Council undertook responsibility for the cost of repairing and rebuilding the bridge described as the 'old bridge' near the site of the ford of the hurdles, and also for repairing the walls of the 'keys'. The 'old bridge' was built in 1210 on the site of an earlier structure dating from the Viking period and it has been rebuilt several times; the present bridge was completed in 1818 and was named 'Whitworth Bridge' in honour of the Lord Lieutenant of the day. In 1938 it was renamed 'Father Mathew Bridge' to mark the centenary of the Father Mathew Temperance movement.

Civic spirit on the part of the citizens generally and of shipowners appears to have been somewhat lacking inasmuch as refuse and stones were continually dumped in the river opposite the 'keys' and old hulks were allowed to rot in the river and in the estuary, particularly opposite Clontarf. In 1593 the city was obliged to order the removal of such hulks under penalty of prison for defaulters. In March 1597 negligence in other quarters led to a disaster involving the death of 200 people following an explosion of gunpowder which had been landed at Wood Quay and was in the process of being removed to Dublin Castle. The report of an official inquiry made several references to laws and ordinances not being put into execution and to misdemeanours on the part of office holders and negligence in attendance to their duties.

In addition to the trade served by the successive wharves, quays and slips in the Wood Quay/Merchant's Quay area, the friars of St Mary's Abbey had a thriving trade with French ports in medieval times, served by a jetty at the Pill (i.e., an inlet of the Liffey where it was joined by the Bradogue) but the Pill had been filled in long before the eighteenth century. A report dated 1590 refers to the depth of water opposite Wood Quay and Merchant's Quay as varying from three to six and a half feet, but no indications are given as to the lunar or tidal conditions when these depths were recorded.

The earliest quay development to the east of Wood Quay would appear to have its origins in a lease, granted by Jacob Newman to the Crown in November 1620, of land between Dame Street and the river for the purpose of building 'a Custom House Crane and Wharf'. In the following July a royal proclamation ordered that this place should be the 'onely, sole and proper Crane and Wharfe for loading, landing, putting aboard or on shore and goods, merchandise or commodities whatsoever to be by sea exported or imported into or forth of [*sic*] the said Port of Dublin'. The proclamation went on to provide that such operations should take place only in the daytime between the rising and setting of the sun. The Custom House seems to have had a relatively short life since in July 1637 it is recorded that the city granted ground to the king to build a new Custom House and extend the Custom House Quay. A third Custom House in this location is recorded as having being built in the 1660s. It contained a Council Chamber for the Privy Council of Ireland. Following the building in 1697 of Essex Bridge, later rebuilt as Grattan Bridge (Capel Street Bridge), another new Custom House was built in 1707 on what is now Wellington Quay. This building features in a number of contemporary pictures, notably that by Tudor dated 1753.

The vessels that could use this Custom House Quay were relatively small by modern standards: the maximum size was about 170 tons burthen. Only four vessels of this size could berth alongside at any one time as the depth at low water was less than five feet at the western end and it was common practice for other vessels to lie in tiers outside those berthed at the Quay. In Sir John Gilbert's history of Dublin, he states that as many as twenty-four ships were berthed in this way, although it is doubtful if the outer tiers could have worked their cargoes in such a position. The level of the quay wall created problems in certain tidal and weather conditions when the level of the river rose as much as nine inches over the quay level with consequent damage to goods lying on the quay. This Custom House was superseded by the present Custom House in 1791.

In 1667 a Dutch fleet under Admiral de Ruyter sailed up the Thames and destroyed English warships anchored near Chatham. To prevent a recurrence, the British government ordered a blockade to be set up by sinking thirteen ships in the river. Sir Bernard de Gomme and Sir Martin Barkman, who were described as the 'Royal Engineers', were instructed to prepare plans to strengthen the defences of the Thames estuary. An uneasy peace with the Netherlands ensued but when war broke out again in 1672, de Gomme reported on the defences in Ireland. He drew up plans for a citadel for Dublin on a site near present-day Merrion Square. As already indicated, navigation west of Ringsend was restricted in this period and Ringsend had become a convenient landing place for vessels whose draught was too deep to allow them to go further upriver; it was at Ringsend that Cromwell landed his 13,000 troops in August 1649. From Ringsend the approach to the city depended on the state of the tide; at low water it was possible to traverse the line of present-day Ringsend Road; when this area was covered at high water, it was necessary to take a more circuitous route via the line of present-day Irishtown, Bath Avenue and Mount Street. De Gomme's projected citadel was intended to cover both sea and land approaches but it did not materialise.

The consequences for the trade of Dublin of the ebb and flow of political fortunes in the Cromwellian and Restoration periods and the wars with France and Holland are somewhat outside the province of this work. It is clear, however, that the merchants and traders of the city were determined that their business would not be prejudiced either by natural hazards to shipping in the estuary and channel or by risks from pirates. In 1674 Andrew Yarranton was requested by the Lord Mayor of Dublin to survey the estuary and suggest some means of defending shipping using the harbour and also of improving the harbour itself. In due course he produced plans for an artificial harbour and fort at Ringsend. Yarranton's proposals suffered the same fate as those of de Gomme but they were important inasmuch as they focused attention on and emphasised the need to improve the port and make it safe for shipping.

The municipal archives contain the following description of the condition of the estuary at the time:

> The Harbour of the City of Dublin in its natural state, wild, open and exposed to every wind, afforded no place of shelter or security to ships except at Clontarf or Ringsend, and even then not free from danger and often inaccessible through contrary winds. The tides uninterruptedly expanded themselves over vast tracts of north and south strands, better known by the names of North and South Bulls, and in their progress towards the city branched out into many channels, both curved and intricate. The entrance from the

bay into the harbour was barred by a bank of quicksand which often shifted and varied with the mutability of the wind and consequently rendered the navigation so uncertain and dangerous as often to baffle both skill and experience. . . . When fortunate enough to escape the danger of the bar, it required the utmost exertion of skill and labour to steer clear of the above-mentioned Bulls [which were] the graves of thousands and immense loss of property of subjects and Crown revenue.

The condition of the harbour and the consequent prejudicial effects on the trade of the city led to a demand for municipal support to establish some form of conservancy authority for the river. But the Corporation had always claimed ownership of the strands of the river under a charter of King John; admiralty jurisdiction was also claimed under a charter of Edward VI as confirmed by a grant of Elizabeth I in 1585. In the late seventeenth century several private persons unsuccessfully sought letters patent authorising them to erect a Ballast Office at the port. In 1685 the Corporation itself sought similar powers on the grounds of the deteriorating condition of the river and its malign effect on shipping and trade. This petition did not receive royal favour due to a conflict between the Lord High Admiral (who happened to be the Prince Consort George) and the Corporation. Both parties claimed admiralty jurisdiction over the port.

In a later petition of 1707, the Corporation added a sweetener in favour of the Lord High Admiral by undertaking to pay him annually a hundred yards of Irish sail cloth. Whether the sail cloth carried the day or not, the fact remains that in the same year an act was passed entitled 'An Act for Cleansing the Port, Harbour and River of Dublin and for Erecting a Ballast Office in the said City'. Power to carry out the various necessary works was vested in the Corporation, the act providing that 'The Lord Mayor, Sheriffs, commons and citizens of the city of Dublin . . . are hereby constituted and ordained keepers and conservators of the Port of Dublin'.

The municipal records describe the preliminary work of the Corporation in relation to its new functions as follows:

> The Ballast Office Act was to take place [*sic*] on the 1st May, 1708 and preparative thereto the Corporation appointed a Committee of citizens, no doubt the most judicious and knowing, and such as were interested in the security of the naval commerce, to consider of and point out the necessary requisites for carrying the Act into execution, and to report their opinion as soon as possible so that no time should be lost in providing the proper materials and appointing officers to superintendent the works.

The committee's report was laid before the General Assembly of the Corporation on 16 January 1708 and its recommendations included the establishment of a 'Committee of Governors or Directors' to manage the business of the Ballast Office; the committee was to report its proceedings quarterly to the assembly and the composition of the committee was to be altered quarterly if thought fit. Officers were to be appointed to carry out the orders of the directors but no salaries were to be settled until after three months. Two lighters were to be built for raising ballast as an experiment on the basis of which charges for supplying ballast to ships could be decided. The report recommended also that the Temple Bar premises be acquired as a Ballast Office.

The committee's report was signed by each of its fourteen members, including Humphrey Jervis, John Rogerson, William Fownes and John Eccles—all prominent citizens but who are probably known nowadays to the man in the street only by the thoroughfares bearing their names.

The committee's recommendations were approved by the General Assembly which appointed the following as the first Committee of governors/directors:

Alderman William Fownes; Alderman John Eccles; Alderman Ralph Gore; Thomas Wilkinson; George Roe; Thomas Curtis; Henry Lee; Thomas Thorne; Edward Verdon

At this period, the Council of the Corporation consisted of an upper house, comprising the Lord Mayor and the twenty-four aldermen, and a lower house usually known as the 'commons' composed of the two city sheriffs, the sheriff's peers (i.e., common council men who had served as sheriffs) together with ninety-six representatives of the city's twenty-five guilds. The city's business was dealt with at four quarterly meetings described as the Easter, Midsummer, Michaelmas and Christmas assemblies. Where pressure of business so required, additional meetings known as post-assemblies were held. To these assemblies, the Ballast Committee or, as they were titled, 'the Directors of the Ballast Office' reported their proceedings.

Meetings of the assembly were held in a building known as the Tholsel which was situated at the corner of Nicholas Street and Skinner's Row; the last named was later incorporated into Christchurch Place. The Tholsel also accommodated a court room, the Trinity Guild of Merchants and the Royal Exchange. Due to the decayed condition of the Tholsel, the assembly was obliged to transfer its meetings for a short time in 1791 to the Tailors Hall in Back Lane and later in the same year the meetings were transferred to the Exhibition Hall in South William Street which now houses the Civic Museum and the Old Dublin Society. A new Royal Exchange was completed on Cork Hill in 1779 but this building was taken over by the Corporation in 1852 and became the present-day City Hall.

Although the Ballast Office Act, as it came to be known, did not come into force until 1 May 1708, the new Ballast Office Committee held its first meeting on 20 January in that year in the Royal Exchange, then part of the Tholsel, and its members displayed their enthusiasm for their work by deciding to order three lighters to be built, one each from three of the Dublin shipbuilders of the day: James Adair, Nathaniel Dyer and Francis Drake. The committee's enthusiasm does not appear to have been damped by any financial considerations since no income could reasonably be expected to accrue for some time but presumably the Corporation's name was sufficient guarantee. The fact that the committee had no legal authority at that stage to enter into any contracts does not appear to have caused any concern.

The committee then adjourned its meeting to the following day when the matter of crews for the lighters was considered. It was decided to write to a Mr Lovett in London to secure his assistance in recruiting 'two lusty, strong men, well versed in the lighters or gabbards for taking up ballast in the river Thames and are masters of the same, and who have no families'. Mr Lovett duly replied but the terms on which the lusty, strong men were prepared to come to Dublin were regarded by the committee as unreasonable and local men were employed instead. It is not unlikely that lusty strong men without families were a rare commodity in those days even in London.

The first officials appointed included William Trydell, Clerk and Secretary to the Committee, Thomas Pearson, Ballast Master and Treasurer, and Thomas Holt, Surveyor and Gauger of vessels. The function of the latter was to measure the tonnage of vessels arriving at the port for the purpose of assessing port dues. The instructions as to the method of measurement were presumably copied from another port, probably London, and they provide an interesting sidelight on early ship measurement based on 100 cubic feet to the ton. The surveyor was required to measure all coasting gabbards by taking 'the length of the keel, the breadth of the beam and half the breadth for the depth of the hold, foreign ships to be measured from the upper deck to the ceiling (i.e., floor of the hold) and that to be accounted the depth of the ship in the hold and that half the depth between decks is to be added to the depth of the ship in the hold, and that to be accounted the depth of the ship; all measurements to be divided by 100'.

The committee was unsuccessful in its efforts to acquire premises in Temple Bar but in July 1708 the General Assembly of the Corporation was informed that a lease had been taken for a period of one year from a Mr Hacken of portion of his house, together with storehouse and yard, in Essex Street. Clearly, proximity to the Custom House, then situated at what is now Wellington Quay, was a major consideration. The committee also referred to a map recently made by the City Surveyor, Mr Moland, showing the estuary of the river. On the basis of this map the committee outlined its proposals for a new direct channel for the river above Ringsend, to be marked out by poles or stakes at hundred yard intervals on both sides of the river; ballast would be raised only from the new channel; the breaking of the river banks by ship masters for the purpose of securing ballast and the dumping of ballast or rubbish would be prohibited.

The committee showed a little more foresight in its approach to the costs of making the new channel than in the case of the lighters. In submitting its proposals it acknowledged that the taking up of ballast and the revenue therefrom would not of itself produce the desired results for many years and accordingly it was proposed that at first the new channel should be restricted in width to twenty feet, 'so as to draw the water from spreading into many branches, and with the aid of the floods enlarge the channel during the ensuing winter, thus making the rest of the work more easy in the following year'. In addition it was proposed that when the gabbards were not occupied elsewhere in raising ballast, they could be used to clean and deepen the river opposite the Custom House, for the benefit of shipping berthing there.

The committee's report concluded with a request that its members be discharged from office and a new committee appointed, since the business of the Ballast Office in its first six months had been very onerous and had interfered greatly with the members' own affairs.

A new committee was accordingly appointed in August 1708 and it lost no time in proceeding with the proposals of its predecessors. Having decided on the line of the proposed new channel, it was found necessary to negotiate with leaseholders of sections of the foreshore along the line of present-day Burgh Quay, as a result of which the leaseholders surrendered portions of the foreshore required by the Ballast Office and were granted other plots in lieu; in addition the leaseholders undertook to build retaining walls along the new river boundaries to their property.

In November 1709, the committee sought the opinion of the Solicitor-General on the interpretation of the 1707 act insofar as it related to the rights of the Ballast Office to prevent any person from taking up and carrying away sand from any part of the strands of the port. In reply the Solicitor-General stated that the inheritance of the strand was in the city and 'they [*sic*] may hinder any person from taking sand or stone or gravel from any part of the strand, whether it be for ballasting ships or otherwise'. This and other legal opinions were factors in later conflicts between the Corporation and various private interests, including the Pembroke Estate and the Vernon Estate, in respect of claims to ownership of the strands.

The Ballast Committee reported quarterly to the General Assembly of the Corporation and these reports were incorporated in the Dublin Assembly Rolls which are included in the Calendar of Ancient Records of Dublin edited by Sir John T. Gilbert. The committee reported generally on the progress of the new works and of various negotiations with owners or leaseholders of land or foreshore adjoining the proposed new channel. From 1711 the reports included a financial statement showing the revenue (i.e., duties imposed on shipping) and expenditure on the new works. In May 1712 the committee reported that 'The easiest and the aptest way (to enclose the channel) will be by the laying of kishes and filling them with stones and backing them with sand and gravel . . . to withstand all the force of the floods that come down the river' and the committee stated that they had entered into appropriate arrangements accordingly. By October of the same year 686 kishes had been laid on the north side of the channel, roughly on the line of present day Eden Quay/Custom House Quay.

Although its main concern at this time was the work involved in the straightening and deepening of the river channel from the city to Ringsend, the committee was conscious of the problems for shipping anchoring in the lower and less sheltered reaches at the river mouth. Consultations were held with Colonel Thomas Burgh, Surveyor-General, and others. Various proposals were put forward to the committee for the creation of more sheltered anchorages, none of which were developed. Incidentally, Burgh was the architect for several important buildings in the city, including the old Custom House on the Wellington Quay site (now occupied partly by Corporation offices and partly by the Clarence Hotel) the Royal Barracks (now Collins Barracks), and the old library in Trinity College.

In July 1713, Captain John Perry offered to survey the harbour and suggest methods for its improvement. Perry's credentials included his employment by the Tzar of Russia 'in making rivers navigable', and his terms for the Dublin project included a guarantee of £2,000 in the event that, having received detailed proposals, the committee decided to dispense with his services and employ another party to carry out the works. While it is not specifically so recorded, Perry appears to have been given some assurances, since in the following September he proceeded with his survey of the river channel and the bar. Nothing further is recorded of his survey until April 1714, by which time the city was without a General Assembly due to political/legal wrangles relating to the appointment of Lords Mayor, Aldermen and City Sheriffs. As it was not possible for the Ballast Committee to submit Perry's proposals (including the guarantee) for approval by the General Assembly, the committee paid Perry the sum of £67 to cover his expenses in coming to

Dublin and carrying out his survey.

In January 1715, the General Assembly approved of the construction by the committee of a boundary wall between foreshore in its owner-ship, known as the City Ground, and that leased to Sir John Rogerson. Subsequently the committee received approval for the building of a wall fronting the channel, to enclose the City Ground now known as City Quay and its hinterland. Sir John Rogerson's obligation to erect a sea wall relieved the committee of the onus of extending the City Ground wall eastwards.

In anticipation of the completion of the embankment of the north side of the river, the City Assembly in 1717 ordered that a survey be made of the strand lying between the Liffey and the Tolka rivers, in area about 440 acres, and a further 77 acres between the Tolka and the Clontarf fore-shore. It was decided to divide the strand notionally into two classes of lots, those along the river front being described as Foot Lots and those in the rear as Acre Lots. A scheme of allocation of the Lots was drawn up and the allottees were obliged to construct and maintain walls enclosing the area to keep out the sea. This obligation was later transferred by statute to the port authority in return for an annual payment from each lot holder. The enclosure of the area between the Liffey and the Tolka by walls was completed in 1728 but the completion of the reclamation of the area, mainly with sand and gravel dredged from the river estuary, took many years. The proposed reclamation between the Tolka and Clontarf was never carried out. The Board's journals record a request from a lot holder in September 1835 for one thousand tons of river mud to fill up a 'low North lot'. In the interim much of the area had been built upon and streets laid out. The erection of the present Custom House (1781-91) and its associated dock system on the land thus reclaimed will be dealt with in greater detail in a later chapter.

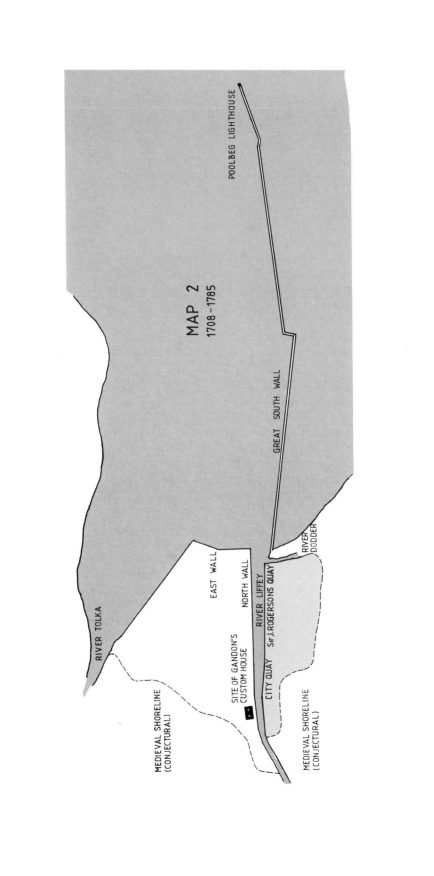

MAP 2
1708–1785

POOLBEG LIGHTHOUSE

GREAT SOUTH WALL

RIVER TOLKA

EAST WALL

NORTH WALL

SITE OF GANDON'S
CUSTOM HOUSE

RIVER LIFFEY

CITY QUAY

Sir J.ROGERSONS QUAY

RIVER
DODDER

MEDIEVAL SHORELINE
(CONJECTURAL)

MEDIEVAL SHORELINE
(CONJECTURAL)

3

The Great South Wall and Poolbeg Lighthouse

THE Ballast Office Committee's continuing concern at the lack of shelter for shipping forced to anchor in the lower reaches of the estuary resulted in a proposal to erect timber piles along the southern margin of the river channel below Ringsend to create an embankment which would give shelter to the channel. In April 1715 the City Assembly approved the suggestion. In its report of October of the same year the committee reported progress on the earlier works on the north side of the channel as far as a point opposite Mabbot's mill. This would be approximately at the junction of present day Memorial Road and Custom House Quay. The work at Ringsend had not yet commenced because of lack of materials.

In the following June, it is recorded that the committee 'together with several merchants and others skilful in sea affairs went down to Ringsend to consider the most proper place for staking out the ground, and out to Poolbeg, and after due deliberation they did on the said day drive down stakes from Irishtown, East by South, to the South Bull in order to raise a bank along a line where the stakes are placed, for the better security of the ships that shall lie in the harbour of Dublin'. In July 1716, it was reported that the staking out of the ground on the south side of the channel below Ringsend had been completed and the area was ready to be piled; two pile driving engines had been ordered, one from Holland and another to be made locally. The committee reported further that 'a man is sent for to Holland that shall be skilled in piling, and making of banks, and to have the overseeing and direction of the said work'. Three months later the committee reported that progress in piling had been made with the engine made locally and it was proposed to transfer operations to the South Bull area in the following spring in order 'to preserve the ships that are most exposed to storms'.

The engine ordered from Holland was delivered later in 1716 but it was found to be incapable of driving piles of sufficient length on the South Bull and it was decided to buy another engine locally for £50 which could drive the longest pile required with half the number of hands required by the Dutch engine. By July 1717 over 300 piles had been driven in three rows, the space betweeen the rows being filled with stones and hurdles.

In 1718 the committee became aware of rumours being spread around the city that the state of the river and the bar had become worse since the Ballast Office was established. The committee decided to find out the position for itself and subsequently reported that it 'went down to sound the harbour and the bar', presumably with the assistance of someone skilled in taking soundings although this is not recorded. The report went on to state that 'at the lower end of Poole Begg and Iron Pool to the perch there was a depth of 30 feet; a little below the perch $27\frac{1}{2}$ to $25\frac{1}{2}$ feet and from thence to the bar 21 to 22 feet; upon the bar there was a depth of 21 feet, and at the buoy of the bar 19 feet'. The committee stated that having compared these soundings with those on Moland's map, it was plainly demonstrable that the harbour and the bar were deeper than they had been ten years previously; the soundings were clearly not low water soundings.

Reports by the committee in succeeding years continued to report progress on the laying of kishes on the north side of the channel as far eastwards as 'opposite to Ringsend Point', and on the piling below Ringsend and on the South Bull. In July 1720 the committee reported that it was becoming impracticable to pile further to the eastwards on the South Bull as the tide seldom left the east end of the piles. One year later the committee reported that a new method had been adopted to overcome the difficulty, by making frames consisting of twenty-four piles, each frame being about twenty-two feet in length and ten feet in breadth, braced and pinned. The frames were made at Ringsend and carried down at full tide between two floats and settled in their appropriate places with 'a sufficient quantity of stone to secure them as soon as they are laid'. By making use of these frames the work could be carried on further eastward than could have been done with the piling engines. In a later report (July 1722) a more detailed description of the frames was given from which it appears that they were box-like structures, twelve feet wide at the bottom and seven feet wide at the top, some framed and braced by dovetailing and pinning; the bottom and sides of the frames were made with planks so that the stones could not fall out nor could sand run through.

In January 1721 the committee reported on the success of the new framing system and the shelter thereby provided for ships lying in 'Poole Begg' and for fishing boats; however, because of the restriction on the tidal flows created by the frames, the water ran with greater force along the ends of the piling, making 'sloughs or greater depths of water at the ends of the piles than in other places'. The problem was overcome by filling in the sloughs which were about $4\frac{1}{2}$ feet deep at low water, thus enabling the piling work to continue eastwards. However, it was reported that persons were carrying away great quantities of sand from the South Bull, a 'practice which was highly prejudicial to the harbour' and the Lord Mayor was requested to issue a proclamation to prevent the practice. Subsequently it was noted that further difficulty was caused to the work by persons digging for mussels among the stones filling up the piling, thus creating spaces for the tide to run through and wash out the filling material.

By January 1723 the Lord Mayor's proclamation had been so successful that the offenders had offered to pay the Ballast Office for permission to take sand from such parts of the strand or the harbour as might be directed by the committee. However, it appears that this proposal had been prevented by Lord Fitzwilliam who had objected to the employees of the Ballast Office hindering any person from taking sand on the grounds that the strand was his and he would maintain his right to it. In April 1723 it was noted that the dispute with Lord Fitzwilliam had 'apparently been resolved since no more sand has been taken off the Strand since then nor was any more sand to be taken off it for the future'.

It was the practice of the members of the committee for the time being, having served for some years, to request to be replaced because of the burdensome nature of their task, particularly in regular visits to the works in progress. In April 1723 the commitee requested the reduction of the quorum to three people, because of the lack of attention of certain members to their obligations. Some of them had never attended a meeting of the committee.

In October 1723 the committee reported that several gabbard men had been found to be 'great rogues' having been detected in cheating the office; the men concerned had been prosecuted and replaced and new rules for regulating and managing the gabbards had been introduced to prevent such practices in the future. The committee also queried the wisdom of continuing the piling in the direct west to east line, pending further examination of the implications of so doing. In January 1724 the committee's report referred to the progress on the wall at the 'North Strand'. This would appear to be the first reference to the construction of a wall on the north side of the channel as distinct from the embankment constructed on the kishes. The committee were authorised to proceed with the piling on the South Bull. However, the General Assembly were informed by the Ballast Committee in April 1724 that there was insufficient money available to carry on both the North Wall and the piling on the South Bull; the assembly instructed the committee to finish the wall on the north side and then to proceed with the work on the South Bull.

In April 1725 the committee reported a diversion of their workmen from the works in progress to assist in raising a man-of-war, the *Aldborough*, which had sunk in 'Poole Begg'. The operation was completed in twelve days which, having regard to the relatively primitive methods available, seems to indicate an expeditious operation which no doubt strengthened the hand of the naval commander concerned when faced with the inevitable official inquiry.

The abortive negotiations with Capt. John Perry in 1713–14 have been noted but in 1725 he returned at the request of the Earl of Carteret, the Lord Lieutenant, to whom he submitted a report entitled 'a method proposed for making a safe and convenient entrance to the Port of Dublin'. Carteret forwarded the report to the Ballast Committee for their observations. In reply the committee indicated that Perry's proposals were by no means new, having been submitted by him on an earlier occasion. They listed objections to Perry's proposals, based not only on their own views but on those of eight pilots and over fifty ship masters using the port. Essentially Perry's proposals were for the construction of a canal from Sutton via Clontarf to join the river Liffey opposite Ringsend.

In April 1726 the committee reported difficulty in procuring suitable stone and requested permission to remove a large quantity of stones which were lying on the strand 'remote from the land near the Black Rock'.

All the reports from the Ballast Committee to the City Assembly included details of the progress of the piling on the south strand and the construction of walls on the north side of the channel from Bachelor's Walk to a point opposite Mabbot's mill. In addition, full details were supplied by the committee of all materials ordered for the works, the purchase of gabbards (sailing barges) for the transport of the materials and the purchase of new gabbards when required.

Following the destruction of a buoy at the bar in bad weather resulting in the wreck of a vessel, the *Friendship* of Bristol, which had stranded on the North Bull, the City Assembly drew the attention of the Lord Lieutenant to the obligation on ships entering the harbour to pay to the Crown a duty for the erecting and maintenance of sea marks, the safety of shipping using Dublin Harbour depending in great measure on the sea marks on the bar and on the North and South Bulls. The destruction of sea marks such as the buoy at the bar was attributed to the neglect of proper maintenance and repairs. The Lord Lieutenant was requested to lay the matter before the new sovereign, George II.

In January 1729, the City Assembly noted that a map of the city and suburbs had been produced by Thomas Brooking and ordered the payment of £10 to Brooking towards the expenses incurred in making the map. While the main thoroughfares shown on this map are named and readily identifiable with those of present-day Dublin, some name changes are important if we are not to be misled by references in contemporary source material. For example, Brooking shows Bachelors Walk as extending on the east almost to the junction with Marlborough Street; on the south side Aston Quay extends to Hawkins Street. George's Quay, which commenced at White's Lane (now Corn Exchange Place beside the *Irish Press* building on Burgh Quay), appears to have included City Quay which is not separately named on the map. Direct access from Aston Quay to George's Quay was not possible due to buildings which intervened and extended to the river bank. These buildings included a brewery owned by a prominent Dublin family of the period—the Sweetmans who, appropriately enough, were also sugar merchants. The map incorrectly shows the river walled on both sides as far east as East Wall on the north side and the mouth of the Donnybrook river (i.e., the Dodder) on the south side, anticipating the completion of these walls by many years. Brooking's map is essentially a map of the city but in the same year Capt. John Perry produced a map of the bay and harbour curiously inscribed as 'curiously engrav'd'. Perry's map shows the line of the canal proposed by him in his earlier submissions to the Lord Lieutenant. Perry also shows the position of 'the buoy' to the south-east of the entrance channel which would appear to be the buoy which was the subject of the petition to the Lord Lieutenant from the City Assembly in 1726.

In July 1729, the committee reported that its income was so small as to prevent the construction of further frames. Consequently a deep gut had been created at the east end of the frames which had carried a spit into the channel, discommoding vessels coming in or going out of the harbour. The committee suggested that the assembly should apply to the next session of parliament for a borrowing clause to be inserted in some forthcoming public act to enable such sum as was necessary, but not exceeding £3,000, in order to finish off the framework on the South Bull. The proposal was approved by the assembly. In October of the same year the committee reported that because of lack of income no further progress had been made with frames but the new gabbards had been employed in dredging ballast out of the channel and used to secure the piles on the South Bull. The committee also reported on Edward Morton, one of the supervisors of the office, who had been appointed to measure all ships; they found that many ships had been measured below their correct tonnage, to the prejudice of the Ballast Office; Morton had been suspended and it was ordered that all ships be measured again.

In April 1730, the committee indicated the urgent necessity of funds to proceed with the works; it would appear that the proposal for legislation had not been successful. The assembly authorised the committee to borrow up to £1,000 to carry on the works. In October of the same year the assembly was informed that £1,000 had been borrowed from Alderman Thomas Howe; twenty-five frames had been finished, of which twenty-one had been laid in position.

Prior to the commencement of the piling on the South Bull, there was a channel known as the Cock Lake extending in a south-easterly direction from the main river channel, near the Salmon Pool, to the bay which was sufficiently deep even at low water to enable the fishing boats to return to harbour. Piling across the Cock Lake was not commenced until late in 1731 and as the piling effectively blocked off the short cut for the fishing boats, the committee recommended that a lighthouse should be fixed at the east end of the frames to assist not only the fishing boats but also other shipping entering the main river channel. The assembly ordered that a lighthouse be erected accordingly.

In October 1734, the committee reported that the gut at the east end of the piles had 'extended itself constantly wider' and was in fact deeper than the bar so that most ships going out and coming in chose rather to make their way through this new channel.

In January 1736, the committee referred to the approval granted in October 1731 for the erection of a lighthouse at the end of the piles; having discusssed the proposal with many ship masters it had been agreed that a floating light would be of great service; accordingly they had bought a vessel and were making the necessary arrangements. In the following May, they reported that the floating light had been fixed at her proper moorings by the advice of the Captain and Master of his Majesty's Yacht. They had agreed that four persons should attend the floating light: 'the first hand at £18 per annum, the second hand at £16 and two lusty boys at £10 per annum'. Lustiness appears to have been a prerequisite of employment on vessels under the committee's jurisdiction. In October 1737 the committee noted that the floating light had been overturned in a violent gale as a result of which the ship had lost two of her 'lanthorns'. No indication is given as to whether the hands or the 'lusty boys' suffered any harm. In January 1738 the floating light was damaged by a passing ship and in April of the following year it was driven on shore near 'Dunleary' in a violent gale of wind. It would appear that this was not the original light since the committee stated that the 'old floating light' had been fitted up as a replacement. In subsequent reports it was reported that the damage to the vessel was such that she was incapable of being used again and it was proposed to build a new one. The new vessel was completed and placed in position in the summer of 1744.

In September 1747 the City Assembly, acting on representations from ship owners, ship masters and traders, petitioned the king for the setting up of a Pilot Office at the port of Dublin for the purpose of authorising 'honest and skilful pilots'. Previous petitions with the like purpose had been unsuccessful and the establishment of an appropriate authority to regulate pilots was not in fact achieved for some years.

Following the completion of piling across the Cock Lake in 1731–2, the committee's subsequent reports were concerned mainly with (a) descriptions of repairs and replacements to the piling and framework due mainly to storm damage and also to damage from vessels being driven upon them, (b) cleansing and dredging the river channel and repairing the gabbards and floats, and (c) the regular statement of income and expenditure which reflected a slow but steady increase in trade in the port.

In April 1748, the committee made a recommendation of major significance by proposing the erection of a double wall from what was known as the Green Patch near the site of what is now Pidgeon House Harbour, to Ringsend as a solution to the perennial expense of repairing and replacing the timber piles. The assembly approved of the proposal that a contract be placed with Benjamin Pemberton for the work at '9 pence per perch'. Reports in the two years following indicated satisfactory progress with the new works and their ability to withstand storm damage. However, in January 1751 the committee reported that it could not proceed with the new walls unless at least £1,500 could be borrowed for the purpose and the assembly agreed to support this. The space between the double wall was filled in, and a roadway made on this filled area became the Pidgeon House Road.

It is curious that one of the primary purposes of the Ballast Office Committee relating to the control of ballasting of ships seldom featured in the committee's reports to the assembly. One report, made in October 1751, referred to a memorial received from masters and owners of vessels, complaining of delays in receiving ballast due to the lack of gabbards (lighters) in use. As a result, three extra gabbards of fifty to sixty tons each were ordered to be built.

Severe storms in the winter of 1752 caused serious damage to the eastern end of the piles although the remainder were only slightly damaged and the new wall escaped intact.

In 1753, the city petitioned parliament for money to complete the rebuilding of Essex Bridge and the new double wall at Ringsend, and in the following year an act was passed granting £10,000 for the bridge and £10,000 for what had come to be described as the 'Ballast Office Wall'. Two years later a further petition was submitted in respect of both projects; in the case of the wall, it was stated that it was to be continued eastwards to the seaward end of the piles. This is the first indication that the piling on the South Bull, as distinct from the western section near Ringsend, was to be replaced by a wall. The money was forthcoming and in the period 1756–9 several further requests for more funds were approved by parliament, but not with any great enthusiasm.

In October 1759, the committee reported that 'the new walls are now finished on both sides and nothing remains to be done but the return to Ringsend'. The term 'new walls' is somewhat ambiguous but it can refer only to the double wall from the piles westward to Ringsend; that portion of the wall subsequently constructed on the South Bull was not completed until 1790. The reference to the 'return' to Ringsend presumably refers to a continuation of the wall in a southerly direction from its western extremity to Ringsend village.

In March 1760 the assembly became aware of a proposed bill to be laid before parliament for the 'securing [of] ships coming into or going out of the Port of Dublin and for the more convenient ordering [of] their anchorage within the said harbour and of the quays of the said City'. The assembly complained to the government that they had been constituted and ordained keepers and conservators of the Port of Dublin and that they had carried out their duties 'with the utmost attention and care to the advantage of this Kingdom in general and this City in particular'. The assembly considered that the proposed bill would affect their rights and deprive them of the franchises enjoyed under a statute of Queen Elizabeth and one of Queen Anne (1707). Accordingly the assembly sought to be heard by the Privy Council 'against the heads of the Bill', and presumably their representations were successful since nothing further was heard of the proposed legislation.

In July 1760 the committee received £1,940 as an instalment of the £5,000 granted by parliament earlier in the year. By July 1761 the balance of the £5,000 had been received but the Committee judged it insufficient to continue the works in hands which included preparations for beginning a foundation for 'an abutment to the east wall'. This was in effect a new wall commencing at the eastern or seaward end of the piles and joining up with the double wall connecting with Ringsend. In October 1761 the committee recommended the framing of a new by-law vesting in the city sufficient powers for the 'better securing [of] ships coming into and going out of the Port of Dublin and for the more convenient ordering [of] their anchorage within the harbour or at the quays of the said City'. Presumably this proposal was intended to anticipate any moves to resurrect the 1760 bill. In December of the same year the assembly were concerned about a petition before the House of Commons for the building of a new bridge over the Liffey eastwards of Essex Bridge. The assembly considered that such a bridge would greatly prejudice the trade of the city by 'interrupting of ships when coming between the walls, that part of the river being full, narrow and scanty for the lying of trading ships and will also be a detriment to the revenue of this City'.

In June 1762 the committee reported progress on the foundation of

John Beresford (1738–1805). Beresford was the prime mover in the replacement of the old Custom House at Essex Bridge (*below*) by the present Custom House.

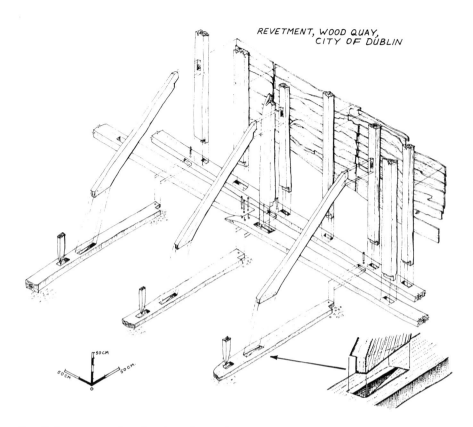

Detailed reconstruction drawing of a medieval revetment at Wood Quay.

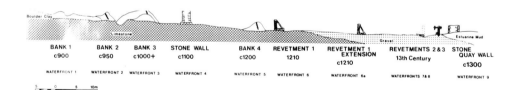

Boulder Clay

Limestone

Gravel

Estuarine Mud

BANK 1	BANK 2	BANK 3	STONE WALL	BANK 4	REVETMENT 1	REVETMENT 1 EXTENSION	REVETMENTS 2 & 3	STONE QUAY WALL
c900	c950	c1000+	c1100	c1200	1210	c1210	13th Century	c1300
WATERFRONT 1	WATERFRONT 2	WATERFRONT 3	WATERFRONT 4	WATERFRONT 5	WATERFRONT 6	WATERFRONT 6a	WATERFRONTS 7 & 8	WATERFRONT 9

5 0 5 10m

Late eighteenth-century river scene showing (*left*) the Hibernian Marine School and (*extreme left*) Cardiff's Shipyard. The foreshore, exposed at low water, can be clearly seen.

The Poolbeg Lighthouse as originally constructed with a gallery, later removed, and the Great South Wall.

Royal Exchange Dublin 9th May 1786
At a Meeting of the Corporation for preserving and
improving the Port of Dublin

Present

The Right Hon. Sir John Parnell Bt.   Robert Black Esqr
The Right Hon. Lord Visct. Ranelagh   Robert Lloyd Esqr
Aldn. Hamilton   John Carleton Esqr
Joseph Wilson Esqr   Sheriff Trevor
Joseph Sandwith Esqr   John Hendrick Esqr
Arthur Bryan Esqr   Aldn. Sutton
Aldn. Howison   Aldn. Alexander
Isaac Weld Esqr

The Right Hon.ble Lord Viscount Ranelagh, The Right
Hon.ble Sir John Parnell Bart, George Sutton, Robert
Black, Arthur Bryan, Isaac Weld, John Hendrick,
Joseph Wilson, John Carleton, & Robert Lloyd Esqrs,
Aldn. James Hamilton, Aldn. Wm. Alexander, Aldn. Henry
Howison & Sheriff Trevor, severally took the Oath, and
Joseph Sandwith Esqr took the Affirmation appointed
to be taken by the Act of Parliament constituting this
Corporation.

Resolved That the House in Essex Street, heretofore called
the Ballast Office, be constituted and appointed the
Ballast Office of the Port of Dublin
                    Adjourned until to morrow at
                    one o Clock to meet at the
                    Ballast Office

Reproduction of the minutes of the first meeting of the Corporation for Preserving and
Improving the Port of Dublin (Ballast Board).

S. F. Brocas' early nineteenth-century view of Carlisle (later O'Connell) Bridge, showing the Ballast Office, Westmoreland St, on the right and Carlisle Buildings on the left.

The seals of the Corporation for Preserving and Improving the port of Dublin and of
the Dublin Port and Docks Board which succeeded it as the statutory authority for the
port in 1867.

Shipping at Eden Quay and George's Quay, c.1843. The photograph is attributed to the Rev. Calvert Jones and is believed to be the earliest photograph of the port of Dublin.

View looking west along Eden Quay showing the new Butt Bridge, c.1880.

Shipping at Burgh Quay and Eden Quay with Carlisle Bridge and Bachelors Walk in the foreground, c.1870.

The early nineteenth-century Dublin Bay lifeboats are believed to have been similar to the *Zetland* lifeboat (*above*) which was in service at Redcar, Yorkshire from 1800 to 1880.

James Gandon (1743–1823), the architect of the Custom House.

the east abutment of the proposed wall on the South Bull from the seaward end of the piles to the wall already built between the Green Patch and Ringsend. They indicated that the foundation of the east abutment might also serve as a foundation for a lighthouse if it should be thought proper to build one at a later stage. The reason for commencing this portion of the wall at its seaward end and then working westwards, instead of picking up where the double wall from Ringsend had finished, was in order that the foundations for the proposed lighthouse could be completed. Work on the lighthouse itself could then proceed as soon as a firm decision should be taken. In addition, this method would afford protection to work on the wall itself as it proceeded westwards.

In December 1763 the assembly became aware of a petition to parliament to vest powers in certain gentlemen to establish a body for the regulation of pilots, haven masters and lighter men at the port. It was conceived that this could affect the rights of the City. The assembly directed the Ballast Committee to meet with the gentlemen referred to and report back. As a result of that meeting it was proposed that instead of creating a new body the proposed powers be vested in the Corporation of the City. These powers included the appointment and removal of pilots, lighter men and haven masters; the powers to be exercised at the nomination and recommendation of a committee to be appointed trienially. The assembly petitioned parliament for the purpose. At a subsequent meeting an amendment to the proposed scheme was suggested whereby the powers proposed to be vested in the city should be delegated to a committee of thirty-three consisting of the Lord Mayor, sheriffs, five aldermen, ten common council men to be elected by the sheriffs and Commons, and fifteen persons to be elected by the freemen of the Guild of Merchants. The assembly directed that an application be made to parliament for the purposes outlined.

In May 1764 the assembly noted that the petition for an Act of Parliament in respect of pilotage at the Port of Dublin had been successful and that the powers sought in the petition were now vested in the Lord Mayor, sheriffs, Commons, etc. In January 1766 a new Committee of Directors of the Ballast Office was elected and, in its first report to the assembly, stated that since their appointment they had made all progress in their power 'in raising the new lighthouse' but were obliged to discontinue the wall on account of the small sum granted by parliament in that session. This is the first indiction that the lighthouse itself was under construction, as distinct from the previous references to foundations and the abutment on which it was built.

In September 1766 the committee reported further progress on the new lighthouse and stated that two new wharves had been ordered to be built 'at the end of the wall near the block house', one at each side, for the more convenient landing of goods. This is a slightly ambiguous report but almost certainly it refers to the eastern end of the double wall (now Pidgeon House Road) from Ringsend to the Green Patch where the harbour known as the Pidgeon House Harbour was later constructed. Rocque's map of 1756, based on his survey in previous years, shows the double wall from Ringsend to the present site of the Pidgeon House and the line of the piles running eastwards from that point. The map gives no indication of any part of the new wall on the South Bull or of the construction of the lighthouse. In this report we find also the first reference to a 'Block House', later to be known as the Pidgeon House.

In June 1767 the committee reported that it expected that the new lighthouse would shortly be finished and that they had advertised 'in the London, Dublin and Amsterdam Gazettes' that there would be a light thereon on 29 September following, and that the old floating light would be discontinued. On that evening, Rogerson's Quay was crowded with people to see the first light shine out from the first lighthouse in the port using candles within a huge lantern; prior to that, lighthouses were in the main coal-fired beacons. The same Ballast Committee report records details of the expenditure (£2,193) on the South Wall and the lighthouse from July 1766 to October 1767, in which the main item of interest is the reference to one year's salary, £200, paid to 'the Architect'. There was also the by now inevitable request for further parliamentary aid to carry on the Ballast Office Wall. As a result of a further petition to parliament, a further £5,000 was granted for the walls. In October 1768 the City Assembly decided to make a presentation to John Smyth, the Architect, in recognition of 'his great ingenuity in planning and his indefatigable zeal and assiduity in carrying into execution that masterly work of the lighthouse so justly and universally admired'. Smyth was presented with a piece of plate to the value of twenty guineas.

In its report to the assembly in April 1769, the Ballast Committee referred to the heavy expenses of building and repairing the gabbards, and had decided to invite proposals from persons willing to build and maintain for twelve years such gabbards as might be necessary. The assembly approved the borrowing of £2,000 to enable work to proceed but called for a report on the general financial situation of the Ballast Office, including details of employees, overseers and pensioners. However, the committee does not appear to have been in any hurry to furnish the information required since no reference is made to it in the records of subsequent meetings of the assembly.

In July 1770 the Ballast Committee reported that they had entered into a contract to build a further fifty feet of the new South wall and requested permission to borrow £1,000. The assembly approved the request but added a slight rap on the knuckles in a stricture that the committee should not in future engage in contracts where money was not already available without prior permission. A further cautionary note was sounded by the City Assembly in January 1772, in connection with a proposal that the Committee of Directors of the Ballast Office should view the progress of the works, when it was ordered that 'no greater sum than the sum of £10 be expended by the foregoing Committee on viewing the works of the Ballast Office'. No doubt, the weather in January was not sufficiently conducive to members to view the works, presumably by boat, without some refreshment to keep the cold out.

In July 1772 the committee stated that a number of labourers had been employed clearing the river between the walls to facilitate navigation to the Custom House Quay. Presumably this referred to the cleaning of the river bed wherever it was exposed at low water in the upper reaches of the harbour.

In October 1774 the pilot committee reported that since their last report three years earlier buoys on banks near the entrance to the harbour had been driven from their moorings, believed to be due to defects in the chains by which they were moored. Favourable reports had been received of buoys fixed on banks at Liverpool and accordingly one of these buoys and chains had been acquired. This buoy together with another made locally had been moored at the Kish bank, one at each end. Notwithstanding the title of the committee, its reports hitherto appeared to deal almost exclusively with the placing of buoys and other navigation marks by haven masters.

In July 1775 the first indications of industrial disputes at the port appeared in a report that the gabbard men employed by the Ballast Office had entered into a 'combination not to work without an advance of price, by which the Committee were distressed for a few days to serve the shipping with ballast'. However, presumably by the exercise of a combination of stick and carrot, the men returned to their work at the existing rates.

By October 1775, 308 tons of stones had been quarried from the river near the Custom House. The channel had thus been considerably deepened, resulting in a safer passage to the Custom House near Essex Bridge.

In December 1775 the first hint of a proposal to erect a new Custom House further down the river was given to the assembly by members of the Commons with a request that a petition against the proposal be presented to the Lord Lieutenant.

The quarterly reports of the Ballast Office Committee in this period make references to timber work around the foundation of the lighthouse being partly decayed and being replaced with cut mountain stone fastened with cast iron. The reports also continued to refer to the removal of shoals and stones in the river near the Custom House.

In November 1776 the pilot committee recommended to the assembly that pilot licences should be granted to eighteen named persons. The list is interesting insofar as it contains names which recur in the lists of pilots and port employees in the following two centuries.

In April 1777 the committee reported to the assembly that the channel in the harbour had shifted and the committee had ordered perches to be removed so as to facilitate the navigation of ships in the harbour. Clearly the erection of the piles and the subsequent construction of the South Wall was having an effect.

An indication of the growth of the city eastwards appears in March 1778 in which the assembly noted a bill before parliament which included a clause 'for establishing one or more ferry boats for carriages and for other purposes over the River Anna Liffey opposite to or near the Marine nursery . . . and also for erecting one or more bridge or bridges over the said river'. The assembly ordered that a petition be prepared to the privy council to oppose the bill on the grounds of the city's right to control ferries under a grant of Charles II and on the grounds that the proposal would 'represent the ruinous consequences to the trade of this Metropolis'. The erection of Essex Bridge and the development of the streets leading to it, in particular Capel Street, meant that any move to transfer the city centre eastwards would be resisted by those who had invested in property or owned businesses in the area. Similar reasons lay behind the opposition of the proposal to build a new Custom House and indeed all subsequent proposals for bridges down river have met with opposition of one kind or another and for varying reasons. The proposal for the new ferry appears to have been amicably resolved since in March 1778 it is noted that all the ferries from Essex Bridge to Ringsend had been leased to John Jones.

The Marine nursery was established by charter in 1766 as a school for boys which was intended to promote recruitment to the Navy. It was first sited in Ringsend but in 1768 a site at Sir John Rogerson's Quay was acquired and a new school opened in 1773. Thereafter it was known as the Marine School.

In April 1780 the Ballast Committee recommended that the assembly apply to parliament for power to impose an additional duty of one penny per ton on all ships resorting to the harbour of Dublin and twopence per ton for all ballast delivered to shipping, the revenue to be applied to the building of the Ballast Office Wall.

The pilot committee appears to have reported annually every October up to 1777, but in 1780 it noted that since its former report of October 1777 there had been no loss of buoys and that there was a balance in hands of over £43. The committee went on to assure the assembly that the whole income of the office was expended 'in the most frugal manner, solely for the purposes of the Act, not one shilling thereof having been lavished in either eating or drinking'. The Corporation, having been saddled with the expenditure involved in promoting the act concerned, was less than pleased with the fact that 'so economical a body as the pilot committee in the course of so many years since the commencement of the Pilot Act (without eating or drinking) had reserved no greater balance than £43 . . . so as to have enabled them to discharge a large debt incurred and due to the city for the passing of the said Act'. The assembly ordered that the pilot committee furnish an account of the receipts and disbursements for the preceding three years and ordered that for the future the pilot committee 'do apply the redundancy of their office in discharge of the said debt'.

4

The Ballast Office Committee and the Wide Streets Commissioners

THE report of the Ballast Office Committee to the assembly in January 1782 was of major significance. It stated that the House of Commons had ordered information to be laid before it regarding the finances of the Ballast Office, its revenue over the previous twenty years, a list of officers and their allowances, an account of the money expended in carrying on the South Wall and an estimate of the cost of completing the work. Clearly the government was becoming tired of the continual requests for money to carry on the wall with no apparent end to the expense, and they were unhappy with the way in which the grants were being managed. The order from the House of Commons is interesting in another respect inasmuch as it contains the first official reference to 'Pidgeon's House', the history of which will be dealt with later in this work.

In March 1782 the assembly noted that two bills which had lately been passed in the Irish House of Commons were likely to be transmitted to London 'in order to their being passed into laws'. In the view of the assembly, provisions in the bills materially attacked the chartered rights of the city; in particular a clause in one bill for the purpose of 'altering the Ballast Office Committee'. It is not difficult to see the connection between this proposal and the earlier request from the government for details of the Ballast Office revenues and expenditures. At any rate, the assembly decided to oppose the bills.

In October 1783 the committee reported that, following receipt from the assembly of a copy of an order of the Lord Lieutenant dated 19 September 1783 in terms similar to those of the House of Commons Order of January 1782, the Ballast Master attended a meeting of the Ballast Committee and laid before them the books and papers required; he was examined concerning the accounts, the manner of building the new wall and the manner of conducting the several branches of the Ballast Office works. Presumably the reason for the order of the Lord Lieutenant dated September 1783 was the delay on the part of the Ballast Committee in complying with the order of the House of

Commons of January 1782. The Ballast Office Committee was not the only organisation to come under government scrutiny where the application of their revenues and government grants was concerned. In 1784 an act was passed providing for the due accounting for all money granted for public works, charities and hospitals and other organisations including the City Assembly insofar as it was responsible for public monies granted for the purpose of the improvement works at the port. The Commissioners of Imprest Accounts were authorised by the act to carry out the inquiries and the Ballast Office Committee reported to the assembly in October 1784 that the commissioners had required an account to be given them of all the revenues of the office since its establishment and its expenditure and also the expenditure of all the parliamentary grants from 1752 to 1781, totalling over £57,000. The committee submitted the information requested to the assembly for transmission to the commissioners under the city seal. The committee pointed out, however, that the pilot committee was responsible for their own account.

In January 1785 the city assembly, undeterred by the deep interest being taken by the government in the finances of the Ballast Committee, petitioned the House of Commons for further aid towards the completion of the South Wall. The petition pointed out that the Corporation, as Conservators of the Port and Harbour, had built a wall of rough mason work 'from Ringsend to the place called the Blockhouse [i.e., Pidgeon House] which has been completed'. The petition proceeded to remind the House of Commons that under and by direction of parliament a lighthouse had been built and a wall commenced from the lighthouse westwards, of which 1,440 feet had been completed; all of the completed works had from time to time been approved of by the House of Commons. The petition pointed out that the government grants were not for a local convenience but as a public work for improving the port and harbour 'in which foreigners as well as the natives of this Kingdom are materially interested'. The petition pointed out that recent grants approved of by parliament had not been received and consequently 'this great national work has been impeded'; as a result, a debt of £4,050 had been contracted for the sole purpose of carrying on the works; but if a sum of £3,500 were granted it would enable the work to proceed and to be completed within a few years.

The reasons for the government inquiry into the finances of the Ballast Committee became apparent in March 1785 when the assembly was notified of another bill being promoted by certain 'Dublin merchants' in regard to the harbour. The assembly ordered that a petition against the bill be presented to the House of Commons.

In April 1785 the committee reported that, as its books were still with the Commissioners of Imprest Accounts, the usual financial abstract could not be submitted. In July 1785 there was another strike by gabbard men but work resumed when it became known that the Ballast Committee were prepared to employ others to carry out the work. No financial abstract was submitted as the books were still with the Commissioners of Imprest Accounts.

The year 1786 was an important one for the port and harbour of Dublin but its significance was not obvious to the Ballast Committee when reporting to the assembly in January regarding contracts which they had entered into for one year for the repair of gabbards and regarding further contracts proposed to be entered into for building gabbards. Dredging had been carried out 'on the bar of the Dodder in order to deepen it', 1,621 tons of ballast having been raised in two weeks in the previous month. The works were the subject of what would appear to have been the first 'notice to mariners' in relation to the Port of Dublin, by the publication of an advertisement 'cautioning all mariners and pilots not to attempt to pass it without a sufficiency of water until further notice'. The committee also noted that the Commissioners of Imprest Accounts had forwarded statements of the Ballast Office accounts and of parliamentary grants for twenty-one years up to 1784. The statements showed that the Ballast Office was 'indebted to the public in a sum of £17,843 0s $1\frac{1}{4}$d, including £386 0s $3\frac{1}{2}$d due by the pilot office'. The report accompanying the statement was sent back to the Ballast Office Committee for their comments. Among the items disallowed by the commissioners were interest on money borrowed £5,937; entertainments of the Lord Mayor and committee £566; pensions and charities £1,599; petitions to parliament £89; abstracts of accounts furnished to parliament etc. £222; gratuities £338; and payments, no purpose mentioned, £56; salaries of officers appointed without the approval of government £4,361. On the credit side the commissioners allowed a sum of £6,437 expended on the Ballast Office wall in excess of that granted by parliament.

In their next report in April 1786, the committee stated that they had contracted with Hugh Murphy, shipwright, to build a gabbard for £440 and to repair old gabbards; in addition, the committee had let to Mr Murphy the yard belonging to the office on Rogerson's Quay. Although Murphy is a fairly common name, it is likely that this yard was the predecessor of the famous Murphy's Boatyard at Ringsend which was established there in the nineteenth century but which was taken over by Dublin Corporation together with adjoining premises in the 1950s as a site for the building of new Corporation flats at Thorncastle Street. To return to the committee, their report proceeded to dismiss rather perfunctorily the statements of the Commissioners of Imprest Accounts. However, the last paragraph of the report is the first indication in the records of the Corporation that the bill promoted by the 'city merchants' and others had been successfully enacted and it is worth quoting in full:

> We presume the Act which has passed both Houses of Parliament will in a few days receive the Royal Assent, by which the management of this office, after being for seventy-eight years under the direction of the Corporation of this City, is vested in a new corporation appointed by the said Act, together with all money, effects, etc., belonging to this office.

The bill had in fact been promoted by John Beresford, no doubt with the assistance of some of the 'city merchants'.

Although the passage of the act through parliament was a subject of public discussion for some time prior to April 1786 it had not previously been referred to in the City Rolls and indeed the order of the assembly on the last report of the Ballast Committee made no comment on the new act nor, indeed, did it make any acknowledgment of the work of the Ballast Office during its seventy-eight years existence. The order was merely 'Report confirmed and made an act of Assembly'. That the assembly was fully aware of the impending transfer of responsibility for the harbour from the Ballast Office is clear in an order of the assembly dated March 1786 in which Alderman Warren, a member of the House of Commons, was requested to move a clause in a bill before parliament 'for the better collecting the public money' to exonerate the city of Dublin from all debts then due by the Ballast Office.

The significance of John Beresford and the Wide Streets Commissioners in the development of the port of Dublin is such that some digression is essential at this point. John Beresford was the fifth son of Marcus Beresford, later Lord Tyrone, who commissioned one of the many great town houses built in Dublin in the eighteenth century. This was Tyrone House in Marlborough Street, which in 1852 became the headquarters of the Board of Education; later, a replica building was erected adjacent to Tyrone House and the two buildings now house staff of the Department of Education. Following the rising of 1798, Tyrone House was the scene of reprisals against captured rebels, involving horrific tortures before they were killed and their bodies exhibited in the Castle Yard.

John Beresford's political and commercial acumen, allied to the powerful influence of his family connections, enabled him to be returned as a member of parliament for Waterford County in both the Irish and English parliaments, and to be appointed a member of both the Irish and English privy councils, and Chief Commissioner of the Revenue in Ireland.

Beresford's first wife died in 1772 and two years later he married for the second time; his second wife, Barbara, was a daughter of Sir William Montgomery whose family had the doubtful privilege of having their name bestowed on a street which later became part of Dublin's red light district, better known perhaps in popular usage as the 'Monto'. Many years later, the street was re-named Foley Street in honour of the sculptor who was born there. One of Barbara's sisters, Elizabeth, married Luke Gardiner, later Lord Mountjoy, and another sister married Viscount Townshend, later Lord Lieutenant. The benefits flowing to Beresford from these relationships were, as may be imagined, considerable.

In 1780 Beresford was appointed Chief Commissioner of the Revenue and later in the same year Lord Carlisle was sworn in as Lord Lieutenant. Carlisle's Chief Secretary was William Eden who became a close friend of Beresford, thus extending the latter's range of influence and facilitating him in bringing about improvements in the thoroughfares, bridges and buildings of the city; Eden requested that in return some thoroughfare should be named after him—hence Eden Quay.

Beresford's concern for the correction of abuses in the management of customs and the improvements he effected in this sector were of considerable assistance to him with the government in his campaign for the building of a new Custom House. While the building is usually described as the masterpiece of its architect, James Gandon, the achievement of Beresford in bringing the project about is not as well known. It was with some difficulty that Beresford persuaded Gandon in 1780 to undertake the design of the new building. We have already seen that the project aroused the opposition of city merchants, through the medium of the City Assembly. When the foundation trenches for the building were opened in 1781, they became a target for a rabble organised by merchants opposed to the project, particularly those with property interests in the older areas of the city and Gandon himself was the recipient of many threats. Notwithstanding later attacks on the works, opposition gradually died out and the new Custom House was completed within ten years, opening for business in November 1791. Beresford had resided in Dominick Street but he had apartments provided for himself in the new Custom House and the large room over the North portico (later used for the hearing of planning appeals in the 1970s) became known as 'Beresford's Ballroom'.

In the meantime, however, Beresford had become less prominent in political matters due to the fluctuating fortunes of successive governments but with the advent of William Pitt the younger as Prime Minister in 1784 Beresford emerged again as a political force, becoming adviser on Irish matters both in Dublin Castle and in Downing Street; in 1786 he was appointed to the Privy Council in London. However, the appointment of Lord Fitzwilliam as Lord Lieutenant in December 1794 was a new check to Beresford's influence. Although the government had adopted a more conciliatory policy towards Catholics, Fitzwilliam appears to have overstepped his instructions in this regard and he came into conflict with Beresford and his circle. Within a matter of months, Fitzwilliam had dismissed Beresford from his position as Chief Commissioner of the Revenue. Beresford appealed to London and as he was too influential to be ignored, particularly in Irish matters, Fitzwilliam received a formal rebuke and was obliged to resign. In July 1795, Beresford was reappointed to his former office and also to the Privy Council. Fitzwilliam's appointment had been a popular one and his departure from Dublin resulted in vicious riots. The resultant ill feeling towards the government pushed Ireland a little closer to the rebellion which followed in 1798. Early in that year Beresford, in a letter to the government in London on conditions in Ireland, stated that the seeds of rebellion were sown far and wide.

After the crushing of the rebels, the long debated proposal for a legislative union between Britain and Ireland was revived. Pitt saw the Union as a stabilising and protective influence. Beresford supported his proposals as a remedy for what he called 'continuing Irish problems'. The Act of Union came into operation on January 1801 and shortly afterwards Beresford, then aged 63, requested to be relieved of his official duties as Chief Commissioner of the Revenue for health reasons. However, he moved to London and continued as a Member of Parliament until his death in 1805. His personal influence as First Commissioner of Revenue during the years from 1780 to 1802 enabled him to promote many great undertakings in Dublin even though these were, directly or indirectly, to his own advantage financially and otherwise. But even his most bitter critics admitted that the city owed a great deal to him.

The main link between the north and south sides of the city was Essex Bridge, giving access from the south side to Capel Street and thence to the main road to the north via Drumcondra Lane, now Dorset Street. On the south side Dublin Castle was situated close to Essex Bridge although with only indirect access via Crane Lane or the lane now known as Upper Exchange Street and described in a 1757 map as 'The Blind Quay'; buildings in Dame Street and in Essex Street then interposed, crossing the site of present-day Parliament Street. In close proximity was Christchurch Cathedral and the adjoining Law Courts, the Tholsel (containing the city corporation's offices and meeting place and the old Royal Exchange) and the Smock Alley Theatre. The convenient situation of these buildings to the main trading centre, Capel

Street, did not dispose those who had business and other interests in the area to look favourably on various proposals to transfer the focus of business life further down river by the erection of a new Custom House and the construction of a new bridge. Divergent views were reflected in the activities of those property owners such as the Gardiner and Eccles estates on the north side and the Fitzwilliams on the south side. The building in the 1740s for the Duke of Leinster of the edifice in which the two Houses of the Oireachtas now sit set the seal of noble approval on that area of the city and society was not slow to follow. In addition, the existence down river of the Houses of Parliament, Trinity College, and other less formal assembly places such as the Rotunda Assembly Rooms and Gardens lent weight to the growing demand for a new bridge east of Essex Bridge and, as a consequence, for a new Custom House.

The additional traffic which the development of the city had propagated resulted in traffic congestion on Essex Bridge and in 1749 a parliamentary committee was set up to examine and report on the problem. As the committee consisted of only two persons, both with links to the estates which favoured the down-river developments, it is not surprising that their report stated that the congestion was due to the lack of a bridge further down river. The problem of congestion was met by the temporary expedient of repairing and widening Essex Bridge, but the campaign for a new bridge and Custom House continued for many years.

In 1757, a commission was set up by statute to produce proposals for a new thoroughfare leading from Essex Bridge to the Castle and also for 'widening or rendering more convenient any other of the ways, streets or passages of the city'. The commissioners were in almost every case holders of high office and, with the exception of the Lord Mayor, all were members of parliament. They included John Ponsonby, speaker of the House of Commons, and Philip Tisdall, Solicitor-General and later Attorney-General; these were two of the most powerful and influential men in the city at that time and both were sympathetic to interests such as the Ellis estate which had large tracts of land on the north side of the river, west of Essex Bridge. Ponsonby and Tisdall used their influence to frustrate successive attempts to promote bills in parliament to authorise the building of the proposed new bridge and Custom House.

Following the completion of the new street (now Parliament Street) leading from Essex Bridge to the Castle, it was decided to build a new Royal Exchange in front of the Castle so as to terminate the view from Capel Street, thus replacing an earlier proposal to have a square in front of the Castle. The new Exchange was completed in 1779, and in 1852 it became the present City Hall. This edifice and the Four Courts on Inns Quay could be regarded as the last major achievements of those who were opposed to the proposed developments down river.

Winds of change followed the appointment of Viscount Townshend as Lord Lieutenant. He had strong objections to the influence and power exercised by the conservative elements. He dismissed Ponsonby from his post of Chief Revenue Commissioner and later he appointed John Beresford and Luke Gardiner to the Wide Streets Commission. Although the dilapidated condition of the old Custom House lent added force to Beresford's case for a new one, it was not until 1780 that he achieved his objective; by that time he had become Chief Revenue Commissioner and indeed the foundation stone of the new Custom House was laid not, as might be expected, by the Lord Lieutenant but by Beresford himself and by all accounts with little formality or publicity. The Custom House was opened in 1791 and in the same year the foundation stone of the new bridge (Carlisle—now O'Connell Bridge) was laid by (who else?) Beresford.

A clue to the change in attitude of some of Beresford's opponents may be found in an agreement whereby the Ellis Estate agreed to drop its opposition to the new developments in consideration of an undertaking whereby the new Law Courts (now the Four Courts) would be built on Inns Quay with obvious consequent benefit to the estate concerned. The foundation stone for the new courts was duly laid at Inns Quay in 1786.

Although the Wide Streets Commissioners were the agents of the changed aspect of the city in pre-Union days, the real battles were fought out in parliament, in the Revenue Board and in the Castle. The Commissioners have been described as an efficient machine for co-ordinating different schemes for the benefit of the Gardiner Estate. However, it has also been said that the political power of the Commissioners, such as it may have been, was combined with cultural enlightenment in regard to the planning and architecture of the city, from which the city was the beneficiary. The evidence is apparent in the enlargement of Drogheda Street (later Upper Sackville Street) to what we know as present-day O'Connell Street, Upper and Lower, the linking of Sackville Street to the 'road to the north' by the construction of North Frederick Street, the long-awaited bridge (opened in 1794) completing the new north/south axis, the building of two new thoroughfares leading from the new bridge to the Houses of Parliament (Westmoreland Street) and to Townsend Street and the south-east (D'Olier Street) the widening of Dame Street and George's Street, and the opening of the quays to provide continuous thoroughfares on both sides of the river by acquiring and demolishing buildings situated on the river bank. An interesting sidelight on this last feature is contained in a memorial by coal merchants and collier captains to the port authority in 1801. The memorialists drew attention to the want of berths for ships between a point opposite present-day Marlborough Street, where it joins Eden Quay, and the Custom House, and between present-day Hawkins Street, where it joins Burgh Quay, and George's Quay. The port authority forwarded the memorial to the Wide Streets Commissioners who decided to proceed with the quays and berths at Eden Quay as requested but progress on the south side had to be deferred for lack of funds. One of the earliest photographs of the port taken about 1860 shows colliers discharging at berths at Eden Quay, just west of the Custom House, before the building of the original Butt Bridge (1878) or the railway bridge (1891).

It is against this background, remote from the port of Dublin as it may first appear, that Beresford's promotion of the bill in 1786 to amend the law in relation to Dublin port must be considered and here we return to the contemporary account of his promotion of that bill, the main thrust of which was the establishment of a new port authority, independent of Dublin Corporation.

In his history of the Dublin Chamber of Commerce, *Princes and Paupers*, Louis Cullen states that trade, manufacture, and parliament were the factors which in combination made Dublin an exceptionally fast growing city and turned it in the course of a century into one of the ten most populous in Europe; London had a similar combination of factors. The circumstances outlined by Professor Cullen emphasise the need which existed in 1786 for a new, energetic and business-like port authority.

The Corporation for Preserving and Improving the Port of Dublin

IN introducing his bill in the House of Commons, College Green, on 1 February 1786, Beresford accused the Ballast Office Committee of serious misconduct in their transaction of the affairs of the port and he quoted the findings of the Commissioners of Imprest Accounts, in particular their reference to a total of £17,000 employed for, among other purposes, entertaining the Lord Mayor. Although the City Corporation were aware of the bill it does not appear that they made any direct objection to parliament and the stages of the bill proceeded. In the course of debate, a curious divergence of interests emerged as between Beresford and his friend Luke Gardiner who had property adjoining the quay walls; the walls were vulnerable to damage from shipping and Gardiner considered that the proposed new port authority should be responsible for repairs to all the quay walls, instead of a section thereof as proposed by Beresford; this section would not have included the wall referred to by Gardiner whose protestations were, however, to no avail. The hand of Beresford in the drafting of the bill is most evident in his proposal for the appointment and naming in the bill of the new commissioners for the port and in a provision for filling vacancies by co-option which was to create virtually a closed shop. It seems likely that approaches were made to Beresford behind the scenes: the Lord Mayor, sheriffs and three of the aldermen were named as commissioners, thus securing representation for the City Corporation. It comes as no surprise to find Beresford himself named in the bill as one of the new commissioners 'for the future direction of the ballast and pilot offices'.

The act named the members of the new board and provided that they 'be and are hereby appointed one body corporate and politick for carrying into execution the purposes of this Act and as such shall have perpetual succession . . . and shall be known by the name of "The Corporation for Preserving and Improving the Port of Dublin".' This title was too cumbersome and confusing for the general public and the new authority was usually known as the Ballast Board.

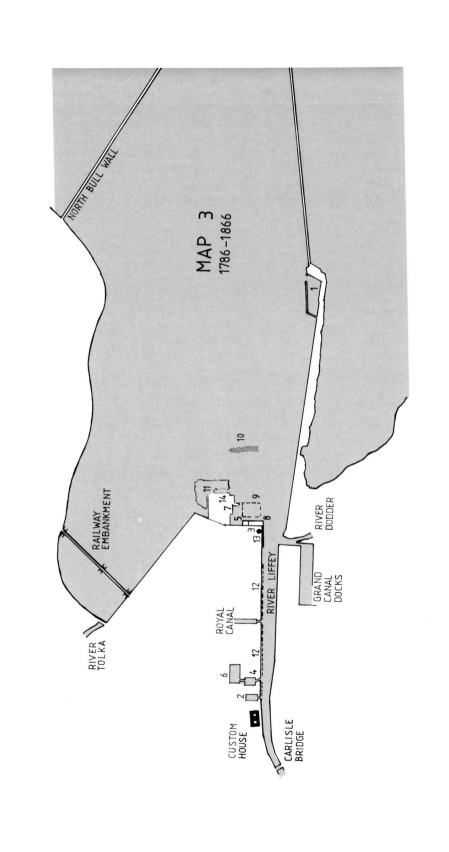

MAP 3
1786–1866

NORTH BULL WALL

RAILWAY
EMBANKMENT

RIVER
TOLKA

RIVER DODDER

RIVER LIFFEY

GRAND
CANAL
DOCKS

ROYAL
CANAL

CUSTOM
HOUSE

CARLISLE
BRIDGE

1

2

3

4

5

6

7

8

9

10

11

12

12

13

14

The provision for perpetual succession was significant, indicating the determination of the promoters to retain control of the new body and indeed the act goes on to provide that vacancies created by the death, resignation or refusal to act of any of the members would be filled by election of suitable persons by the remaining members. Although the Lord Mayor's membership was ex-officio, as was that of the two city sheriffs, a vacancy caused by the death or resignation of an alderman was required to be filled by the Municipal Corporation but clearly six Corporation representatives could not hope to outweigh the combined voting power of the other seventeen members.

Many of the provisions of the act were in effect a re-enactment of previous statutory provisions under which the Ballast Office Committee operated and others were such as might be expected on a rationalisation of the arrangements for the maintenance and improvement of the harbour. For example, existing officers and employees continued in office or employment; revenues of the new authority were to be applied in the first place towards the payment of salaries and necessary expenses and the residue to be applied in improving and cleaning (i.e., dredging) the harbour, keeping the river walls in repair and in carrying on the new South Wall. The new board had power to borrow money and issue debentures and all such transactions were subject to annual inspection by the Commissioners of Imprest Accounts. The act included clauses for governing the licensing and appointment of pilots and of a pilot master to supervise their conduct, and also of haven masters whose duty it would be to regulate and station all vessels in the harbour and to see that buoys and floating perches should be maintained at the sandbanks of the approach to the port.

The act recognised the harbour of Dunleary as being within the port of Dublin and the board was empowered to carry out improvements and to raise and supply ballast to vessels there, under the same arrangements and regulations and subject to the same charges as at Dublin. In addition, the board was authorised to lay and maintain buoys in the channel between Dalkey Island and the mainland, known as Dalkey Sound.

At that time Dunleary was a village consisting essentially of the thoroughfare on which the well-known hostelry 'The Purty Kitchen' stands. In fact the official name for this portion of the road, as shown on the street nameplate, is 'Old Dunleary'. A small cove which then extended to the foot of the rise on which Cumberland Street stands was cut off by the construction of the Dublin and Kingstown Railway in the early 1830s but the road running parallel to the railway at this point, known as Dunleary Road, was not constructed until 1904. A small pier built between 1756 and 1767 still exists within the present Dun Laoghaire harbour and this small pier was the original Dunleary pier.

Together with the cove it formed the Dunleary harbour to which eighteenth-century records refer. The present East and West Piers of Dun Laoghaire were built in the period 1816–36.

The many references in the act to ballasting operations emphasise the importance to sailing vessels and to the port itself of proper regulation of the raising (i.e. dredging) and supplying of ballast to ships and also the control of dumping of ballast from vessels loading outward cargoes; the act made detailed provisions in this regard, including the construction of new ballast wharfs.

As already noted, the sandbank at the confluence of the Dodder river with the Liffey estuary had been a problem for many years, and the new act empowered the board to divert the course of the Dodder through a new cut or canal to be constructed from the river at a point between Ballsbridge and Ringsend and discharging on the south strand. Local inhabitants were to be authorised to draw fresh water from the new cut and compensation was provided for in the event of claims from the owners of local salt refineries if the fresh water upset their operations by mixing with the sea water used for the making of salt. However, the proposed diversion of the Dodder was never carried out partly as a result of improved methods of dredging which enabled the sandbank to be removed.

A rather interesting provision in the new act would be unlikely to receive approval in a modern parliament. This was the vesting in the new board of power to hear, try and determine summarily all offences against any clause of the act and to impose penalties ranging from fines to distraint and sale of goods and chattels of the offender. In the case of any person found guilty of cutting away or damaging a rope attached to a buoy or an anchor, the board had power to commit the offender to 'the house of correction' for up to six months; alternatively, he could be publicly whipped and the board's journals record numerous cases where such punishment was ordered. The board could not be accused of sex discrimination in this matter since we find that in 1802 Lucey Bates was sentenced to three months with hard labour in the house of correction, for casting loose a lighter. No indication of Lucey's age or of the reason for her offence is given; the thought comes to mind that her motive may have been similar to that of some modern young car thieves—temporary exhilaration—without any concern for the possible consequences.

The bill received Royal Assent on 8 May 1786 and the new Commissioners lost no time in getting down to work for on the following day they had their first meeting in the Royal Exchange. The first meeting was something of a formality at which the new commissioners took an oath or affirmed as provided for in the act constituting the new body.

The assiduity of the new board was evident from their decision to meet on three days a week, Tuesdays, Thursdays and Saturdays, at the office in Essex Street formerly used by the directors of the old Ballast Office Committee. It is a curious fact that, notwithstanding his interest in the establishment of the new port authority, Beresford did not attend the first five meetings. This does not appear to have hindered the board from proceeding to appoint various committees to organise the financial arrangements, administration, duties of employees, identification of property taken over from the Ballast Office and the pilot office and the making of new regulations for measuring tonnage of vessels by the board's supervisors; in addition, a revision of the harbour bye-laws was undertaken. Progress was made in all these matters within one month of the first meeting of the new board together with proposals for repairs to breaches in the quay walls on both north and south sides of the river, in particular Sir John Rogerson's Quay where serious breaches had occurred.

At this stage the board had no direct responsibility for the maintenance of much of the older quay walls. It will be recalled that the wall known as City Quay, protecting the City Ground, was constructed by the municipal corporation acting through the Ballast Committee and the responsibility for erecting and maintaining the remainder of the existing walls was that of the leaseholders of the foreshore. The new board was concerned at the ruinous conditions of some of the quay walls and took up with the Privy Council the need for repairs to 'the quay between the Marine School and Ringsend, known as Sir John Rogerson's Quay'. The Privy Council in turn forwarded the board's request to the municipal corporation. They replied that the onus was on Sir John Rogerson's successors in title to the lease of the foreshore in this area: the Right Honourable Luke Gardiner and the estate of another former Lord Mayor, Alderman Richard Benson. This controversy resulted eventually in the transfer to the board of the title in and responsibility for all the quay walls east of Carlisle Bridge under an act of 1792.

The members of the new board were named in the act, as follows: The Right Honourable the Lord Mayor and Sheriffs (2) of the City of Dublin for the time being.

Rt Hon. Lord Viscount Ranelagh	Leland Crosthwaite
Rt Hon. John Foster	George Macquay
Rt Hon. John Beresford	Isaac Weld
Rt Hon. Sir John Parnell	Joseph Sandwith
Rt Hon. John Monk Mason	John Hendrick
Ald. James Hamilton	Joseph Wilson
Ald. William Alexander	John Carleton
Ald. Henry Howison	Robert Lloyd
George Sutton	John Patrick
Robert Black	Arthur Bryan

In October 1786 the staff of the new board were recorded in the board's journal as:

Secretary;
Pilot Master;
Two haven masters;
Two supervisors for measuring ships' tonnage;
Storekeeper;
Five boatmen;
One messenger;
Labourers, seamen, etc. employed ad hoc on the new Great South Wall and other port development, usually from March to October in each year.

Curiously no mention is made of a supervisor of the port works or of the men employed on the gabbards in raising ballast.

It is not clear what the arrangements were for nominating a chairman for the new board although it may be that in these early meetings originated a practice noted in later years whereby the third member to arrive at the meeting was voted into the chair. It would appear that the proliferation of meetings created difficulties for some members since at the end of the second month of its existence, the board ordered that 'before any Gentleman takes the chair, he be asked whether he can stay while there was business to be done'.

In August 1786 the board decided that one general meeting be held each Tuesday to which all members would be summoned; in addition meetings would continue to be held on Thursdays and Saturdays to which three members would be summoned on a rotation basis.

Responsibility for pilotage had passed from the Ballast Office to the new board which proceeded to arrange for the drawing up of new licences for pilots, owners of lighters and, strange as it may seem, for dealers in old rope!

After the preliminary work of organising working arrangements and identifying priorities, clearly the major work to be tackled was the completion of the South Wall and in the following two years various contracts were entered into to complete the wall in sections, the contract for the last hundred feet being awarded to Mr G. Myers in 1788.

John Pidgeon's House and Eighteenth-Century Dockland

IN August 1786 the new port board noted that one of its employees, John Pidgeon, was infirm and unable to work and it was ordered that an allowance of five shillings per week be paid to Pidgeon for one month. It does not appear that Pidgeon survived long enough to receive the full allowance since early in September the board ordered that one of its supervisors, John Mullarkey, be paid two pounds to defray the expenses of burying Pidgeon who had for twenty-five years been employed by the Ballast Office committee before being transferred to the board's service.

The original piling extending for one and a quarter miles seawards from Ringsend had been replaced by a double wall filled with gravel, as will be recalled, and this wall was completed by the Ballast Office committee in 1759. In 1760 the committee arranged for the construction of a blockhouse at the eastern end of the wall where it joined the timber framework across the South Bull. Pidgeon's duties included acting as watchman on the committee's property and he was allowed to reside in the blockhouse which appears to have been a substantial building according to a report made by the new board's supervisor of works, Mr Francis Tunstall, in August 1787; in this report the building is described as having eight rooms, with lofts over three of these rooms. Pidgeon was permitted to sell refreshments to passsengers from the packet ships and because of his association with the building, it became known as 'Pidgeon's House' and is so described in contemporary newspapers as early as 1766. Prior to the construction of the new wall extending from Ringsend to Pidgeon's House, passengers arriving or departing on the sailing packet ships were obliged to employ boatmen to row them between the packet ship anchorage (east of the present Pidgeon House harbour) and Ringsend or City Quay. Strictly speaking, the term 'packet ships' refers to vessels owned or chartered by the Post Office for mails, the term deriving from the description of mails in the sixteenth century as 'pacquets of letters'. Only government officials were permitted to travel on packet ships and the vessels used by ordinary passengers were described as 'passage boats'.

With the construction of the new wall it soon became a thoroughfare for passengers using the packet ships. The discomforts of sea travel, particulary in bad weather, were such that Pidgeon's liquid refreshments were no doubt in great demand to revive drooping spirits after passages from North Wales which sometimes lasted a week or more in adverse conditions; similar sustenance was available for those about to embark and suffer the inconveniences, hardships and hazards of the packet ships. Pidgeon's duties included assisting at the lighthouse amongst other things and no doubt exposure to bad weather conditions brought on the illness from which he died. An account of Pidgeon and his family appeared in the *Dublin Penny Journal* in 1833. Under the heading 'A story of the last century' the article described the initiative of Pidgeon in his efforts to increase his income by supplying refreshments not only to packet ship passengers who landed or departed from the new wall near the blockhouse but also to those citizens who desired to take the sea air on fine Sundays. Pidgeon and his son would row such persons down river from Ringsend, land them at the Blockhouse for refreshments and take them back to Ringsend later in the day. Pidgeon was believed to be a 'snug man' but this appears to have been an ill-founded belief since he seems to have died penniless, as we have noted.

The Penny Journal stated that one night four men were admitted by Pidgeon to his premises on their plea of distress, but having entered they attacked Pidgeon and his wife. The younger Pidgeon had his hand very severely slashed by a sword in attempting to defend his parents but he managed to escape and summon assistance. Before he returned the thieves had disappeared, having taken any article of value they could find, and having damaged Pidgeon's boat beyond repair. Pidgeon's daughters, Mary and Rachel, were also present in the house but they were not molested. When the news broke, Pidgeon's regular patrons organised a collection to provide a new boat for him. The son's injury was not so easily remedied and his hand was permanently disabled. However, he could steer the boat when accompanying his father on fishing trips in the river. One day, they found their hook fouled by an object which turned out to be the body of one of the robbers. Later the Pidgeons heard that the thieves had fallen out; one had been killed and his body thrown into the river. Another of the gang was later captured but this was little consolation to the family since Pidgeon senior died soon after, to be followed a short time later by his son whose injury eventually proved fatal.

The girls were left to fend for themselves and as they could not afford to employ men to row the boat, they put their own limited experience of boats to good use by resuming the ferrying of people down river at the weekends. They soon became objects of curiosity and sympathy and it was said that their boat was more popular then ever before with men of all ages, all anxious to row themselves so that eventually the girls seldom had to exert themselves. However, they became sufficiently capable of handling a boat to attempt the rescue of three persons following a shipwreck in the harbour one stormy evening. They took the unfortunate trio (one of whom was a child) ashore, provided them with blankets, food and warmth, and looked after them until they were fully recovered. During that time the child became very attached to one of the sisters, Mary. The child's father, a widower, was the second member of the rescued party and he was an American of some substance with business to attend to in Dublin. He was happy to leave the child with the sisters until he had attended to his affairs. It appears that the child's attraction to Mary was matched by that of its father who later proposed marriage, and was accepted; he returned to America with his new bride, his young son and his sister-in-law, Rachel, who was reported to have found a husband for herself in the New World. It is, unfortunately, difficult to reconcile the finale of this story with the records although it may indeed have some factual basis.

Although the South Wall was not completed when the new board came into existence in 1786 the lighthouse (later to be known as the Poolbeg lighthouse) had been completed in 1767 and was operational from 29 September in that year, using candles as the illuminant. In July 1786, the new board decided to experiment with oil and patent lamps instead of the candles and the masters of the packet ships were asked to observe and comment on the results. The improvement was so marked in the opinion of the masters that the board decided that the lighthouse should thereafter be lit with oil and it became one of the first lighthouses in the British Isles to be so lit.

We have noted how the new port works, including the lighthouse, were of great interest to the citizens at large and how boatmen, including Pidgeon and his family, were kept busy at weekends ferrying passengers from Ringsend down river in fine weather on tours of inspection. Sometimes the drunken behaviour of some unruly elements in forcing their way into the lighthouse was such that the board ordered that no person was to be admitted to the lighthouse 'except those of decent appearance and masters of vessels'. Further, no liquor was to be sold, consumed or brought into the lighthouse and hawkers were forbidden to sell liquor on the South Wall, to the benefit, no doubt, of Pidgeon and his successors.

In August 1787 the board had under consideration the future use of the blockhouse and it was decided that two of the eight rooms should be reserved to the use of the board and its committees, thus facilitating inspection of the works in progress. Two other rooms were reserved for the Inspector of Works, Mr Tunstall, and two more for the use of contractors working on the walls. The remaining two rooms were allotted to Mr Patrick O'Brien and his wife to act as housekeepers of the premises, on their undertaking to keep the board's rooms clean and 'provide breakfast when directed' for any member of the board. The O'Briens were given no salary but were permitted to continue Pidgeon's business of 'retailing spirituous liquors'.

The new board soon became aware that certain of its employees were being paid their wages in taverns and inns. Presumably the board regarded arguments put forward by the supervisor justifying the practice as specious, since in 1787 it ordered that 'on no account or pretence whatever shall wages be paid to gabbardmen or labourers in any house where ale or spirits are sold'. This order foreshadowed the campaign waged by James Larkin more than 120 years later against a similar practice in the payment of dockers' wages by some stevedores. The board also found time to investigate allegations of fraud by the gabbardmen in respect of their claims for payment for delivering ballast to ships which had not in fact received the full required amount.

The board was conscious of the potential of the new South Wall between Ringsend and the blockhouse, or Pidgeon House as it was by now generally known, and in May 1792 a committee was appointed to treat with the Fitzwilliam (now Pembroke) Estate for the purchase of a strip of the foreshore on the river side of the new wall. Under a legal process common in those days and known as an inquisition, the ground was valued by a jury at £640 and the board was entitled to acquire the property on payment of this amount to the owners. However, the municipal corporation put the board on notice of the city's claim to the title to the foreshore, stating that the city should be the recipient of the £640 awarded by the jury. A legal wrangle between the Corporation and the Fitzwilliam Estate dragged on for many years and it was not until May 1800 that the foreshore was eventually conveyed to the board under an order of the court. In 1814 a further strip, adjoining and north of this foreshore, was acquired by the board from the estate. Although development of this foreshore did not commence until the 1950s, the decision of the board to acquire the fee simple title was justified since it was on this foreshore that the new South Quays were constructed between 1950 and 1975, including a large container terminal, a roll on/ roll off facility, a dry bulk cargo quay and a quay for the ESB for the discharge of fuel for its Ringsend generating station before the advent of the Poolbeg station in 1970.

However, one project in this area undertaken by the board in June 1791 was regarded as being of considerable importance in its day. This was the construction of a small tidal harbour, or 'bason' as it was described, at the Pidgeon House, which became known as the Pidgeon House Harbour. The purpose of this harbour was to facilitate the packet ships and their passengers by obviating the need for boatmen who had previously been required to ferry the passengers to and from these vessels lying in their anchorage in the river channel. Contracts for the walls of the new harbour within a harbour were placed in April 1792 and the work was completed in 1793. The fact that the new harbour dried out at low water eventually outweighed the advantages to the packet ships of its relatively sheltered berthage; the consequent delays to the vessels led to the transfer of the packet station to a new harbour at Howth in 1818.

In August 1793, the board decided that the arrangements previously undertaken by Pidgeon and his successors for the shelter and sustenance of packet ship passengers were no longer adequate and it was decided to build a hotel at the new Pidgeon House harbour for a sum not to exceed £2,000. Work was commenced later that year and the building was completed in 1795.

The outbreak of the rising of 1798 in May of that year coupled with the threat of a French invasion resulted in a request to the board from the Lord Lieutenant for the temporary use of the 'quays, buildings and adjoining land at the blockhouse for military defence purposes'. The board had little option but to agree; however, they were sufficiently conscious of their responsibilities to the port to insist that the premises be returned 'as soon as the public exigencies allow and all damage being paid for'. The public exigencies were such that the premises were never returned to the board. Instead a fort was constructed on the site and the premises became known as the Pidgeon House Fort but the only record of any military action involving its guns was in 1843 when they were trained on the site of O'Connell's proposed mass meeting at Clontarf. The fort was one of the premises proposed by Robert Emmet to be captured and occupied during the short-lived revolt of 1803.

The continued use of the Pidgeon House premises by the War Department was formalised by a lease in 1802 and two years later the board agreed to exclude all commercial shipping from the harbour, thus making it available exclusively for government purposes which, of course, included the Post Office packets. However, the matter of rent for the premises became a focus of considerable controversy which was eventually referred to arbitration. Before agreement was reached on the arbitration award, the government decided to purchase the premises but agreement could not be reached in regard to the purchase price, and the board proposed that this question be likewise referred to arbitration. The War Office officials continued to drag their collective feet for many years and as the board could not get a decisive reply to its continued reminders of the outstanding negotiations it served notice to quit on the Board of Ordnance in 1810. Although negotiations were resumed and arbitration agreed on, the matter was not concluded until 1814 when the premises were transferred for the sum of £100,183.

The blockhouse was removed in 1835 but the Pidgeon House Fort remained in government hands until 1897 when it was purchased by Dublin Corporation in connection with its proposed main drainage scheme; most of the harbour area was converted into sewage settlement tanks, leaving only a small channel at the east end where the old packet ships had berthed. In 1902 Dublin Corporation opened its new electricity generating station at the Pidgeon House harbour, the coal for the station being discharged from colliers lying at the old packet ship berth. Following the establishment of the Electricity Supply Board in 1927, it took over responsibility for the Pidgeon House generating station in 1929. This station continued in operation until 1975, although in its later years it was used mainly as a stand-by. The hotel building, which was used by the War Office as officers quarters, is still in existence and is at present (1988) used by the ESB as offices. Portions of the old walls of the fort with their embrasures may still be seen together with some of the barracks buildings in which the troops were quartered.

In a paper read to the Old Dublin Society and reprinted in the *Dublin Historical Record* (vol. V, no. 2) Joseph W. Hammond gives a colourful description of dockland in the eighteenth century, as a community practically independent of the rest of the city. It was the home of mariners, shipbuilders, shipbrokers, rope and sail makers, ship chandlers and outfitters as well as doctors, apothecaries, confectioners, grocers, brewers, in addition to a floating population of packet ship passengers, sailors, revenue officers, smugglers, military patrols, and press gangs for whom the many inns and taverns provided creature comforts. Fights between sailors and press gangs were commonplace as indeed were those between smugglers and revenue men, or excisemen as they were sometimes known. A fresh corpse discovered following a fracas of this kind was a prize sought after by medical students. George's Quay was the place of embarkation for prisoners being transported, in many cases for relatively minor offences, to the Virginia tobacco plantations. Following the American War of Independence, the destination of such prisoners was usually Botany Bay. There were also prison ships anchored off Ringsend or in the anchorage which later became the modern Alexandra Basin; sometimes, these prisoners were offered the choice of service in the British army or navy in return for their liberty.

For those in peril on the sea, whether seamen or prisoners, there were always anxious families awaiting news of the ships carrying their loved ones, and the hazards of seafaring and sea transport is reflected in a report of 1769 which stated that twenty houses adjoining George's Quay and Luke Street contained between them thirty-six widows.

One paragraph of Hammond's, although highly-coloured in the style of a Victorian novelist, deserves to be quoted in full:

> In the last decade of the eighteenth century, Rogerson's Quay was a pleasant suburb, affording a delightful panorama of sea and country. There was a touch of glamour and romance around this quiet locality, enlivened now and then by the passing of military patrols in their scarlet and buff uniforms, the sinister press gangs swaggering with musket or cutlass, and the boys of the Marine School in their dark blue jackets and white ducks. Florid topers in the brandy-fumed taverns looked out over their tankards at the spreading canvas of ships going by and the only sounds on the air were the cry of the gull and the curlew, or the refrain of sailors at the capstan. Time there went by ship's bell or the bugle and drum of the Marine School. Nightfall brought forth the mellow strains of the violin or the notes of a harpsichord from behind closed shutters and bolted doors, and the only sounds outside were the steady tramp of the patrol, and an occasional call of 'Halt!' or the scurrying patter of the press gang after a pedestrian who had changed his mind and turned back.

Further illuminating sidelights on the period are provided by the *Freeman's Journal*. In November 1793, it was reported that over 100 seamen had been 'pressed' from vessels in port, including packet ships, and as a result the packet ships for Parkgate and Liverpool were unable to sail until new crews had been recruited. A week later, the press gang were attacked and stoned by a large crowd of coal porters who were 'armed with Pikes and Adzes'. The crowd disappeared on the arrival of a troop of cavalry, no doubt to the great relief of the press gang. In the winter season it was not unusual for fleets of up to forty colliers to arrive in the estuary; it was likewise not unusual for the coal merchants to delay ordering the ships up to unloading berths so as to keep up the price of the coal.

Although not directly related to the port of Dublin the following extract is worth noting (November 1792): 'Lord Fitzwilliam, it is said, has let all the gound undisposed of between the Circular Road and Merrion on building leases of sixty-one years at five shillings a foot. We may look for a continuation of the metropolis to the BlackRock'.

The reference to the sound of harpsichords is no doubt due to the fact that John Hammond, foreman shipwright with the shipbuilding partnership of Matthew Cardiff and Michael Kehoe, forsook the shipbuilding business in 1797 and became a harpsichord maker. It is unlikely that many harpsichords can be heard in this neighbourhood today, music being generally supplied by ballad groups in the local pubs. Cardiff's name is enshrined in the street known as Cardiff Lane which joins the quays near the large gasometer, a major landmark in the older part of the port. One of Malton's pictures shows shipping in the Liffey opposite the Marine School on Sir John Rogerson's Quay in 1796 and nearby may be seen the stern of a ship under construction in Cardiff's shipbuilding yard.

7

The Port Authority's Lifeboat Service, 1801–62

LONG before the establishment of the 'National Institution for the preservation of life from Shipwreck', later to be renamed the Royal National Lifeboat Institution, locally operated lifeboats had been in operation in many places in the United Kingdom and elsewhere late in the eighteenth century. In the year 1800, the port board decided to place lifeboats around Dublin Bay and the first boat was built by John Clements of Ringsend, at a cost of '105 guineas'. It was delivered in February 1801 and the board decided that it should be stationed at the 'Sheds' of Clontarf, under the care of Thomas Murray, an employee who lived in the neighbourhood. The choice of Clontarf may at first seem strange but it must be remembered that before the construction of the North Bull Wall (1819–24) the north shore of the estuary, generally referred to as the North Bull, was the scene of many shipwrecks. The term 'Sheds' of Clontarf does not refer to a modern public house known by that name but to shelters provided for fishermen on the seafront at the site of the present-day junction of Clontarf Road and Vernon Avenue. They have long since been removed.

A second boat, also built by John Clements, was delivered early in 1803 and stationed at Sandycove. A third boat, built in 1805, was stationed at Sutton. A fourth boat was ordered in 1815 and stationed at the Pidgeon House. Following the report of the loss of a vessel off Howth in October 1816, the board decided to place a lifeboat at Howth, although this was, strictly speaking, outside the Port of Dublin.

Each of the board's lifeboats was placed under the care of an employee of the board living in the locality, the lifeboat service as a whole being under the general supervision of the Pilot Master. There were many changes in the location of the lifeboats and eventually only three were retained—Kingstown, Howth and the Pidgeon House which, incidentally, was later known as the Poolbeg station.

No detailed records or pictures exist of the early Dublin Bay lifeboats but it is likely that they were similar to the famous Redcar Lifeboat, the

Zetland, which was built in 1800 by one of the pioneers in lifeboat design and construction, Henry Greathead. This boat was in service for over eighty years and is now preserved at Redcar in Yorkshire as a historical relic. In these early years, crews for the Dublin Bay lifeboats were mustered ad hoc from local fishermen, pilots, coastguards or even military personnel.

Reports of services rendered by lifeboats were usually accompanied by a memorial from the crew requesting some remuneration for their services. Awards to the men concerned were usually made by the board, depending on the particular circumstances of each case. The caretaker for each lifeboat received the sum of six guineas per year for his services.

In 1824, the National Institution for the Preservation of Life from Shipwreck was established; in 1854, the name was changed to the Royal National Lifeboat Institution. Many improvements were effected in the design and construction of lifeboats following the establishment of the RNLI and the port board was not slow to profit from the experience of the newer but broader-based organisation. Indeed, a number of lifeboats were purchased by the port board through the RNLI.

The nineteenth-century lifeboats were very vulnerable, even when crewed by men experienced in the ways of small craft and rough seas; they were, after all, open boats dependent on oar propulsion. For some stations, lifeboats were designed and rigged for sailing, in particular the larger craft such as at Howth and Kingstown. The development which revolutionised the service early in this century was, of course, the internal combustion engine, but without diminishing in any way the respect and admiration due to the modern lifeboatmen, the risks and hardships undertaken by the crews of the early open lifeboats are almost beyond comprehension. If the term 'cockle-shell heroes' has any meaning, surely it must refer to the early lifeboatmen.

In 1860, a new lifeboat for the Kingstown station was acquired by the port board from the Royal National Lifeboat Institution but on her first trial in November of that year, the Pilot Master found many faults with her and considered her 'cumbersome and ill-formed'. He stated that she was so heavy that it took 30 men to launch her and he did not think she could ever be pulled to windward in a gale. A request was made to the builders, Messrs. Forrest of Limehouse, to take her back and to substitute a more suitable craft but this request was refused. The boat's deficiencies constituted one of the factors which prevented her from being used when she was most needed during the disastrous storms of February 1861.

In 1861, the port board entered into negotiations with the RNLI to hand over the remaining three lifeboat stations at Kingstown, Poolbeg and Howth and these negotiations culminated in an agreement whereby in 1862 responsibility for these stations was taken over by the Institution. Thus ended the direct involvement of the port board in the provision of lifeboats in Dublin Bay, although its harbour craft, pilot cutters and tugs have, down the years, continued to contribute their share to the saving of life in the bay.

One man dominated the lifeboat service in Dublin Bay, both before and after the advent of the RNLI to Dublin. In the sixty odd years from 1817 to 1880 his name continually recurs in references not only to lifeboats and shipping but to many other aspects of local history. This was William Hutchison who was born in Dublin in 1793 and at the age of thirteen joined the Navy as a midshipman. At the age of twenty, he reached the rank of lieutenant and such information as exists on his career in the intervening years on the Mediterranean and West Indies stations reads like pages from a Hornblower novel. In common with many other naval officers in 1816, Hutchison found himself ashore on half-pay. He returned to Dublin where he found that a vacancy existed in the service of the port board for the position of harbour master of Dunleary harbour and inspector of the board's quarries at Bullock harbour. The Dunleary harbour referred to was not the modern harbour but the pier and cove described in Chapter 5. The quarries at Bullock formed part of lands at Bullock and Sandycove leased in 1804 by the board from the Carysfort Estate. Stone drawn from the quarries was transported by gabbards from Bullock harbour across the bay for use in port works at the Great South Wall, the Great North (Bull) Wall and also at Howth harbour. It was the duty of the inspector of quarries to supervise and tally the output of stone from the quarries and arrange transport. In December 1817 at the age of twenty-four Hutchison was appointed to the vacant position at an annual salary of £100 and he was also provided with a substantial house which now forms part of the complex known as Our Lady's Manor at Bullock Castle. Hutchison's duties also required him to supervise the lifeboat established at Sandy-cove in 1803. Space does not admit of any detailed account of the many rescues in which Hutchison was involved as coxswain of the lifeboat, but his reports illustrate the hazards which he and his volunteer crews faced when called out to attend stricken ships. In attempting to take the crew off a brig named the *Ellen*, ashore at Sandycove point in December 1821, four of the lifeboat's crew were drowned when she was capsized. Hutchison regained the shore with the remainder of the crew where they waited all night for the storm to abate, thus enabling them to rescue the brig's crew. His report was as follows.

Gentlemen.   28th December 1821
I beg leave to state that on Friday evening between the hours of eight and nine o'clock, I was informed by some of the Pilots that a Brig was ashore near Sandycove and that they would accompany

me in the lifeboat to save the crew from a watery grave, their cries being most affecting. It blew a most violent gale from the south-east and on my arrival at Sandycove, numbers of men were ready to launch the Life Boat and with a volunteer crew of 14 men [I] embarked and with much difficulty reached the stern of the vessel where we received a hawser to hold by. At this time, the vessel was lying nearly head to the sea which broke completely over her and while the crew were in the act of getting into the Life Boat she filled with water. But perceiving our perilous situation the crew desisted. While we were bailing out the water with our hats, a sea of which I shall never forget the aspect, overwhelmed the Life Boat and washed 6 of us out of her. Two, fortunately, caught hold of the rope they had been holding the boat by and 3 then unfortunately perished. With difficulty, I regained the Life Boat and with the remainder of her crew we were drove among the breakers without oars and most providentially we got on shore having received many contusions and the loss of another of my brave companions who from exhaustion let go his hold and was washed out among the rocks.

Two of the unfortunate Pilots have left widows and children who will be in a most desolate state without the humane grant of small pensions from your Honourable Board.

I remained on the beach all night for the purpose of rendering assistance; during the flood tide the violence of the sea had driven the vessel so high on the rocks that at low water we were enabled to get the crew out with safety.

The vessel's name was the *Ellen* of Liverpool with a valuable cargo.

I beg leave to subjoin the names of the men who assisted me.

The names of the Life Boat's crew on the evening of 28th December, 1821:

Denis Mooney, Hugh Byrne (Drowned), Thomas Byrne, John Byrne, Charles Archbold, Laurence Murphy, Thomas Fitzsimons (Drowned), John Archbold (Drowned), Thomas Grimes (Drowned), Michael Mooney, William Rogan, Philip Cullen, Laurence Tallant, John Tallant.

As a result of Hutchison's appeal on behalf of the families of those who were drowned, the board granted small annuities to the widows of the married men and to the destitute parents of the others.

As a result of his efforts in rescuing the crew of another brig, the *Duke*, on 14 August 1829, Hutchison was awarded the Gold Medal of the Institution later known as the RNLI.

Following the decision of the government in 1815 to build a harbour of refuge in Dublin Bay, responsibility for the project was entrusted to a body which, following the visit of George IV in 1821, was described as 'the Commissioners for the Royal Harbour of Asylum at Kingstown.' In the following year Hutchison became aware of the proposed appointment of a harbour master for the new harbour and he promptly asked the board for a letter of recommendation to the commissioners. Since it was intended that the new harbour would come under the control of the board when completed, it seemed to the board logical to agree to Hutchison's request. Hutchison was duly appointed as the first harbour master of Kingstown harbour.

In 1828 a vacancy arose for an assistant pilot master in the Dublin pilotage service which was then based at Kingstown. Hutchison applied for and was given this position; later he was appointed pilot master.

One of the worst storms recorded around the coasts of the United Kingdom occurred on 9 February 1861. One hundred and thirty-five vessels were posted as missing around the Irish and British coasts. Fifteen were wrecked in Dublin Bay, eight off Howth, one off Bray, five off Wicklow and three near Arklow. A memorial on the east pier at Dun Laoghaire records the heroism of Capt. John McNeill-Boyd, commander of the naval guardship *Ajax* and five of his crew on that Saturday. In an attempt to rescue the crew of the schooner *Neptune*, one of two vessels which had struck the rocks off the east pier, the six men were caught by a heavy sea which washed them off the seaward slope of the pier and drowned them. Two of the schooner's crew of four were also drowned, as were two of the crew of the second vessel—the brig *Industry*.

Hutchison and others were involved in the efforts of Capt. McNeill-Boyd at the east pier that day and Hutchison was awarded the Silver Medal of the RNLI for his services. He was then sixty-eight years old.

In the following year, 1862, control of the lifeboat service in Dublin Bay was transferred from the board to the Royal National Lifeboat Institution. A branch of the Institution was established at Kingstown and Hutchison was appointed as the first honorary secretary.

In 1863, the board decided that the duties of its pilot master were such as to require the whole-time service of the person concerned and that Capt. Hutchison, having now reached the age of seventy and having had over forty-five years service with the board, must now decide whether he wished to continue as harbour master in the service of the Kingstown Commissioners, in which case the board would retire him on pension; alternatively, if he wished to continue as pilot master he would have to retire from the position of harbour master of Kingstown. Capt. Hutchison elected to continue as harbour master of Kingstown and was succeeded as pilot master by Captain Wilcox, RN.

In 1871, Hutchison was appointed a Justice of the Peace and, although retired from the position of pilot master under the Dublin board, he continued as harbour master of Kingstown for another eleven years until 1874 when, at the age of eighty, he retired.

He continued to attend meetings of the lifeboat committee until October 1880. He died in the following year, aged eighty-seven. Shops in Kingstown were closed and flags on ships in the harbour were at half mast during the funeral cortege, but although the obituaries in the newspapers referred to his long service as harbour master of Kingstown, no mention whatever was made of his work with the lifeboats for over fifty years. A paper read to the Old Dublin Society in 1979, and on which this chapter is based, was intended to rectify this omission albeit almost one hundred years after his death.

8

The Port Authority and Irish Lighthouses, 1810–67

UNDER a statute of 1810 (50 Geo. III Cap. 95) responsibility for lighthouses, beacons and seamarks around the coast of Ireland was vested in the Corporation for Preserving and Improving the Port of Dublin, but before dealing in more detail with this apparently anomalous arrangement it may be helpful to sketch in the earlier history of lighthouse administration.

Prior to the nineteenth century many lighthouses had been built by private persons acting under letters patent granted by the crown. The motives of such persons were not altogether altruistic since they were authorised to collect tolls from shipping benefiting from the lighthouses. An early example was Sir Robert Reading who in 1665 was granted a patent to erect such lighthouses in Ireland, including two on the 'Hill of Hoath'. The enterprise appears to have been unprofitable since in 1704 the patent was surrendered and responsibility for the upkeep of those of Reading's proposed lighthouses which had been built was taken over by commissioners specially appointed by Queen Anne for the purpose.

In 1717, title in lands on which barracks and lighthouses stood or were to be built was vested in the king by an Act of Parliament (4 Geo. 1. Cap. 3) compensation being paid to the owners of the lands. The act provided for the appointment of new commissioners (later described as 'trustees of the barracks in and throughout the Kingdom of Ireland'), to carry out the provisions of the act, and these powers were amended and extended in a later act of 1767 (7 Geo. III Cap. 6). In 1796 the Revenue Commissioners were empowered to build three lighthouses at Wexford, Mayo and Galway, and responsibility for all lighthouses in Ireland passed from the 'trustees of the barracks' generally known as the Barrack Board (not to be confused with the Ballast Board) to the Revenue Commissioners.

The work of building and renovating lighthouses was carried out for the Revenue Commissioners by a contractor named Thomas Rogers. His work included the building of three new lighthouses (Cranfield at the entrance to Carlingford Lough, Kilwarlin near Strangford Lough, and Arran Island off the coast of Donegal) rebuilding or renovating two more (Howth Head and Loop Head) and altering the lantern system from candles to oil in five others (Copeland Islands, Old Head of Kinsale, Kinsale Harbour, Hook Head and Waterford Harbour).

As in the case of Ireland, the early lighthouses in England, Scotland and Wales were erected mainly by private persons but by the end of the nineteenth century, the pressure of public opinion was towards their control and operation by a public authority. The Corporation of Trinity House, London, was established by royal charter in 1514 as a charitable institution concerned with the well-being of seamen and their dependants; under later charters and Acts of Parliament, the functions of this body were extended to include the erection of lighthouses and beacons; it also became the principal pilotage authority. By the middle of the nineteenth century all private lighthouses in England and Wales had been taken over by Trinity House; the last to be acquired was the Skerries Lighthouse, near Holyhead, in 1841. Later the jurisdiction of Trinity House in respect of lighthouses was extended to the Channel Islands and to Gibraltar. However, Trinity House had no jurisdiction over Ireland or Scotland and because of complaints regarding the unreliability of lighthouses in Scotland, a new lighthouse authority was established by statute in 1786 and vested with responsibility for all lighthouses, buoys and beacons in Scotland and the Isle of Man, under the title of Commissioners of Northern Lights.

Returning to the Irish situation, we find that early in June 1810 the Corporation for Preserving and Improving the Port of Dublin became aware of a bill which was about to be placed before parliament for the purpose of transferring to the board responsibility for all lighthouses around the coasts of Ireland. The matter had been brought to the notice of the board by some of the members as a result of a newspaper report, no formal notice of the proposal having been received by the port board from the government at that stage. The newspaper report referred to gave the impression that the port authority was to be 'assimilated' into Trinity House, London, and not unnaturally this created something of a stir at a special meeting of the board summoned to consider the matter. The matter was clarified in subsequent correspondence with the Right Honourable John Foster (Chancellor of the Exchequer and former speaker of the Irish House of Commons). He forwarded a copy of the bill from which it emerged that there was no intention to interfere with the board's statutory functions as harbour authority; the new lighthouse functions would, however, be subject to the overview of Trinity House. The board was placated and signified its approval on 5 June.

As the bill was enacted shortly afterwards and signed by the king on

A view of the banquet held in Stack A, Custom House Docks, on 22 October 1856, for Irish regiments returned from the Crimean War.

Loading Guinness barges at the brewery wharf, Victoria Quay, 1898.

The Baily Lighthouse, Howth, designed by
George Halpin Senior, in operation from 1813.

Richard Martin's barque *Howth* photographed off Cape Horn on 24 January 1897.

A letter from Michael Davitt (*above*) to Nicholas Proud, secretary of the port board, dated 1 June 1886, in which he explains his absence from board meetings. The date of the letter is significant: it was written exactly one week before the opening of the debate on the First Home Rule Bill which explains why he was detained in London.

The *Great Eastern*, berthed at the then new North Wall extension in 1886. In the foreground, some of the Ringsend fishing fleet. The photograph below shows the main deck of the *Great Eastern*.

The twin opening bridges over the entrance to the Royal Canal at North Wall under construction, c.1890.

The newly erected 100-ton crane at North Wall extension being tested, 1905.

The ship in the foreground (*above*) is the paddle steamer *Shamrock*, one of the four new passenger ships operated by the London & North Western Railway Company between Dublin and Holyhead in the mid 1870s. By 1883, the company purchased the Prince of Wales Hotel, North Wall and changed its name to the North Western Hotel. To accommodate the increased number of passengers, they built a new hotel starting at the rere of the old structure (*below*). The old structure was subsequently demolished and the new hotel occupied the entire site.

The Harbour Master's staff, May 1911. Capt. George Graves (bearded) photographed with pilots, berthing masters, dock gatemen and (last two rows) harbour police.

An early oil tanker the *Balakanai*, discharging gas oil for the Alliance Gas Company at Great Britain Quay, 2 April 1900. Note the primitive oil pipeline and the timber half barrels used for spillage.

The *Wicklow*, one of the ships transferred from the City of Dublin Steam Packet Company to the B & I in 1919. She served for fifty-four years on the cross-channel service.

North Wall, 1920.

15 June 1810, it is obvious that the proposal had been in train for some time before the newspapers got wind of it. Having regard to the influence and standing of many members of the port board, it is difficult to understand how such an important proposed addition to the board's functions could have been drafted without their knowledge.

In August 1810, the Lord Lieutenant requested that the board place a floating light on the shoal known as the Kish and also that the lighthouse on Howth Head be removed to a more advantageous position. His Lordship stated that these proposals were intended 'to render every possible security to His Majesty's Packets and the trade of the St George's Channel'. On the advice of their haven masters, the board agreed to both proposals. A suitable vessel was procured in Holland, taken to Dublin and fitted up as a floating light (or, as it would now be termed, a lightship). Named the *Richmond* in honour of the Lord Lieutenant, the vessel was placed at the north end of the Kish bank on 16 November 1811.

The lighthouse on Howth Hill referred to by the Lord Lieutenant was one of these for which Sir Robert Reading had received his patent in 1665. It was situated on what is colloquially (but incorrectly) described as the 'summit' on an eminence overlooking Dublin Bay, near the site of the present car park. The original light was a brazier burning on a squat tower which was taken down by Thomas Rogers in 1790 and replaced by a circular tower about six metres high, displaying an oil light. However, because of its height over sea level, the light was frequently obscured in cloud and therein lay the reason for the request of the Lord Lieutenant for its removal to a more advantageous location. The promontory then known as the 'Green Bayley', now the Baily, was chosen as the new position and the work of erecting and fitting out the new lighthouse was completed in 1813 under the supervision of George Halpin, the board's Inspector of Works, who had also designed the structure. Halpin was responsible for the design of a number of other lighthouses, including that on the Tuskar Rock, during his service with the port board, but the detailed history of these and other lights on the coasts of Ireland are outside the scope of this work.

In 1854, the government decided that the lighthouse responsibilities of Trinity House, the Commissioners of Northern Lights and the Corporation for Preserving and Improving the Port of Dublin required to be more explicitly stated and appropriate provisions were included in the Merchant Shipping Act 1854 (17/18 Vic. Cap. 104). Under that act the port board in its capacity as lighthouse authority for Ireland would act under the name 'Port of Dublin Corporation'. While Trinity House continued to have the final decision for the placing of new lights or alterations thereto, a new feature was introduced in the form of certain appelate functions vested in the Board of Trade. The exact limits of the latter board's responsibilities were somewhat indeterminate and led to considerable controversy in the succeeding decade.

The expansion of the sea-borne trade of the United Kingdom in the early years of the reign of Queen Victoria brought greater demands for improved navigational aids for shipping and greater attention focused on existing deficiencies. A Royal Commission was appointed to examine the existing systems of management, operation and maintenance of light-houses on the coasts of the United Kingdom. The commissioners duly visited not only the United Kingdom lighthouses and light vessels but some of those in France and Spain. The Commission presented its report in 1861 and in that report the Board of Trade came in for strong criticism for the manner in which it had exercised its functions under the 1854 act; whereas the three lighthouse authorities had appeared to be striving continually to improve the lighthouses, the objective of the Board of Trade appeared to be solely that of economy and not progress. That board was castigated also for interfering unnecessarily in proposals for new or improved lighthouses and, in some cases, for exercising its authority in such a manner as to involve far greater expenditure than had been proposed by the local lighthouse authority but to far less effect. However, although the report recognised the excellent work done by the three authorities, it considered that the system of control laid down in the 1854 act was cumbersome, inefficient and leading to false economies and criticism was also expressed at the lack of 'scientific element' in the composition of the managements of the three authorities.

The Commission's recommendations were few but drastic; they proposed the transfer of the functions of the existing authorities to a new central authority to be known as 'the Trinity Commissioners for Lights' consisting of ten members, four of whom would be elected by Trinity House, four by the government and one member each from Ireland and Scotland.

The recommendations of the Commission pleased no one although the report provided a most informative and useful survey of the state of the lighthouse services of the United Kingdom at that time, together with a mass of scientific and statistical evidence. At any rate, no action was taken on the recommendations. It is a curious fact that whereas the 1854 act provided that the Dublin port authority when acting as lighthouse authority should be known as the 'Port of Dublin Corporation', nowhere in the Commission's report was this title used, all relevant references being to the 'Ballast Board' or occasionally to the Corporation for Preserving and Improving the Port of Dublin, or the 'Dublin Board'.

The Commission noted evidence given by the 'Dublin Board' regarding George Halpin junior (who had succeeded his father as

Inspector of Works and Superintendent of Lighthouses) and of the burden imposed on him by reason of his necessary attendance on new lighthouses or those being renovated in various parts of the country. The strain consequent on overwork had been such that the board had felt it necessary to reduce Halpin's duties in respect of the port of Dublin to enable him to concentrate on the lighthouses. None the less, Halpin had become seriously ill and had to take extended leave of absence. It seems likely that Halpin's illness was symptomatic of the difficulties encountered by the board itself in the carrying out of its dual functions. Although a change was slow in coming, when it did arrive in the form of the Dublin Port Act 1867 (30 Vic. Cap. 81) it went to the root of the problem by severing the lighthouse authority from the port authority. This is dealt with in more detail in Chapter 15.

When the Corporation for Preserving and Improving the Port of Dublin took over responsibility for the Irish lighthouses in 1810 there were only fourteen lighthouses; by 1867 there were seventy-two, an indication not only of the responsible manner in which that body carried out its lighthouse functions but also of the work of the Halpins in designing and supervising the construction of many of the fifty-eight lighthouses provided between 1810 and 1867.

9

The Ballast Offices

BY the end of the eighteenth century, the development downriver of new facilities for shipping, the construction of the new Custom House, the work of the Wide Streets Commission in Sackville Street and Westmoreland Street and the construction of the new Carlisle Bridge combined to alter the focus of the port administration and of other activities associated with shipping. One of the consequences was the need for larger offices for the board and its staff, situated in a more convenient location than at the rear of the Old Custom House. On the suggestion of some of the board members a lease was secured of premises in the new Lower Sackville Street, near Carlisle Bridge, for a period of three years from 1 January 1794 at a rent of one hundred guineas a year, the new offices 'to be constituted and appointed the Ballast Office of the Port of Dublin'. The office in Essex Street was vacated and the first meeting of the board in its new Ballast Office was held on 24 January 1794. The board was the first of many tenants in these premises at No. 6 Lower Sackville Street, which were considerably altered in later years. They eventually became the DBC restaurant which was destroyed by fire in Easter Week 1916. The premises now form part of the Bank of Ireland at Lower O'Connell Street.

Notwithstanding the convenience of the new offices, some members of the board considered that the growth of trade at the port and its development together with the importance of the port in the economy of the country warranted premises more in keeping with the board's status, and a suitable site for new offices to be specially built was a continuing objective of the members. In 1795, consideration was given to a site in Cope Street which the Wide Streets Commissioners had at their disposal but although the freehold interest was purchased by the board it appears to have been a fallback position from the start, situated as it was in a relatively backward situation off Anglesea Street. In the modern phrase, the Cope Street project was put on the back burner while enquiries continued elsewhere.

The proliferation of imposing new buildings in the city at that time, both public and private, together with the possibility of a more appropriate site no doubt influenced the board in the matter. When such a site became available at the junction of the new Westmoreland Street and Aston Quay in 1801, the board moved in quickly to acquire the site at No. 21 Westmoreland Street under a lease of 175 years and the third Ballast Office was built on this site.

The adjoining building comprised two narrower sites, Nos. 19 and 20 which had two shops on the ground floor; one was a hatter's shop with a workroom at the rear and the other was occupied by James Delaney, a tailor. The first floor of Nos 19/20 was occupied by a firm of solicitors and the upper floors were used as a residence by Delaney and his family, Delaney holding the lease of the whole building. On Friday, 7 June 1866 while Delaney and his son were out rowing on the river, fire broke out in the workroom of the hatter's shop about 8 p.m. but although the fire brigade were soon on the scene their efforts were hampered by lack of water pressure and the collapse of a ladder. Mrs Delaney, her three daughters, a servant girl and a visitor were trapped on the top floor where they had sought refuge from the smoke. In a very short time, the upper floors collapsed and the six people lost their lives. The tragedy provoked a public outcry regarding the failure of the fire brigade to rescue the victims. Questions were raised in parliament and the Dublin Corporation held its own inquiry. The Ballast Office escaped with only minor damage.

Understandably, Delaney had no heart for rebuilding and he offered to sell his interest in Nos 19/20 to the board, the other tenants having sought alternative accomodation. The offer came at an opportune time since it had long been evident that the accommodation in the existing Ballast Office had become inadequate for the dual function of port authority and lighthouse authority and the availability of the site at Nos 19/20 appeared to be the solution of the problem. Delaney's offer was accepted and a new lease was negotiated with the ground landlord of Nos 19/20. A contract for the rebuilding of the burnt out premises and their incorporation into the Ballast Office was placed with the firm of Samuel Bolton.

Following the passing of the Dublin Port Act, 1867, the severance of the board's two functions became effective on 17 June 1867, and on completion of the rebuilding work in 1868, and after some controversy as to which portion of the combined premises the new lighthouse authority (the Commissioners of Irish Lights) should occupy, it was eventually agreed that they should rent the older section, i.e. the original Ballast Office, from the port board and the latter would occupy the new section. The Commissioners of Irish Lights remained in the building as tenants of the port board until 1898 when they moved to new offices in Carlisle Building.

In 1870 the board decided to erect a time ball on the roof of the Ballast Office for the benefit of ship masters who wished to check their chronometers; such a time ball was a common feature in other ports. The time ball consisted of a copper sphere about four feet in diameter sliding on a vertical wooden pole which formed the axis of the ball which was normally positioned at the top of the pole. A control clock in the board room was connected by telegraph wire to Dunsink Observatory; by means of this wire an electrical impulse was received every second by the control clock. A local circuit connected the control clock to the time ball, arranged so that when Dunsink relayed an impulse at 1 p.m. Greenwich Mean Time, the time ball was released and dropped to the bottom of the pole.

As GMT did not apply in Ireland until 1916 the time signal in those days caused not a little confusion to the general public since at 1 p.m. GMT the local time was 12.34 p.m. While shipmasters could no doubt cope with the time difference the signal could not be seen from deepsea vessels berthed downriver. Suggestions were made for the adoption of another signal such as used in Leith, the port of Edinburgh. This was a signal gun timed for noon local time. A story is told of pressure being exerted on the authorities by clergymen in the neighbouring churches to suspend the signal on Sundays because they found their sermons disturbed not so much by the sound of the gun but by the simultaneous action of every gentleman in the congregation taking out his timepiece to check its accuracy. It is not known how successful the clergymen were in their efforts but the suggestion of a signal gun was not adopted by the port Board in Dublin. Eventually the ball was removed to the Berthing Master's Office at the east end of Sir John Rogerson's Quay where, it may be said, it was still out of sight of deepsea vessels in Alexandra Basin. The almost universal use of radio by ships at the end of the Second World War was a clear indication that the ball served no further purpose and it was removed and given to Dunsink Observatory as a souvenir.

The control arrangement in 1870 linking Dunsink with the Ballast Office was extended to clocks at Trinity College and to the Royal Dublin Society's premises then situated in Kildare Street. Later the control was extended to the public clock at Amiens Street railway station but this was discontinued in 1921.

The control clock in the board room of the Ballast Office showed Greenwich time and it was matched by a similar clock showing Dublin time. Both clocks have magnificent mahogany casework and they now form an interesting historical souvenir in the entrance foyer of the board's new headquarters at Port Centre, Alexandra Road.

The feature of the Ballast Office best known to the general public was the famous public clock on the Westmoreland Street facade which was installed in September 1871 and, like the time ball, was connected to the control circuit from Dunsink. The effects of wind and weather on the exposed hands of the clock caused slight irregularities and this reacted on the control clock. The latter required an accuracy within one-fifth of a second whereas the public clock did not require such fine limits and the control was eventually disconnected from the public clock in 1902. However, the clock's reputation for accuracy does not appear to have been affected by the removal of the Dunsink control nor, indeed, by the fact that, situated as it was at about 17 feet over ground level, the position of its hands could hardly be accurately judged by passers-by looking upwards.

The Ballast Office was probably known to generations of Dubliners by reason of its clock rather than from any awareness of the identity or business of its occupiers. Callers to the office from time to time have included those who thought it was the General Post Office; others assumed it was Westland Row railway station. These misapprehensions were not assisted by the fact that until the 1960s no name plate or other identification appeared on the facade of the building. The favourite story of the hall porter of the building in the 1930s and 1940s, Jack Barnes, relates to a gentleman who had dined not wisely but too well and was anxious to pawn his boots.

The Ballast Office was not particularly distinguished from an architectural point of view although it and its look-alike, Carlisle Building, were sufficiently imposing in their early days to feature in the series of views of Dublin by Samuel Brocas dated 1817. In later years, the Ballast Office ranked with Nelson Pillar as a popular rendezvous prior to visits to the theatre, cinema, sporting events, or in the case of the impecunious a simple promenade from O'Connell Bridge to St Stephen's Green.

As with so many Georgian buildings which were and are dear to the hearts of Dublin people, the functional qualities of the Ballast Office were somewhat lacking and behind its famous façade lay a conglomeration of rooms unsuited to present day office requirements and not susceptible of modernisation without considerable expenditure. In addition the development of the port downriver had resulted in the headquarters becoming more and more remote from the activities of the port and of the other departments of the board.

Various proposals were considered over the years for a central headquarters in which all the departments could be housed and in 1954 an architectural competition was held for the design of such a building to be located in the Custom House Docks complex, but the financial climate at the time did not favour proceeding with the project, having regard to more immediate requirements for the accommodation of shipping and the modernisation of facilities. The view had been held in many quarters over the years that the proper place for the board's headquarters was the deepsea area of the port, but the Westmoreland Street offices remained the headquarters until the expiry of the ground lease in 1976. Pending a decision on a new building in the port area, the board took a lease of part of a new building, Gandon House, in Amiens Street. In 1978 the long-awaited decision was made to build a new headquarters building to accommodate all departments, with the exception of the staff associated with the warehousing department in the Custom House Docks. In August 1981, the board moved into the new building, Port Centre, which is situated on part of the former Liffey Dockyard premises at Alexandra Road.

10

The Bull Wall and the Bull Island

BECAUSE of its importance to the development of the port, it seems appropriate to deal with the construction of the North Bull Wall in some detail. Notwithstanding the improvements in the administration, development and operation of the port under the new authority, Dublin Bay continued to take its toll of seamen, ships and their cargoes in bad weather, and in Chapter 7 we saw that the authority was impelled to establish a lifeboat service in the bay.

The government, however, was concerned rather with preventative measures and, accordingly, in an act passed in 1800 (40 Geo. III, Cap. 51) responsibility for the improvement of the port (as distinct from its operation, maintenance and administration) was temporarily vested in a body known as the Directors General of Inland Navigation. Their function was concerned not only with inland navigation but also with the improvement of the port of Dublin and other ports and the creation of an efficient interface between the port of Dublin and the Grand Canal and Royal Canal.

The new directors sought the advice of engineers, surveyors and others with experience in the construction of harbours; these included Sir Thomas Hyde Page and Captain Daniel Corneille. Captain William Bligh was also invited to survey the harbour and to make proposals for its improvement. His survey was meticulous and indicated that earlier charts were deficient, particularly that made in 1686 by Captain Greville Collins whose distances were proved to be inaccurate, thus throwing doubt on the exact location of the bar as shown on his chart and consequently on the extent of changes in it in the intervening years.

Bligh took the view that as the depths in the river channel and at the quays were considerably less than those at or near the bar, attention should be concentrated in the first instance on improving the situation upriver and he envisaged an extension seawards of the north quays to effect the desired objective. The chart of his survey shows a proposed extension from the existing termination of the north quays at the junction with the East Wall, and running parallel with the Great South

Wall, to provide a protective wall along the north side of the channel in the lower harbour.

Suggestions proposed by Hyde Page and others included a canal along the south shore from Dunleary to Ringsend and a similar canal along the north shore from Sutton to Clontarf and thence to East Wall.

Bligh's proposal was recommended to the Lord Lieutenant by the Directors General in August 1801 but the matter was deferred following a request from the port board for consideration of a proposal by two members of the board, George Maquay and Leland Crosthwaite. Their suggestion envisaged a pier running in a south-easterly direction from Clontarf and terminating at a proposed new lighthouse to be built opposite the Poolbeg Lighthouse. In support of this proposal it was pointed out that it had the advantage not only of preventing sand from the northern shore of the bay being washed into the harbour but also of impounding a great volume of water at high tide which, on the ebb, would be concentrated on the relatively narrow space between the Poolbeg lighthouse and the proposed lighthouse at the end of the proposed pier. A scouring action would thereby be created in the ebb tide which would deepen the entrance channel. It was contended that under Captain Bligh's proposal an easterly swell would be confined between his proposed wall and the Great South Wall; such a swell, combined with an easterly gale, could endanger ships at anchor in the channel or moored at the upper quays and could possibly cause flooding in the city. A pier from Clontarf would create a wider area over which the effects of an easterly swell through the narrow entrance would be dissipated. Most important from the point of view of shipping entering the port was the shelter which the new pier would afford, bearing in mind the number of vessels which at that time were obliged to anchor in the river channel, awaiting high water to move further upriver to discharge or discharging overside into lighters while so anchored.

The proposal for a pier running from Clontarf was not a new one, a similar proposal having been made in 1786 by William Chapman, an engineer from Newcastle.

The Directors General asked their consultant, Captain Daniel Corneille, to report on the board's proposal. He expressed support for it and was asked to prepare plans and estimates for the project which he duly did but it would appear that the divergent views of the various experts created a problem for the Directors General and the board's proposal was allowed to lie dormant for a number of years.

While the various proposals were in transit between the parties, an important appointment was made by the board in the person of George Halpin who became the board's Inspector of Works in 1800 following the death of Francis Tunstall. His salary was fixed at one hundred pounds per annum and he was allowed 'ten guineas' to purchase a horse to enable him to supervise more easily the various port works which extended from Sutton on the north side of the bay to Bullock harbour on the south.

Notwithstanding that Halpin was a builder by trade, with no academic engineering qualifications, his contribution to the development of the port cannot be overstated, as will appear.

The sale of the Pidgeon House premises in 1814 enabled the board to pay off debentures and to set aside funds for future port development but although the 'Great North Wall' project, as it was described, was considered on a number of occasions over the intervening years, no real progress was made until 1818 when Halpin was instructed to carry out a new survey of the outer harbour with particular reference to the site of the proposed new wall. Halpin decided to visit Plymouth where a new breakwater had been constructed across the entrance to Plymouth Sound, using almost four million tons of local stone but, presumably because of the differences in scale, situation and local conditions, Halpin found little to assist him in his calculations. However, he recommended that the board apply to the Directors General for the plans and estimates which had been prepared by Captain Corneille. He also proposed that Francis Giles be commissioned to carry out the proposed new survey of the outer harbour and bar. Giles was a hydrographic surveyor in the service of the Admiralty and had already carried out a survey of Howth harbour for the government. On hearing of the proposed survey, the Commissioners of Customs suggested that the survey be extended to include the whole river channel as far upriver as Carlisle Bridge, the cost to be borne 50/50 as between the parties and this was agreed. The survey commenced on 1 June 1818 and was duly carried out with the assistance of Halpin. A joint report by Giles and Halpin to the board in May 1819 recommended that work on the new wall be commenced along a line indicated in an accompanying drawing. The board instructed its law agent to proceed with the necessary legal procedures for the acquisition of the foreshore required for the wall from the reputed owners, the Vernon Estate. The foreshore required was valued by the inquisition process at £450 and, pending clarification of the Vernon title, this sum was lodged in court.

Corneille's plan had proposed a wooden bridge to connect the proposed new wall with Clontarf, thus permitting the passage of water along the channel to the north of a sandbank which was later to grow into the Bull Island as we now know it. In September 1819 a contract for the bridge was awarded to a consortium of builders, Richard Bergan, Arthur McKenna and Andrew Woods, in the sum of £1,582 and the work was reported completed in April 1821. Stone for the main work of constructing the wall was purchased at three shillings per ton (15p in decimal currency) delivered to the site, and this was supplied by various local quarries, mainly those in Howth. Construction of the wall itself commenced and in November 1821, Halpin reported that 6,000 feet had been completed. By July 1822, when inspected by Thomas Telford at the board's invitation, it had been extended by a further 1,500 feet, and on his advice, a further 500 feet was added giving a total length of 8,000 feet. Of this, a length of 5,500 feet was constructed to a height of 18 feet over Low Water Ordinary Spring Tide on the seaward side of the wall, the next 1,500 feet to the level of high water of neap tides and the remaining 1,000 feet to half flood level. The foreshore has altered greatly since those days; areas which were then under water at low tide are now dry and in addition the many improvements to the road surfaces altered the level of the top of the wall.

Further extensions were deemed unwise until the effects of the wall as thus constructed had been observed, although a survey had already shown an improvement in the depth over the bar of from 6 feet 6 inches to 9 feet, and the bank in the river channel known as the North Bank (the site of the present North Bank Lighthouse) had been lowered by three feet. In 1823 further extensions totalling 1,000 feet were approved, bringing the total length to 9,000 feet. The reason for the restriction of the height of the last 2,000 feet of the wall to half flood level was to prevent possible damage to the outer end of the wall by the increased pressure of spring tides if the wall had been continued at full height. The half flood (or, as it is generally termed, half tide) wall acts as a safety valve in allowing the higher spring tides to pass over it instead of being contained between the end of the wall and the Poolbeg Lighthouse on the south side of the harbour entrance. Thus, the 'Great North Wall' or as we know it the 'North Bull Wall' was completed in the year 1824.

Because of the propensity of the skippers of fishing vessels, and indeed larger ships, to use the new breakwater as a convenient and cheap source of ballast on outward trips, the board was obliged to employ watchmen to prevent this practice and also to discourage other depredations such as the removal of the timbers of the wooden bridge connecting the breakwater to the shore. Two small cottages were provided for the watchmen near the bridge.

In 1838 the Admiralty decided to establish a coastguard station at the breakwater and for this purpose they sought a lease from the board of one of the watchmen's cottages together with an adjacent plot of ground on which it was proposed to erect five further cottages for the coastguards. The board agreed, subject to a formal agreement whereby the coastguards would, where possible, aid the watchmen in their duties.

The new breakwater achieved the desired objectives, including the prevention of sand being washed or blown into the previously unprotected northern part of the harbour. The sand which thus accumulated on the seaward side of the breakwater gradually grew into what we now call the Bull Island. An Admiralty chart dated 1838 shows the breakwater, including the watchmen's cottages and the embryo Bull Island which was described as the 'Clontarf Bank'.

Local residents were not slow to recognise and appreciate the amenity provided literally at their doorstep by the Bull Wall, as it came to be generally described, and it soon became a popular attraction for Sunday walks and a convenient place for the more energetic to display their swimming prowess. For those living further away and of sufficient means to have a carriage it was a popular drive. Even for those of more modest means, a walk from the city to the Bull Wall in summertime was by no means unusual and the advent in 1873 of horse trams from the centre city to Dollymount made the Bull Wall an even more attractive venue for the family outing in fine weather. The electrification of the Dublin tramway system commenced in 1896 when the first electric car operated from Haddington Road to Dalkey; the second line to be electrified was that from Annesley Bridge to Dollymount in November 1879 and it was extended to Nelson Pillar in the city centre in March 1898. Not surprisingly, the consequence was an even greater increase in the popularity of Dollymount, the Bull Wall and the adjacent beach.

The increased use of the wooden bridge linking the Bull Wall with Clontarf Road was a matter of concern to the port engineer in 1873 following the introduction of the horse trams. He reported that the bridge was then fifty years old and showing signs of decay; he was concerned lest the structure should collapse when a crowd of people were crossing. The board's reaction was to propose the removal of the bridge since its original purpose of providing access to the causeway during its construction no longer existed; in any event access by boat was available to workmen if required. Public opinion was outraged at the possibility of the loss of such a popular amenity and the board was prevailed on to rebuild the bridge. However, the board decided that the bridge as rebuilt should be only half the original width of twenty feet, so as to restrict it to pedestrians, and barriers were placed at each end of the bridge to prevent vehicles crossing. In 1906 the board decided to complete the reconstruction of the bridge to its original width of twenty feet but motor cars and motor cycles were forbidden to cross unless in special circumstances and with prior permission. The restriction on motor cycles was lifted in 1912 when they were permitted to use the bridge for an annual licence fee of 'one shilling', five pence in modern currency. Later the restrictions on both cars and motor cycles were removed.

The growing popularity of sea bathing in Victorian times involved the provision at the major seaside resorts of bathing boxes or 'machines' as they were known, in which intending bathers could change into bathing costume, thus preserving the existing conventions in the matter of modesty. Although some local residents had received permission to place private bathing boxes on the beach, such facilities were not generally available at the Bull Wall and many complaints were made to the board that visitors to the Wall in the 'bathing season' had been shocked by 'the primitive, not to say indecent, exhibitions taking place there'. The complainants went on to describe the attitude of 'certain males' who displayed no consideration for passing females in the matter of changing into bathing costume. Subsequent complaints referred to the scandalous conduct of those of the male sex who preferred to swim *au naturel* and the board was obliged to post a notice requiring swimmers to wear costumes and not to bathe within 500 feet of the Clontarf Road.

In 1899 John Lumsden applied to the board on behalf of the Dublin Golf Club for permission to use portion of the ground adjoining the Bull Wall on which 'three greens' could be laid out; the club had already received permission from the Vernon Estate to lay out the remaining fifteen greens on the estate's property on the island. Lumsden was the first captain of the club and had been the moving spirit in its establishment in 1885, using a course laid out in the Phoenix Park on the area usually known as the Fifteen Acres. The board duly granted permission and in later years the club purchased the fee simple of the areas leased. In 1921 a second golf club, St Anne's, was established on the north-eastern end of the island. The Royal Dublin Club has been the venue for many championship golf matches, both Irish and international.

Following the outbreak of war in 1914, the Bull Wall and Bull Island were taken over by the British military authorities in September of that year for use as a training camp; the clubhouse of the golf club was used as the officers' mess. When the army evacuated the area in August 1921 it left a useful legacy in the form of water and electricity supplies laid on during the occupation. The coastguard cottages were transferred by the British Admiralty to the new Irish government in March 1922 and were handed back to the board by the Office of Public Works in July 1926.

In later years, bathing shelters, public shelters, toilets, drinking fountains, and terracing at the bathing places were provided by Dublin Corporation. Because of the increase in cars using the Bull Wall for access to the two golf clubs and to Dollymount Strand (as the beach on the Island is usually known) the Corporation also resurfaced the roadway and provided footpaths, and in 1955 the port board provided traffic lights at the approach bridge.

Dollymount Strand was the scene of a number of drowning tragedies over the years by reason of deep channels and gullies running through the foreshore where the depth of water otherwise was relatively shallow and safe for non-swimmers. Although the area concerned was outside the board's lands, it arranged for warning notices to be erected in the location of what to the public was generally known as 'Curley's hole'; the name is believed to derive from that of one of its first victims. However, the notices sometimes caused difficulties in that there was not one 'hole' but several and their position was not constant; almost every tide, particularly in strong easterly winds, brought about a change in position. The number of tragedies has, happily, decreased very much in recent years and few, in any, are due to 'Curley's hole'.

During the 'Emergency', as the period of the Second World War was officially described in Ireland, the Department of Defence established an anti-aircraft battery at the seaward end of the Bull Wall at the point where it gives way to the half tide wall. The battery was removed in 1945 and the site was put to a more peaceful use when it was handed over by the board in 1972 to a committee of port workers for the erection of a statue of Our Lady Star of the Sea, on the top of a concrete tripod 60 feet high. The erection of the statue was the culmination of many years of work by an indefatigable voluntary committee based on the City Quay parish.

The lagoon between the Bull Island and the coast road was the subject of several proposals by Dublin Corporation over the years for its development for boating, swimming and other aquatic pastimes. The matter was first proposed in 1929 and reviewed again on a number of occasions. In 1946 the Corporation commissioned Sir Claud Inglis, an eminent consultant engineer, to advise on the various proposals which had been made and which differed from each other mainly in regard to the area proposed to be impounded. Inglis estimated that an impounded lake extending from Bull Bridge to Sutton creek would cost almost £1 million but he considered that there were several technical imponderables which could only be evaluated on the basis of detailed specialised investigations. As a result of these investigations, it was found that the maintenance of the required depth of water at all times was not feasible due to the existence of a stratum of gravel under the lagoon and the island which would allow the water to percolate; further, biological tests showed that notwithstanding tidal flows which would occur at certain times in the tidal cycle, the impounding of the proposed lake would produce a 'green lagoon' instead of a 'blue lagoon' as the scheme had come to be described, and eventually, the Corporation dropped the proposal. However, the construction in 1962–4 of a causeway from the coast road opposite Watermill Lane to a point roughly half way along the island enabled many citizens to have easier access to the eastern section of the beach and sand dunes whether by private car or, in summertime, by bus.

In 1931 the island was designated a bird sanctuary and in subsequent years it has received international attention; over 150 different bird species have been identified on the island. In 1986 an Interpretive Centre was provided by Dublin Corporation to provide visitors to the island with information on its flora and fauna.

Halpin, Giles, Telford and company would no doubt be pleasantly surprised to find that their prosaic harbour breakwater had brought in its wake such excellent amenities within a half-hour's journey from the city centre.

11

The West Quay Walls and the Bridges

THE progressive development of the city eastwards from the early town was, as we have noted, accompanied by the continuing growth in trade and commerce with the consequent need for additional bridges over the river Liffey to accomodate the increase in traffic. The effect of building each new bridge was to cut off a stretch of the river previously used to berth ships and discharge their cargoes; thereafter these sections of the the river were confined to small craft such as lighters and barges. The knock-on effect was to require the construction further down river of new shipping quays to accomodate the shipping thus displaced, apart altogether from the new berthage required to handle the increased trade to the port.

The Act of 1786 under which the port authority was established provided that it should be responsible for repairing or rebuilding the existing quay walls which at that time extended as far to the east as the new Custom House, then in course of building on the north side of the river, and to the Marine School on Sir John Rogerson's Quay on the south. Later statutes extended this responsibility to include all the quays and walls on both sides of the 'River Anna Liffey', as the acts describe the river, from Barrack (now Rory O'More) Bridge to Sutton on the north side of the bay and to Dalkey on the south.

In addition to vesting responsibility for the maintenance of the quays and walls, the last named act, passed in 1811, also vested in the authority full title in the 'quays and walls called the North South and East Walls'. These functions and title were extended also to 'all the bridges now over the said River Anna Liffey or which hereafter may be built or erected within the said limits over the same'.

In as much as the river was in constant use for the transport, by lighter or barge, to the upper reaches of goods landed from ships berthed lower down the river or anchored in the estuary, it was clearly desirable that the port authority should have jurisdiction over the areas concerned and hence the fixing of Barrack Bridge as the western limit of the port. In later years the steam barges of the Guinness brewery were to travel further westwards to Victoria Quay but the western limit of the port was never altered. Responsibility for the quay walls and the bridges upriver of the ordinary shipping berths was, in the circumstances of the times, a logical addition to the authority's functions.

Since the public at large and the occupiers of premises situated on the upper quays were the main beneficiaries of these upper river works, it was considered inequitable that expenditure thereon should be borne by the shipping using the port, and accordingly the statutes provided that this expenditure should be recouped from the city and the county by means of an annual levy to be known as the 'West Quay Walls and Bridges Tax'.

Following the building of Carlisle Bridge, the obligations of the city and county in respect of this tax were applied to all the quays and walls westwards of this bridge and likewise to all the bridges, including the new bridge. The remaining quays downriver from Carlisle Bridge continued to be the direct responsibility of the port since they were used primarily for shipping and the costs of their maintenance continued to be borne by the general revenues from shipping.

Within twenty years of its construction, Carlisle Bridge came under criticism as being too narrow for the traffic which required to use it and various proposals were put forward in later years for widening it; other suggestions were for another bridge further downriver. A census of traffic taken in 1860 showed that 1,037 vehicles per hour passed over Carlisle Bridge, compared with 1,091 vehicles per hour over London Bridge. Public meetings were held to gain support for improving Carlisle Bridge and for a new bridge to cross the river either immediately to the west or immediately to the east of the Custom House. The existing legislation was found to have certain loopholes so far as the financing of these proposals were concerned and eventually in 1876 an act (39/40 Vic. Cap. 85) was passed to authorise the rebuilding of Carlisle Bridge and the construction of a new bridge crossing the river to the west of the Custom House; the new bridge was to be an opening structure operated by hydraulic machinery to enable vessels to continue to berth at Eden Quay and Burgh Quay. The design for both bridges was produced by the port engineer, Bindon Blood Stoney.

In April 1877 contracts for both projects were placed with the firm of William J. Doherty of Belfast and Dublin who had also been the contractors for most of the re-building of Sir John Rogerson's Quay. The new opening bridge, named Butt Bridge at the request of the Municipal Corporation, was opened to the public in September 1879 and a census taken in the following month showed that an average of 3,177 vehicles passed over the bridge daily together with '6,308 pedestrians, 55 equestrians and 223 cattle'. While vessels continued to pass through to the upriver berthage at Eden Quay and Burgh Quay, the use of this berthage gradually declined, due mainly to the lack of water for the larger vessels using the port and also to the difficulty of loading and unloading cargoes on quaysides which had become major thoroughfares. The bridge opened for shipping for the last time on 13 December 1888. With the completion of the 'Loopline' railway bridge in 1891, it would not in any event have been possible for ships to pass under this bridge which, it should be stated, is not the responsibility of the port authority but of CIE.

The rebuilt Carlisle Bridge was opened to the public in August 1880 but not without something of a controversy, or more accurately a storm in a teacup, regarding the name of the bridge. The port board had erected a tablet on the bridge showing the years of its erection and rebuilding but the Municipal Corporation considered that the bridge should be renamed O'Connell Bridge because of a project then in hands for the erection of a statue to Daniel O'Connell in Sackville Street, close to the rebuilt bridge; the Corporation also desired that the names of the Lord Mayor, the high sheriff, the port engineer and the contractor be included. The port board was not greatly disturbed by the proposal which, when it came before it, was approved without much discussion, and a new plaque was placed over the original tablet. The statue was unveiled in the following year, 1881.

By the 1920s it had become apparent that Butt Bridge could not cope with the traffic requiring to use it. Its replacement by a new and wider fixed bridge was authorised by the Dublin Port and Docks (Bridges) Act 1929 and this bridge, designed by the port engineer at that time, Joseph Mallagh, was completed in 1932. The act made provision similar to that of the earlier statutes whereby the costs of erecting and maintaining the rebuilt bridge would be recouped as before from the city and county. As Eden Quay and Burgh Quay had not been available to shipping since 1888 the maintenance of these quay walls was thenceforth paid for in the same manner as the other 'West' quay walls.

Anticipating future demand for another bridge further downriver, the port board secured powers in the 1929 Act for the construction of a transporter bridge to cross the river near Cardiff Lane. The bridge was intended to be so built that shipping would pass underneath but in the event the bridge was never built.

The construction of the Talbot Memorial Bridge, completed in 1978, marked a fundamental departure from existing statutory provisions in that, by agreement between the Municipal Corporation and the port board, the bridge was built by the Corporation under powers granted by a statutory instrument known as a bridge order. The order provided that the cost of erection and maintenance of the bridge would be borne directly by the Corporation and since sections of Custom House Quay and George's Quay would no longer be available to shipping, their maintenance would fall under the existing provisions relating to the maintenance of the West Quay Walls.

Considerable controversy followed a proposal by Dublin Corporation in the 1970s to erect a new high level bridge across the Liffey as part of a major road development plan. The location was to be that proposed by the port board for the transporter bridge in 1929, but the proposal was shelved.

In 1975 a proposal by a private company to erect an opening toll bridge to connect East Wall with Ringsend was made to the board. The project was attended by long delay due to the many legal and practical difficulties which had to be overcome but eventually agreement was reached as between the promoters, the port board, Dublin Corporation and the relevant government departments, and following the passing of legislation necessary to permit of the construction of a toll bridge and approach road, the East Link Toll Bridge was opened in 1984. As the bridge has a lifting span to allow of shipping passing through, it does not interfere with the use by ships of the quays up as far as the Talbot Memorial Bridge and the port board still continues to be responsible for the costs of maintaining these quays.

The following is a summary of the history of the other Liffey bridges situated within the port limits.

Rory O'More Bridge (at Watling Street)

A wooden bridge, built in 1670 on this site, was the scene of a violent fracas between factions supporting and opposed to its situation, resulting in the deaths of four people. Thereafter it was known as Bloody Bridge. It was rebuilt in stone in 1704 and named Barrack Bridge because of its proximity to the then new Royal (now Collins) Barracks. In 1812, an ornamental gateway was erected on the southern side of the bridge but following the opening of the new Kingsbridge railway station in 1846 the gateway became an obstruction to the increased traffic along the south quays; it was removed and re-erected at the entrance to the Royal Hospital at Kilmainham. The bridge was rebuilt once more, this time as an iron bridge to a design by George Halpin junior; following a formal re-opening by Queen Victoria in 1863 it was re-named Victoria Bridge and the adjoining quay between the bridge and Kingsbridge was named Victoria Quay.

In 1929, the centenary year of Catholic emancipation was celebrated with ceremonies in Dublin, culminating with Benediction at an altar erected on the bridge. Thereafter the bridge was known for some years as Emancipation Bridge but it was later given its present name of Rory O'More Bridge.

Liam Mellowes Bridge (at Queen Street)
The first bridge on this site was built between 1683 and 1688. It was swept away by a flood in 1763 and it was rebuilt between 1764 and 1768. The bridge has been called by various names over the years, including Arran Bridge, Bridewell Bridge, Ellis Bridge, Queen's Bridge and Queen Maeve's Bridge before receiving its present name.

Father Mathew Bridge (at Church Street)
See Chapter 2.

O'Donovan Rossa Bridge (at Winetavern Street)
The first bridge on this site was built in 1682–3; named Ormonde Bridge, it was situated slightly to the east of the present bridge. Ormonde Bridge was destroyed in a flood in 1806 and the present bridge was built in 1816 and given the name Richmond Bridge, later renamed as O'Donovan Rossa Bridge.

Grattan Bridge (at Capel Street)
The first bridge on this site was built in 1676; known as Essex Bridge it was widened in 1753–5, rebuilt in its present form in 1873–5 to Stoney's design and named Grattan Bridge.

Liffey Bridge (at Liffey Street)
Originally called Wellington Bridge, but better known to Dubliners as the Metal or Ha'penny Bridge; although within the limits of the port the port board has no responsibility for its maintenance. In March 1816 the port board received a submission from William Walsh who stated that he had obtained a lease of the Liffey ferries from the Dublin Corporation. He proposed to replace one of the ferries with an iron toll bridge for pedestrians only across the river near the new Wellington Quay. The board agreed subject to the condition that if at any time the bridge was considered to be 'objectionable or inconvenient' it must be taken down and the quay walls restored within twelve months of being served notice to do so. It was soon apparent that John Claudius Beresford, a member of the board and son of John Beresford of Custom House fame, was a partner in the project since later in the same year he sought and received the board's consent to the erection of toll houses at each end of the bridge. As soon as the toll houses were erected they were seen to be an eyesore and their removal was ordered by the board on the grounds that 'all obstacles should be removed which in any way impede the view of the walls and the bridges'. The toll houses were removed and replaced by turnstiles. The toll for the bridge and the ferries at the time was one halfpenny from whence the bridge derived its popular name. The lease of the bridge and ferries expired in 1915; the

turnstiles were removed and the bridge was declared open to the public in 1919. In 1920 the Corporation ordered new motor ferries to be built at the boat building yard of John Hollwey at Ringsend; these ferries were operated by the Corporation itself until 1984 when the service was withdrawn.

12

Packet Ships and
the Advent of the Steamship

DURING the reign of Elizabeth I, it was found necessary to establish a regular means of communication with the Queen's representative in Ireland. Ships chartered for the purpose were known as 'pacquet' ships as we have noted and until 1657 they generally operated between Dublin and Liverpool or Chester, and sometimes Parkgate on the estuary of the Dee. Although a harbour had been in existence at Holyhead for many centuries, the difficulties of traversing the North Wales terrain discouraged most travellers from using that route. One of the more difficult stretches involved using a track along the sands skirting the mountain at Penmaenmawr when weather and tidal conditions permitted; in unfavourable conditions travellers were forced to dismount from their coaches and follow a precipitous and dangerous track over the mountain.

Following the restoration of Charles II in 1660, a new General Post Office was established and a new Postmaster-General appointed. The statute under which these arrangements were made provided that all other persons were forbidden 'to set up or employ any foot-posts, horse-posts or pacquet boats'. This act has been described as the charter for the British Post Office. A year later John Swift was appointed as the sole contractor for the provision of packet ships to Ireland, to carry general mails as well as state papers.

An account of the difficulties to be encountered by travellers to Ireland in the seventeenth century is given by John Bingley, a government official who travelled to Dublin in January 1605. His ship had made four attempts to cross to Dublin in bad weather; on the fourth venture, they ran into a storm which damaged the ship severely and she had to return to Beaumaris. He noted that when crossing through Chester, he saw a great many people waiting to cross to Ireland; because of the continuous bad weather conditions, the ships had been delayed for many weeks resulting in a backlog of about 400 persons waiting to embark. As late as the end of the eighteenth century, the packet ships and passage boats were small sailing craft of no more than sixty or seventy tons, but their size had the advantage that when weather or tidal conditions made it impossible to beat into Dublin harbour, they could use the small harbour at (old) Dunleary.

From March 1768, six packet ships were employed, enabling a daily service to be maintained on weekdays. In 1772, the system of awarding the mail contract was altered; instead of one contractor being appointed, a contract was entered into with the master-cum-owner of each of five packets, thus reducing the service by one vessel. In the same year, improvements were carried out to much of the road system along the North Wales coast, particularly at Penmaenmawr, and the Holyhead route became gradually more acceptable to travellers, involving as it did a shorter sea journey than that from Parkgate, Chester or Liverpool.

In 1796, the Post Office decided to maintain small vessels of about forty tons, known as wherries, at Holyhead and Dublin. The wherries were described as being 'handier than the cutter-rigged packets and able to beat out of Holyhead Bay when the regular packets could not do so'. If conditions were against packets trying to enter the Liffey estuary or Dunleary the mails could be transferred to wherries in Dublin Bay to be taken ashore.

Wilson's Almanac for 1797 contains advertisements for the various 'H.M. Pacquets'—the *Bessborough, Leicester, Hillsborough* and *Loftus* on the Holyhead route, passages to be booked at the Marine Hotel, 72 Sir John Rogerson's Quay. Five other 'packets' (actually passage boats) on the Parkgate route had their Dublin agent in Rogers' Hotel at 85 Sir John Rogerson's Quay. For those passengers wishing to go to Liverpool, Messrs Wybrants at 37 George's Quay were ready to make the necessary arrangements on five vessels on that run—*Duke of Leinster, Beresford, Thetis, Ponsonby* and *Viceroy*.

One of the best known of the Post Office packets was the *Bessborough* which had two cabins, one with eight berths for ladies and the other containing twelve berths for the gentlemen; servants, carriages and horses were 'accomodated' on the deck. Although the vessel was described as being fitted up with mahogany 'and every convenience a traveller could desire', these attractions did little to alleviate the misery of a rough crossing in winter weather; even in fine weather, passengers sometimes had to undergo the discomfort of being carried ashore at Holyhead on the backs of labourers employed for the purpose when the packet could not come alongside the pier at low water at certain spring tides.

The passage boats were not always as well found and maintained as the Post Office packets and it was not unusual for unscrupulous passage boat owners to skimp in various ways; a common way of saving money (and one not always obvious to passengers) was to employ a smaller crew than was desirable for the safe working of the ship. In an act of 1800 (40 Geo. III, Cap. 47) this scandal was tackled head-on. The act referred to the necessity for the protection of the lives and properties of H.M. subjects 'a great number of whom constantly pass in passage boats between Dublin and different ports in Great Britain'. The act provided that no passage boat should be less than sixty tons burden, excluding H.M. vessels, packets or wherries. The appointment of inspectors by the Dublin port authority was authorised , with the duty of inspecting all passage boats to ensure that they were maintained in good and sufficient condition for their purpose and 'well provided with all the necessary tackle and materials, properly manned and with sufficient water for passengers and crew'. Exclusive of the vessel's master, mate and ship's boy, one able seaman was required to be employed for every twelve tons of the ship's burden. If a passage boat satisfied the requirements of the act and those of the port authority her master was issued with a licence enabling him to operate the vessel as a passage boat.

In November 1807 the board were informed that when the packet *Bessborough* was on passage in bad weather, the master Captain Edmund Browne was found to be 'dead drunk in his cabin'. The vessel had received damage in the storm and was in grave danger of becoming a total wreck; however, the crew managed to get the vessel into Parkgate. Not surprisingly, the master's licence was withdrawn.

Following the Act of Union of 1800, further improvements were made both in the roads and in the ships, due to some extent to the influence of Irish Members of Parliament arising from the necessity to travel to London on parliamentary business, thus bringing them in closer contact with the harsh realities of the journey between the capitals. Somewhat larger packets of about 100 tons were introduced and by 1808 all the older packets, including the *Bessborough*, had been replaced.

In 1818 the packet station was transferred from Dublin to Howth and this is dealt with in more detail in Chapter 13.

The advent of the steam engine and its adaptation for ship propulsion led to the establishment of the first regular service by a steamship, the paddle steamer *Comet*, which operated regularly between Glasgow and Greenock from 1812 to 1820. The first steamship seen in Dublin was the *Argyle*, later renamed the *Thames*, which called en route from London to the Clyde in May 1815. In the following year a company was formed in Dublin under the title 'The Steam Packet Company' to operate a passenger service between Howth and Holyhead with two paddle steamers, the *Hibernia* and the *Britannia* built in the previous year on the Clyde. The vessels were identical, with an overall length of 77 feet, beam 24 feet and in addition to their steam propulsion they were schooner-rigged. Accomodation below deck was somewhat more spacious than in the sailing packets, cabin accomodation for thirty being provided with the usual arrangements on deck for the passage of horses and carriages. Two further vessels were proposed with the intention of competing with the Post Office packets for the passenger trade. After a short trial trip along the coast on 6 September 1816, the first voyage from Howth to Holyhead took place a week later, on Friday 13 September. The service operated spasmodically for some months during which the advantages of steamships were demonstrated by passages of eight hours from Holyhead, compared to an average of fifteen hours in good weather by the sailing packets. However, dissension among the members of the company led to litigation, resulting in the sale of the vessels and the disappearance of the company.

In 1820, a company called the 'New Steam Packet Company' made its appearance with a new paddle steamer, the *Talbot*, and efforts were made by this company to obtain the mail contract between Howth and Holyhead but without success. The *Talbot* had a tonnage of 150 tons and at 93 feet overall she was somewhat longer than the earlier *Hibernia*; with a narrower beam and a more powerful engine than the *Hibernia*, the *Talbot* reduced the time for the voyage to $7\frac{1}{2}$ hours soon after she commenced her service on 3 May 1820. Within three weeks the company's second vessel arrived to complement the *Talbot*; this was the *Ivanhoe*, somewhat longer and with an engine of 60 h.p., and a daily service was inaugurated.

The Post Office was kept fully aware of the success of the new steamers by its local agents, and although the masters of the sailing packets were, not surprisingly, somewhat contemptuous of the abilities of the steamers to perform in safety throughout the winter months, the authorities chartered the *Talbot* to carry the mails for some months later in 1820. The experiment satisfied them that steamships were commercially viable and it was decided to order two new steamers which would operate in conjunction with two sailing packets. The new Post Office steamers arrived in Howth on 31 May 1821 and they commenced operations on the following day. They soon proved their superiority over the *Talbot* and the *Ivanhoe* which is not surprising in view of their size and power. The first ship was the *Lightning* of 205 tons and with two engines of 40 h.p. each; the second was the *Meteor* which was slightly smaller and with two 30 h.p. engines.

The *Talbot* and the *Ivanhoe* were withdrawn from the Howth run and transferred to Dublin to operate a service to Liverpool from Sir John Rogerson's Quay. In accordance with the statutory requirements governing passage boats operating from Dublin the two vessels were obliged to undergo inspection and on 21 July, an application was accordingly made to the board by Thomas Boyd on behalf of the owners for the relevant licences. The board had doubts as to the propriety of granting licences to steam vessels but were advised by the attorney-general that the statute concerned gave them no power to discriminate between sailing vessels and steamships, provided the latter complied with the requirements of the statute and the port regulations. The board's haven masters who were also the Inspectors of Passage Boats reported that with the exception of some minor deficiencies the vessels *Talbot* and *Ivanhoe* were well-found in hulls, rigging, sails and gear; however, they were not competent to report on the engines and machinery. Appropriate certificates were duly produced in respect of the engines and machinery from Richard Robinson of the Phoenix Foundry and the board ordered that the necessary licences be issued.

In the early 1800s a number of sailing ships were in operation on cross-channel passenger and cargo services from Dublin. Some of these ships were owned by George Langtry and in 1820 he acquired two new paddle steamers, *Waterloo* and *Belfast* with which he commenced a service to Liverpool. The competition for this traffic was extended in 1822 with the advent of the St George Steam Packet Company which put three steamships on the route, but in 1824 a new Dublin company appeared on the scene that was eventually to become the largest company operating on the Irish Sea routes. This was the City of Dublin Steam Packet Company founded by a remarkable man, Charles Wye Williams, whose abilities and interests extended far beyond the realm of shipowning. By 1826 the company owned fifteen ships and for a time it extended its operations to the Liverpool-New York route and through its holding in the P. & O. Co. it was involved in continental and Mediterranean trade. The company became interested in a new development for steamship propulsion by propellor (or screw as it was then known) instead of paddles, and it acquired a number of schooners equipped with screw propulsion for cargo and livestock work. One of its competitors in this field was the Dublin and Liverpool Screw Company, the 'Screw' company as it was generally known, and rivalry between the two led to cut-throat competition with shameful consequences in the years of the famine and its aftermath. Thousands of people fled the country, many with no possessions other than the clothes, or in many cases rags, in which they stood. The Screw company offered to take passengers on deck for one shilling and demand for passages was so great that frequently several ships a day were despatched to Liverpool. Scenes of near riot were witnessed at the Dublin quays as the intending passengers rushed the gangways.

The City of Dublin company responded by offering the same fare to passengers willing to use its screw schooners; the normal fare by the company's paddle steamers was three shillings but cheap as the fare by screw ship may seem, the facilities on board were minimal, consisting of the use of such space on deck as could be obtained between the cattle pens, no under-deck shelter for passengers being provided. Toilets were non-existent and the consequences of the sea sickness of humans and animals were appalling. Passengers on screw schooners were usually known as 'deckers' or 'paupers' by the authorities at Liverpool and many were in very poor health due not only to the ravages of famine but also of typhus. Deaths on voyages were not unknown as were births in unbelievable conditions. In bad weather the voyage from Dublin to Liverpool could take from twenty to thirty hours.

In 1859 a committee of inquiry into the conditions in which the 'deckers' travelled was headed by Captain H.M. Denham, a consultant marine surveyor at Liverpool. The committee's report noted that in the year 1848 almost 300,000 people were landed at Liverpool from Irish ports. Of this total, over 130,000 were en route to the USA and of the balance 120,000 were found indeed to be paupers. The average number of 'deckers' per ship arriving from Dublin over a three month period in 1848 was given as 600 and quarantine officers reported that fever and disease were rampant among them. The infection spread to doctors, social helpers and clergymen at Liverpool who tried to give some assistance but many of them contracted the fever and died. The citizens of Liverpool became so alarmed that eventually local magistrates were obliged to order the return to Ireland of many of the paupers.

In 1838, a new steamship company was established by a group of Dublin businessmen under the title 'British and Irish Steam Packet Company' with an office at Eden Quay. The directors included Wiliam Carleton who was also a director of the City of Dublin company, and Arthur Guinness, a descendant of the founder of the famous brewery. The new company took over the business of an existing company, the Dublin and London Steam Packet Company.

The proliferation of shipping companies operating out of Dublin throughout the nineteenth century and their amalgamation, absorption or disappearance, although a most interesting story, is somewhat outside the scope of this book. However, one major failure was that of the City of Dublin company, due to the misfortunes of war in 1914–18 and the loss of the mail contract (see Chapter 13). In 1919 the company's operations and ships were taken over by the British and Irish company together with those of Tedcastle McCormick and the Dublin and Manchester Steam Shipping Company.

13

The Harbours of Howth and Kingstown

ALTHOUGH the harbours of Howth and Kingstown/Dun Laoghaire are outside the limits of the Port of Dublin, the statutes authorising their construction provided in each case that when they were completed they would come under the control and jurisdiction of the Dublin Port authority. It seems appropriate, therefore, to deal with their early history.

The building of Pidgeon House harbour brought some improvement for the sailing packet ships and their passengers, but these ships were still faced with the difficulty of getting into Dublin harbour in strong adverse winds; on the other hand, when running for the harbour with following winds there was always the hazard of the lee shore to contend with in storm conditions. Even when these difficulties had been overcome, there was insufficient berthage to accomodate all the packet ships and passage boats requiring to berth there and as a result some ships could be forced to stand off and anchor in the river until a berth became available. As if these problems were not enough for the shipmasters to contend with, Pidgeon House harbour dried out at low water spring tides and had very little water on the neap tides and the consequent delays to the mails was a matter of considerable concern to the Post Office authorities.

In 1800 Thomas Rogers, the contractor to the Revenue Commissioners for building and repairing lighthouses, suggested that a harbour be built at Howth and connected by a canal along the north side of the Sutton isthmus and cutting through to the Sutton/Kilbarrack foreshore and thence via Clontarf to Dublin. In the same year, Sir Thomas Hyde Page outlined proposals for a new harbour at Howth and another at Dalkey, with the object of providing a more suitable packet station than the Pidgeon House. However, it was not until the year 1807 that the government decided that a harbour should be built at Howth. In that year, commissioners were appointed under an act (45 Geo. III Cap. 113) to oversee the construction of the new harbour. The Earl of Howth was appointed Chairman of the Commissioners who were vested with powers in relation to Howth similar to those of the Corporation for preserving and improving the port of Dublin in relation to the Port of Dublin. The plan which was adopted for Howth was prepared by Captain George Taylor and the early stages of the construction were supervised by him. Taylor resigned from the project in 1808 and he was succeeded as superintendent of the work by John Aird, acting under the direction of John Rennie.

Considerable controversy preceded the commencement of the new harbour because of the belief among many interested parties that its position in relation to the tidal currents must inevitably lead to silting. Although John Rennie was appointed to direct the operation in 1809, work had already started and he had not a free choice as to the site of the new pier (the present east pier) as proposed under the original plan. Not surprisingly he was pessimistic as to the likelihood of the success of the project.

The Earl of Howth was in the happy position of being able to supply the stone for the work from his nearby quarries and this he proceeded to do without the benefit of formal contract or authorisation. No query was raised by the other commissioners until they received a bill from Lord Howth for 91,000 tons of stone already supplied. The earl indicated his intention to continue to supply a further 500,000 tons necessary to complete the work, but the claim was resisted by the other commissioners and the work was stopped. The opinion of the attorney-general was sought as to the validity of Lord Howth's claim and the commissioners were duly advised that there had been no obligation on him to supply the stone and no obligation on the commissioners to pay for the quantity already delivered. Subsequently, large quantities of stone were procured from the Dalkey quarries and elsewhere to complete the work.

Following a recommendation by Rennie, the original proposal was enlarged in 1810 to provide for a second (west) pier. The harbour was completed in 1813 but it was not formally established as the mail packet station until 1818. In the meantime, an Act of Parliament passed in 1811 (50 Geo. III, Cap. 72) provided that the works when completed should be vested in the Corporation for preserving and improving the port of Dublin.

Deficiencies anticipated by the parties opposed to the harbour became apparent soon after the arrival on the scene of the steam mail packets; complaints were made of damage sustained by bumping or actually taking the ground at low water due, it was alleged, to the high level of rock in the bed of the harbour. Siltation at the entrance and in the berths was also a problem.

Developments on the south side of Dublin Bay which were in progress before Howth harbour was completed were ultimately to evoke

George Halpin Junior, chief engineer to the port board, 1854–62.

The Scottish square rigger, *Queen Elizabeth* (*above*) at City Quay, c.1895. She can also be seen on the right-hand side of the photograph below, taken on the same occasion, showing a general view of the river and in particular the old timber jetties at Custom House Quay.

Two views of shipping at the North Quays and the North Wall extension, 1929.

Bindon Blood Stoney, chief engineer to the port board from 1862 to 1898. The illustration (*below left, opposite*) shows the title page of his textbook on the theory of stresses.

Alderman Alfred (Alfie) Byrne, Lord Mayor of Dublin, at the opening of the reconstructed Butt Bridge in 1932.

THE

THEORY OF STRESSES

IN

GIRDERS AND SIMILAR STRUCTURES,

WITH

PRACTICAL OBSERVATIONS ON THE STRENGTH AND OTHER
PROPERTIES OF MATERIALS.

BY

BINDON B. STONEY, LL.D., F.R.S.,

MEMBER OF THE INSTITUTION OF CIVIL ENGINEERS, MEMBER OF THE INSTITUTION OF NAVAL ARCHITECTS,
AND ENGINEER TO THE DUBLIN PORT AND DOCKS BOARD.

Priusquam incipias, consulto ; et ubi consulueris, mature facto opus est.

With Illustrations on Wood by Oldham.

NEW EDITION, REVISED,
WITH NUMEROUS ADDITIONS ON GRAPHIC STATICS, PILLARS, STEEL, WIND PRESSURE,
OSCILLATING STRESSES, WORKING LOADS, RIVETING,
STRENGTH AND TESTS OF MATERIALS.

LONDON:
LONGMANS, GREEN, AND CO.
1886.

[The Right of Translation is reserved.]

The present Poolbeg Lighthouse.

The Eucharistic Congress of 1932 created an unprecedented challenge for Dublin port. Among the eight liners which berthed at the quays were the *Sierra Cordoba* and the *Dresden* (*above*) which were moored in Alexandra Basin and the Dutch liner *Marnix Van St Aldegonde* (*below*) at Sir John Rogerson's Quay.

The four lighthouses on the north side of the river channel. These four photographs show the lighthouses at the North Wall extension (*above left*), the Eastern Breakwater (*above right*), the North Bank (*below left*) and the North Bull (*below right*).

Sir Richard Martin, one of Dublin's leading commercial figures in the late nineteenth and early twentieth centuries.

acknowledgment that Howth harbour had been a failure so far as the mail packets were concerned. These developments were the construction of a 'harbour of refuge' at what was then known as Dunleary, and of the first railway line in the country which ran between Dublin and Kingstown, as Dunleary was later re-named.

The hazards of Dublin Bay had been once more illustrated in November 1807 when the troop transport *Rochdale* and the packet ship *Prince of Wales* were wrecked between Blackrock and Seapoint in a north-easterly gale, with the loss of 380 lives. The disaster provoked a public outcry and a demand for a harbour of refuge. The government was still considering the various proposals put forward originally in 1800 and subsequent years including the building of a canal along the south shore of the bay, and it was not until 1815 that statutory provision was made (55 Geo. III, Cap. 191) for the appointment of commissioners with powers to make surveys, plans and estimates for the erection of a 'harbour or place of refuge which would be of great advantage as well to the ships trading to the port of Dublin as to the ships and vessels of His Majesty's Navy which may be in the Irish Channel.' In the following year, authorisation was given to proceed with the work of building the new harbour (56 Geo. III, Cap. 62) and it was provided that on completion of the new harbour it should, as in the case of Howth harbour, become vested in the Corporation for preserving and improving the port of Dublin. The new harbour was not therefore primarily intended or designed as a place for landing or loading passengers or goods but as a harbour of refuge in which ships trading to Dublin and elsewhere could shelter in bad weather, and also as a naval station.

The original designs were by John Rennie, and like those for Howth harbour, they provided originally for only one pier, the present East Pier. Work commenced in 1816, the stone for the project being drawn from Dalkey quarries by a special tramway devised for the purpose. However, it became evident at an early stage in the work that the shelter afforded by a single pier would be inadequate in north-westerly gales and in a further act of 1820 (I Geo. IV, Cap. 69) sanction was given for a second pier, the present west pier. This act referred to an accumulated surplus in the Dublin port authority's lighthouse revenues account, and went on to provide that an annual sum of £4,000 should be applied from that fund towards financing the new piers until they had been paid for. George IV had succeeded to the throne in 1820 and following his coronation in 1821 he visited Ireland. At the conclusion of his visit, his departure from the new harbour was made the occasion of re-naming the town and its harbour 'Kingstown'.

The developments at Dunleary/Kingstown had been closely watched by the Post Office authorities and in 1826 they decided to experiment with a mail packet service from Liverpool to Kingstown, calling at Holyhead en route to pick up mail from London. The delay involved in the call at Holyhead resulted in the experimental service being withdrawn and two new services established instead, one from Liverpool and the other from Holyhead. The existing mail packet service to Howth was, however, maintained. The only berth available at that time in Kingstown was the old Dunleary pier and although it was used for a time it was clearly inadequate for the packet service. In 1827 a small timber jetty was constructed at the new east pier, near the site of the present band stand, and a watering jetty to supply the boilers of the packet ships and drinking water for the passengers and crew was built on what was later the site of Carlisle pier.

Blunders and inefficiency continued to mark the management of the mail packet service by the Post Office but it must be said that the decision, based on a recommendation by the British Postmaster-General in 1833, to close down the Howth station and transfer the mail packets to Kingstown was a wise one in the long run since Howth could not have accommodated the larger vessels which were to operate the service in later years. The completion of the new railway was seen as facilitating the movement of mails between Kingstown and Dublin, having regard to the poor state of the roads generally. The first sailing to the new station in Kingstown took place in January 1834.

In the same year, the Board of Works proposed to the Dublin port authority that a bill be promoted to repeal all existing statutory provisions whereby old Dunleary harbour and the new Kingstown harbour were or would be vested in the Dublin Port & Docks Board. The Dublin authority had a great deal on its own plate at this period and assent to the proposal was quickly forthcoming. Accordingly, in August 1836 an act was passed (6/7 William IV, Cap. 116/17) carrying these proposals into effect and vesting both Dunleary and Kingstown harbours in the Kingstown Harbour Commissioners. In effect, the area enclosed between the two new piers, and for the space of 500 yards outside the entrance, became an enclave within the port of Dublin but not part of it except in relation to the pilotage and lighthouse functions of the Dublin board.

Victoria, niece of George IV, succeeded to the throne in 1837. A new masonry wharf was completed in Kingstown in the same year and named after the young queen. The mail packets used this wharf until the construction of Carlisle pier which, together with its rail extension from Kingstown railway station, was completed in 1859.

Following a highly critical report by a committee appointed to enquire into the management of the mail service, responsibility for the operation of the mail packets was transferred to the Admiralty in 1837. Although it was an established fact that the standards of accommodation offered by the vessels owned by private contractors were far ahead of those on the Admiralty's mail service, no efforts were made for many years by the Admiralty to court the passenger traffic by improving the accommodation on their ships.

With the completion of a railway line linking London and Liverpool in 1838, the Post Office decided to send mail for Ireland via Liverpool and the City of Dublin Steam Packet company succeeded in obtaining a contract to provide a nightly mail packet service between Liverpool and Kingstown, thus entering on an association with Kingstown and the Post Office which was to last for over eighty years. The Admiralty continued to operate a day service from Liverpool and while the use of Holyhead was temporarily suspended so far as the London mails were concerned, this harbour was still used for mail from Chester and other places.

The City of Dublin company placed four new ships on their new mail service, *Royal William, Queen Victoria, Duchess of Kent* and *Duke of Cambridge*. Before she entered the mail service, the *Royal William* was one of the earliest paddle steamers to make a transatlantic crossing, completing the outward passage from Liverpool to New York in nineteen days in July 1838, and the return trip in just over fifteen days. The *Queen Victoria* also made headlines but for a very different reason; when entering Dublin Bay in a snowstorm in February 1853, she was wrecked just under the Baily Lighthouse with the loss of sixty lives.

In 1848, a rail link between Chester and Holyhead was completed with the exception of a bridge over the Menai Straits, this stage of the journey being accomplished by horse-drawn omnibus across the suspension bridge built by Telford and completed in 1825. In August 1848, the Chester and Holyhead Railway Company, in association with the London and North Western Railway, commenced an express rail service between London and Holyhead; the trains on this service were the first to receive a name—the 'Irish Mail'. The Liverpool mail service was discontinued and the contract with the City of Dublin company terminated. Holyhead once again became the pick-up point for the transfer of the London mails to the packet ships and the Admiralty commenced a new daily service with four ships specially acquired for the purpose. At a somewhat late stage the Admiralty had seen the advantage of increasing its share of the passenger market, as distinct from its Post Office responsibilities, and the new ships had been built and fitted out to standards far in advance of those of any previous vessel specially built for this service. The new ships were four times as large as the early *Ivanhoe* and *Talbot*, and they had engines six times as powerful. One of the new ships, the *Banshee*, set a record for the crossing from Holyhead to Kingstown of 3 hours 40 minutes, which is little more than the scheduled time for the crossing by modern car ferries. The *Talbot*'s best time was 7½ hours.

The completion in 1850 of Stephenson's tubular railway bridge across the Menai Straits enabled through trains to be run between London and Holyhead without the necessity of changing at Bangor to make the crossing by the old suspension bridge.

The efficiency and financial results of the mail packet service as operated by the Admiralty were no better than had been the case under the Post Office management. In the time honoured fashion, the government set up another committee of inquiry and its report confirmed that the operational costs of the ships were far in excess of those of private contractors. It was a case of history repeating itself since the decision to employ contractors to operate sailing packets some sixty years earlier had been based on much the same reason. As a consequence, tenders were invited publicly for a contract for a period of ten years from 1850 for the carriage of the mails between Holyhead and Kingstown.

In anticipation of securing the contract, by somewhat unethical means it may be said, the Chester and Holyhead company ordered four ships to be built and named them *Hibernia*, *Scotia*, *Cambria* and *Anglia*—the four kingdoms as they were later known. These names were given to successive vessels on the route over the following century. Despite its preparations, the railway company was unsuccessful in its bid for the contract which was awarded to the City of Dublin company. The railway company decided to make the best of a bad job by operating their ships for passengers only.

When the contract came up for renewal in 1859, the City of Dublin company was again successful and to meet revised conditions in the contract requiring a faster service, four new ships were ordered and named after the four Irish provinces. Each generation of ships arriving on the scene had set new standards of comfort and speed and the new 'provinces' were no exception. The *Ulster* established a new speed record for steam ships, reaching 18 knots on her trials and later she set a new record for the Kingstown/Holyhead crossing of 3¼ hours which stood until the arrival of the next generation of 'provinces' in 1897 when each of the new ships achieved a passage time of under 2½ hourse on trial trips before entering service.

The City of Dublin company continued to hold the mails contract until 1919. In the meantime, the Chester and Holyhead company had been absorbed by the LNWR company which had decided in 1861 to transfer its Irish passenger terminal from Kingstown to North Wall, Dublin. Subsequently, the company built a railway station adjoining its berthage at the North Wall; rail links were built, giving access to the Irish railway system for both passengers and goods. In 1883, the company bought a hotel known as the Prince of Wales which was situated at the junction of (old) Wapping Street and the North Wall. The name was changed to the London and North Western and the hotel was later superseded by a new hotel, the construction of which commenced on a site at the rear of the old structure which was later demolished. The new building was extended to its present frontage on the North Wall. The LNWR ships on the North Wall/Holyhead route, described as 'express' steamers, continued to compete with the City of Dublin company's Kingstown service for the passenger traffic, always with the objective of breaking the Dublin company's monopoly of the mail contract.

In the early 1900s a dispute arose between the LNWR and the Dublin Port and Docks Board regarding the dues chargeable on the company's ships at Dublin. In 1908 the company stated its intention of transferring its passenger service back to Kingstown on the grounds that the dues at Dublin were excessive (see Chapters 16 & 17); since Kingstown was obliged to charge the same rates as at Dublin, the true reason was probably because the company was still hopeful of capturing the mail contract. The hotel was converted into offices which nowadays are occupied by CIE.

The subsequent rivalry between the LNWR and the City of Dublin company regarding rights to berthage at the Carlisle pier developed into a dispute which became known as the 'Battle of the Pier'. This pier normally accommodates only two ships, one on either side and each company had three vessels in service with one on stand-by at any one time. Contemporary photographs show both sides of the pier occupied with other steamers anchored between the Carlisle pier (or as it was usually known, the Mailboat pier) and the east pier. The controversy developed into litigation which ended with a House of Lords decision in 1909 granting rights to the LNWR to use the pier as well as the City of Dublin company. An uneasy peace followed until the outbreak of war in 1914 when the four railway ships were requisitioned by the Admiralty as troop ships, leaving the City of Dublin company in sole occupation of the pier. Following the demise of the latter company in 1919, the LNWR, which had already four new ships under construction, was finally awarded the mail contract and their first ship took over the service in 1920, to be followed by her sister ships shortly afterwards.

On the reorganisation of the British railway system in 1921, the LNWR became the London Midland and Scottish Railway company and it was soon realised that the service could be operated with three ships of the standard and speed of these new 'kingdoms'. The *Anglia* was laid up; the *Scotia* was requisitioned for trooping in the Second World War, leaving the *Hibernia* and *Cambria* to maintain the service until they were replaced in 1959 by motor ships of the same names.

14

The Early Victorian Period, 1830–67

BECAUSE of the increased duties and responsibilities which devolved on George Halpin as a consequence of the board's dual functions as port authority and lighthouse authority, the board in 1830 appointed an assistant to Halpin in the person of his son, George Halpin Junior, who was a qualified civil engineer.

At this time the foreshore alongside the quay walls was exposed at low water in many places; in other locations only five feet of water was available at low tide. The impetus to trade which followed the opening of the steamship era brought demands from the shipping companies for deeper water alongside the quay walls to enable their vessels to remain afloat at low water and thus avoid risk of damage to the vessels' paddleboxes. In 1834 the board sought the advice of William Cubitt, a London civil engineer of high repute. Cubitt suggested that the best, although admittedly expensive, solution would be to rebuild the quay walls further out into the river with deeper foundations, thus enabling dredging to the required depth to be carried out without endangering the stability of the quay walls. However, he recognised that the costs of such a scheme might not be acceptable to the board and as an alternative he proposed that piling be carried out at a suitable distance in front of the walls with the same objective. Here again, the board found the estimated costs too high for their resources but the problem became so urgent that, following sustained pressure from the shipping companies, the board was forced to review the situation in 1836.

Eventually, it was decided to build a timber wharf 'at the end of the North Wall' to accomodate the 'larger' steamships which could not take the ground at low water in the existing berths. The new wharf could, perhaps, have been more accurately described as being at East Wall since it was constructed on a north/south line at the junction of East Wall and North Wall, on the site of what was later known as the 'Crossberth'. A basin or 'pond' was dredged outside the wharf to a depth of twelve feet at low water; this was sufficient to enable the largest steamers then using the port to remain afloat at low water. By modern standards these would have been relatively small vessels of 300 or 400 tons with an overall length of 150 to 180 feet.

In 1839 the masters of the steamships using this wharf complained that access to the wharf had become difficult because of the number of Ringsend fishing vessels mooring in the pond, presumably to avail of the comparative shelter from the prevailing winds which was afforded by the East Wall, the wharf and the steamers berthed there. The harbour master was instructed to ensure that the pond was kept clear of the fishing vessels at all times and to direct them to moor on the south side of the river channel at Ringsend, parallel to Pidgeon House Road, where dredging had recently been carried out. This was the origin of the description of this stretch of the river as the 'trawlermen's pond'. The pond provided on the north side for the steamships became known as 'Halpin's pond', the derivation of which is obvious. Halpin's pond or pool were names which continued to be applied to the large basin later dredged in this area, known as Alexandra Basin. The original pond was deepened and extended in the 1840s to provide a depth of sixteen feet at low water, enabling foreign-going vessels to moor to buoys and discharge into lighters while awaiting a vacant berth at the quays.

While on one of his lighthouse inspections in July 1854, Halpin senior collapsed and died. His son was appointed inspector of works and superintendent of lighthouses, and another engineer, Thomas Ramsey, was appointed as his assistant.

Notwithstanding the protection afforded by the North Bull Wall, vessels moored in the pond or berthed at the new wharf were still exposed to risk in extreme weather conditions, particularly in easterly gales. In 1856, a breakwater 700 feet long was constructed on a north/south line, parallel to and 1,000 feet to the east of the new wharf. The breakwater was in effect an island created by the dumping of dredged spoil and protected by rubble facing; it was removed many years later when the pond was being developed into the Alexandra Basin.

When the port authority was established in 1786, the total tonnage of vessels arriving at the port in that year was about 300,000 tons. By 1836 this figure had increased to 400,000 tons of which just over half was attributable to the operations of the companies engaged in the cross-channel trade, and by 1840 the demand for improved berthage for these vessels was such that Halpin reported the urgent need for timber wharves further upriver, similar to that built at the pond. The board approved, and by 1842 two wharves had been constructed at the North Wall, one on each side of the entrance to the Royal Canal Dock. Each wharf was 500 feet long but although the benefit was immediately manifest it was overtaken by the increase in the number of additional companies joining in the competition for cross-channel traffic. More timber wharves were inevitable and by the early 1860s timber wharves had been constructed in front of the north quays from the east side of the entrance to the Old Dock as far as Fish Street, now known as Castleforbes Road. Gaps were left at the steps used by the ferries.

The shipping companies' demands were not confined to berthage; in 1846 the City of Dublin company drew attention to the provision at other ports of shelters on the quaysides for the protection of goods discharged from ships or awaiting loading. The board agreed to erect one such shelter on an experimental basis but this was soon followed by a succession of similar shelters as each company sought the same facility. The shelters were somewhat primitive, consisting merely of a roof supported by iron columns but without side or end walls. In later years, the shelters were removed and replaced by larger enclosed sheds.

Halpin's assistant, Ramsey, resigned in 1856 and the board appointed Bindon Blood Stoney to the position of assistant engineer not, be it noted, assistant inspector of works. Stoney was destined to have a brilliant career as a port engineer which was later recognised by the bestowal of an honorary Doctorate of Laws and election to the Royal Society. He also became a fellow of the Institute of Naval Architects and, in his own discipline, he was a member of the Institute of Civil Engineers. Like his father, Halpin junior was obliged to devote most of his time to the lighthouse work, involving long absences from Dublin and of necessity Stoney was the *de facto* port engineer.

Facilities for repairing ships were a necessity in a port like Dublin. In 1825 the board had ordered the construction of a graving slip on which its dredging craft could be hauled up for repairs but following repeated requests by shipping companies to be allowed to use the slip, the board agreed in 1830 to provide a larger slip for public use. Known as Nos. 1 and 2 graving slips, these are still in use. A gridiron was provided at the end of the North Wall in 1835 for the use of smaller ships. This was a rather primitive method of enabling ships to take the ground safely at low water for the purposes of hull repairs. It consisted of a timber and iron framework or grid, about 100 feet long by 35 feet wide, laid on the river bed beside the quay wall, the site having been previously levelled off. The foreshore and the gridiron were exposed at low water, thus facilitating hull repairs and painting.

By the late 1840s, it was clear that the larger slip was no longer adequate for the requirements of the shipping companies and by 1850 Halpin senior had produced a set of plans for a graving dock to be located close to the No. 2 slip which was situated on the north side of Halpin's pond, opposite the junction of East Wall and Lr Sheriff Street. At this period, the Admiralty was empowered to examine all proposals for new harbour facilities and considerable delay ensued before the new graving dock proposal was approved. The original design had provided for a dock 350 feet long by 70 feet wide at its entrance but after consultations with the City of Dublin Steam Packet company, who had pressed for the provision of the dock and whose new mail steamers were about 340 feet in length, the board agreed that the length of the dock should be 400 feet. In 1853, the board accepted the tender of William Dargan for the construction of the dock. Dargan had already established a reputation in the field of building railways, and indeed he was also involved as a director of some of the railway companies. The foreshore at East Wall on which the graving slips had been constructed had been acquired from Dublin Corporation under inquisition in 1812 and most of the site of the new graving dock lay within the area thus acquired. However, the board ordered that a further inquisition be sought to acquire the necessary additional foreshore in this vicinity and this was effected in 1850. Part of the additional area was acquired from the Corporation and the remainder from the Vernon Estate which claimed ownership of all the foreshore lying between the river channel and the Clontarf seafront.

The construction of the dock was a slow process. Access to the site from East Wall was by means of a short breakwater road originally built in connection with the No. 2 slip and this breakwater road was extended for the purposes of the graving dock contractor; it was subsequently absorbed into a road leading from East Wall to the ship building and repairing yard later opened in this location.

The new dock was opened on 9 February 1860 when the sailing ship *Agnes Anderson* was docked for repairs. The vessel was owned by the timber firm of Thomas Martin, later known as T.&C. Martin. This vessel was followed by one of the City of Dublin mail steamers on the Kingstown/Holyhead route and the dock was soon in continuous demand.

During the construction of the dock a retaining wall, 2,300 feet long was built on an east/west line along what is now the line of Tolka Quay Road and indeed the wall was to be the source of this name since it deflected the course of the Tolka eastwards to the end of the wall. At its eastern end the wall continued at right angles towards the main river channel for a further 2,000 feet. The area thus enclosed by the new graving dock and the retaining wall was reclaimed by dumping material dredged from the river channel and it formed the nucleus of what is now the main area of the port estate, bounded on the west by East Wall and on the east by the Sealink container terminal. Almost all of this area was reclaimed by the same method.

The unending cycle of more and larger ships and the problems of accommodating them with berthage was well illustrated in a report of the harbour master in the early 1860s in which he stated that every berth on both north and south quays was occupied, with a further forty coasters, both steam and sail, moored in tiers or anchored in the river awaiting berths; some of these vessels were discharging their cargoes into lighters for transport upriver, or into the canals.

Stoney foresaw the need for berths with up to twenty-two feet depth at low water and in 1861 he put forward a proposal for the continuation of the North Wall Quay seaward beyond its existing termination at the junction with East Wall. Instead of the older method of quay construction within a piled cofferdam, Stoney proposed to build large concrete blocks each weighing 350 tons at a special wharf to be erected near the graving dock. When each block was ready it would be lifted by a special floating crane consisting of a shear legs on a barge or float, and transported to the site of the new quay extension. The foundation for the block would be excavated by dredger, with the final clearing and levelling carried out manually by men working in a diving bell. The bell consisted of an iron chamber twenty feet square, and access to the bell was by an iron shaft with an airlock. By this method, Stoney contended that considerable savings would be made over the cost of construction by traditional methods. A further advantage would be a substantial saving in the time taken for completing the work.

Halpin was away from Dublin on lighthouse duties when Stoney submitted his report and when he became aware of the report on his return a controversy arose between the two men. Halpin informed the board that in his opinion the proposed method of construction was not feasible because of the size of the blocks proposed by Stoney. Halpin's health had deteriorated partly because of the strain of his duties and partly by the hardships of continual travelling on his lighthouse inspections. The board was aware of Halpin's condition and the members were concerned on his account; it was for this reason that they had agreed that he should delegate most of the port work to Stoney, while he concentrated on the lighthouses. Halpin's caution was no doubt primarily based on the engineering considerations but it is difficult to avoid the suspicion that his objections were to some extent coloured by pique at his assistant's decision to submit to the board a report of major significance without prior consultation.

Stoney's forceful personality is evident in a supplementary report to the board, rebutting Halpin's arguments and pointing out that blocks of the size he proposed had been used in the port of London many years previously and were also in the process of being used at Southampton. The board was clearly embarrassed by the undignified wrangle between its principal engineering officer and his assistant; approval in principle was given for Stoney's proposals but no immediate action was ordered. The controversy clearly did nothing either for Halpin's confidence or for his health and some months later in March 1862 he retired and Stoney was appointed as 'engineer'.

In 1864 the board's financial situation had improved to the extent that it became possible to make a start on the plan proposed by Cubitt thirty years earlier, the re-building of the quay walls. The first section to be undertaken was the stretch of quayside immediately west of the present North Wall Extension gates and the new quay was intended for the use of 'deeply laden vessels from foreign ports with cargoes of grain and timber' which required a depth at low water of sixteen to eighteen feet. By the late 1860s this section, 740 feet long, had been rebuilt.

In 1864 also, the board decided to proceed with the North Wall Extension and Stoney was instructed to obtain tenders for the shear float and diving bell. In October of that year, the tender of Harland and Wolff, the Belfast firm, was accepted for the shear float and that of Grendon and Company of Drogheda for the diving bell. The plant was delivered in 1866 but by that time legislation was in progress for the re-constitution of the port authority and the project was left in abeyance.

Good berthage facilities with graving slip and graving dock accommodation are of themselves not sufficient without a safe navigable approach to the harbour and a river channel deep and wide enough for the vessels which use it. The construction of the North Bull Wall had effected a considerable improvement in the depth of water on the bar but the effect on the depths in the river channel, though substantial, was not so spectacular. Continuous dredging was required to reach and maintain the necessary depth. The early methods of dredging in the port, as described in a contemporary account, indicate that they were slow and laborious, requiring 'eighteen large lighters, each of 60 tons capacity and containing a crew of nine men. [The lighters] take station over an appointed place. A spoon, consisting of a strong ring of iron to which is attached a net, is fixed to the end of a long pole. This is let down to the bottom, perpendicular to the bow of the boat and, by means of a rope fastened to the spoon and passing over a windlass, dragged along and raised at the stern filled with sand or gravel which it has scooped up in its passage.' The loading of each lighter took four hours.

Halpin senior had kept in touch with dredging developments in other countries and in 1812 the board accepted his proposal for the purchase of a steam engine to be used in dredging, similar to that in operation at the port of London. The engine was duly supplied by the firm of Fenton, Murray and Wood of Leeds, together with the plans for a suitable vessel to be built to accommodate the engine. The engine was used to drive an endless chain of buckets in place of the primitive spoon. The new vessel was built by a Dublin shipbuilder named Anthony Hill. She was 60 feet long, 21 feet beam and $8\frac{1}{2}$ feet draught but although she was usually referred to as the 'Steam dredging vessel *Patrick*', she was not capable of self-propulsion and had to be towed into position for dredging but could then manoeuvre within limits by hauling on her four anchors. Although the steam engine had been introduced into Dublin in 1791 no local man could be found capable of working the dredging engine and eventually an Englishman, Thomas Ashby, was recruited for the job. To enable the new dredger to operate at her maximum efficiency, four new lighters of 35 tons each were provided and her first operation was to dredge the channel known as Ringsend Gut leading to the Grand Canal Docks, in the year 1815.

By 1829, the *Patrick* was reported to be worn out and the board placed a contract for a replacement vessel with Garwood and Co. of Glasgow. The new vessel was delivered in 1830 and her output was so impressive in her first year of operation that a second vessel was ordered, with a capacity to dredge 1,500 tons per week compared with 1,000 tons by the existing dredger. The new vessel was 100 feet long with a beam of 26 feet but, unlike her two predecessors, her engine was used not only for driving the chain of buckets but also for self-propulsion by means of paddle wheels. The floats used to transfer the dredged material, or 'spoil' as it was known, were usually propelled manually by the method known as 'poling' but this manoeuvre could be almost impossible in bad weather. A private company was operating a towage service in the port in the 1830s, principally for towing sailing ships in and out of the harbour and in 1835 Halpin was authorised to hire the tug to move the floats in bad weather. Apart from this occasional use of tugs, however, there were otherwise no major changes in the system of dredging methods until the 1860s.

The disposal of surplus dredged material was not a major problem in the early years of the spoon dredging since the spoil was generally suitable for ballast for ships, a commodity always in demand and the provision of which had been an important function of the port authority since the old Ballast Office Committee days. Surplus material was also made available to the owners of those lots which adjoined Custom House Quay and the North Wall, for reclaiming and levelling their ground. The increased output of the new dredgers and the fact that the lots had been substantially reclaimed obliged the board to seek another outlet for the spoil. This consisted in dumping it on the Pidgeon House Road and then transferring it by wheelbarrow to the south side of the road to form an embankment along the south strand. By 1860 the dumping had become a source of bitter complaint from residents in the Sandymount and Merrion district, all of whom were tenants of the Fitzwilliam/Pembroke Estate which took up the residents' complaint with the port board. The problem was that in the absence of a retaining wall some of the spoil was being washed away by the tide and deposited on the beach at Sandymount and Merrion.

A new solution was proposed by Stoney in June 1860, namely the adoption of the hopper-float system which was in operation at the ports of Liverpool, Hull and elsewhere. The hopper-float had bottom-opening doors and when loaded by the dredger, the vessel could be taken out to sea, the bottom doors opened and the spoil dumped in a suitable location offshore where it would be dispersed or carried away by tidal currents. It would thus be possible to dispose of spoil not suitable for reclamation or for ballast and Stoney submitted figures showing that the cost of providing and operating the hopper-floats could in a very short time show a substantial saving over the existing method of dumping across the Pidgeon House Road. While the board was generally favourable to the proposal it was not until 1863 that tenders were invited for five hopper-floats and a new dredger. The first two floats were delivered late in 1864 and in the following year Stoney reported that the new arrangement was working very satisfactorily. Suitable spoil was still being used for reclamation of foreshore near East Wall and close to the graving slips and graving dock.

The advantages of using a steam tug for towing the floats had been demonstrated during the short-term hire of a tug in bad weather and in June 1864 the board accepted the tender of Grendon & Co. for the building of a steam tug for the dredging fleet. Pending delivery of the new tug, Stoney was authorised to hire a local tug. The new tug arrived in 1864 and in the following March Stoney reported that the new system had proved highly efficient and had justified the outlay involved.

The continuing growth of the port's trade can be judged by the figures for 1866 which showed that a total of almost 1.4 million tons of shipping had arrived, compared with 400,000 tons in 1836. Cross-channel shipping in the general cargo trade, steam and sail, accounted for 850,000 tons compared with approximately 200,000 tons in 1836. Foreign shipping totalled 163,000 tons in 1866, the figure for 1836 being 36,000 tons. Colliers reflected the increasing need for coal for industrial and domestic purposes; at 335,000 tons in 1866, the total was almost twice that for 1836. Whereas ships of 400 tons had been regarded as large in relation to the port of Dublin in the 1830s and 1840s, deep sea vessels of 1,000 tons were commonplace in 1866.

Before the board was replaced by a new authority under the Dublin Port Act of 1867 (30. Vic., Cap. 81) it formulated a number of suggestions to be laid before the incoming board, the most important of which was that Stoney's project for the North Wall extension should proceed.

15

The Dublin Port and Docks Board

THE brief given to Gandon in 1780 for the proposed new Custom House provided for enclosed docks accessible by locks, together with warehouses and stores; John Rennie was the consultant for the docks, but only one dock was built at first and it was opened in 1796. A second dock was opened in 1821 and it was named George's Dock in honour of George IV who, following his coronation, visited Dublin in August of that year.

The king's marital problems are outside the scope of this work but it may be noted that while in Holyhead en route to Dublin he was informed of the death of Caroline, his separated and disowned wife. The king's reaction was to announce that he did not expect mourning to be worn by the people during his visit to Ireland. Adverse winds delayed his departure from Holyhead on the royal yacht, a sailing vessel. The king became impatient at the delay and he decided at short notice to cross to Ireland on one of the new Post Office steam packets operating between Holyhead and Howth. His unexpected arrival at Howth on a quiet Sunday afternoon was witnessed by a mere handful of surprised local people which was just as well since it appears that he had to be helped ashore; presumably his coronation celebrations were still in progress while at sea. In fact the celebrations continued for two weeks and whereas it had been intended that the king should open the new dock on Monday 27 August, a social engagement at Slane over the preceding weekend delayed his return to the city and the dock was opened in his absence by Lord Castlecoote.

A third dock leading off George's Dock, and known as the Inner Dock, was completed later in the 1820s. Warehouses were built adjoining each of the docks with the intention that all goods liable to customs duty should be discharged there and if necesary stored under bond in the warehouses or in the vaults below them, within the overall security provided by a high security wall which still (1988) forms part of the Custom House Docks complex.

In June 1832, the Chamber of Commerce sought the board's consent and support for a memorial to the government, proposing the transfer of the Custom House Docks to the board. The board agreed and the chamber duly submitted its proposals to the government. The matter lay dormant for over eight years but in October 1840 the Treasury Commissioners in London asked the board if it would take over the control and responsibility for the docks, excluding the warehouses which had been leased by the Scovell brothers, warehousekeepers, for a term of forty-five years from 1824; the docks premises would continue to be the property of the crown and the arrangement with the board would be by lease at a nominal rent of five shillings per annum. Although the board consented to the proposal, negotiations dragged on for almost five years, being completed eventually in 1845. Implicit in these negotiations was the mutual understanding that the deal would eventually be completed and it was arranged that pending the completion of the formal lease the board should take over the docks in September 1841. The clauses of the lease were finally agreed and included a provision for a term of eighteen years from 1844. On the termination of the lease in 1852 the Treasury agreed to its continuation from year to year.

The bulk of ships using the port in the 1830s and early 1840s were between 200 and 300 tons and because of their dimensions they had no difficulty in locking in and out of the docks. Although the early paddle steamers could enter the lock without difficulty, the fact that entrance and exit could be effected only over a three hour period at high water meant that those vessels engaged in the regular cross-channel services were not disposed to risk the potential delays involved. The average size of vessel using the port was growing year by year and it soon became clear that limitations on the size of vessel that could use the entrance lock constituted a major obstacle to the optimum use of the docks complex. The board and its officials were fully aware of the potential value of an improved dock system which could take the largest vessel then envisaged as likely to use the port, in particular foreign-going vessels desirous of taking advantage of bonded warehousing. The cost of the necessary improvements were recognised as being out of court, particularly in view of the board's tenure, but as a first step towards the target the board opened negotiations with the Treasury in 1865 for the pur- chase of the docks. Reversing the procedure of 1832, the board sought the support of the Chamber of Commerce which was quickly forthcoming but equally promptly withdrawn when the board indicated its intention to promote a bill in parliament which would not only authorise the purchase of the Custom House Docks but also empower it to levy dues on goods landed or loaded at the port. Hitherto the only commodities on which such charges were levied were timber and stone, the board's main revenue being derived from charges on the ships themselves.

The trading community and the shipowners had long agitated for representation on the board which under its 1786 constitution filled vacancies in its membership by co-option. In November 1865 the board offered to include provisions in the bill for representation of both trading and shipping interests, but this was not sufficient inducement to win over those opposed to the bill. The board was eventually forced to withdraw its proposals for dues on goods, but the shipowners continued to oppose the bill, their chief spokesman being William Watson, the forceful and influential managing director of the City of Dublin Steam Packet Company. Finally the board agreed that if the bill were not opposed, it would promote another bill in the following session of parliament to provide for the representation sought by the traders and shipowners. This commitment was entered into during the committee stage of the bill which was eventually enacted as the Dublin Port (Docks) Act 1866 (29 Vic., Cap 25). Ownership of the Custom House Docks complex was vested in the board, subject to the unexpired term of the Scovell lease, with effect from 1 October 1866. On the expiration of the Scovell lease in 1869 the board took over the operation of the warehouses on 1 September in that year.

In fulfilment of its undertaking given during the progress of the bill, the board appointed a committee in October 1866 to examine and report on how the proposed representation of the trading and shipping interests could be organised. The committee recommended the reduction from seventeen to twelve in the number of members which the board itself had the right to nominate, i.e. as distinct from the Lord Mayor and those members nominated by the Municipal Corporation; it was proposed that triennial elections should be held by duly qualified electoral panels for four members representing the trading interests and four for the shipowners. This proposal was not acceptable to the shipowners who decided to promote their own bill for the reconstitution of the board. Meetings were held between the parties in an effort to arrive at an amicable settlement whereby one bill acceptable to all the parties would be promoted unopposed. The Chamber of Commerce was not happy with either the board's bill or that of the shipowners; it held the view that the board's bill provided for a preponderance of members to be elected by the board itself while the shipowners' bill proposed too many shipping representatives for the chamber's peace of mind. The chamber proposed a compromise whereby the three groups, board, traders and shipowners, should each have seven representatives, the Municipal Corporation retaining its existing representation of the Lord Mayor ex-officio and three aldermen. The compromise bill was duly promoted and accepted by parliament with the amendment that the Corporation representation should consist of the Lord Mayor and three citizens not necessarily council men.

The government took advantage of the bill to include provisions for the severance of the lighthouse and port functions of the board, giving the title of 'Commissioners of Irish Lights' to the lighthouse authority and 'Dublin Port and Docks Board' to the port authority. The existing constitution and statutory arrangements governing membership provided for in the 1786 act continued to apply to the new lighthouse commissioners, the port authority being re-constituted as outlined above.

Although the separate authorities came into being with the passing of the bill into law on 17 May 1867, the re-constitution of the new port authority could not take place until arrangements for drawing up electoral panels of voters could be made and the elections held. Accordingly, the act provided that the powers and functions of the Dublin Port and Docks Board as re-constituted would come into force in January 1868.

Reverting to the Custom House Docks, several schemes for improving the entrance locks and the docks themselves were proposed over the ensuing years but it was clear that to effect any material improvement would involve expenditure out of proportion to the advantages to be gained, particularly since attention had been focused on the potential for deepwater berthage at new quays further down river unhampered by entrance locks and therefore accessible at all stages of the tide. Gradually, direct discharge from vessels to the warehouses in the Custom House Docks declined although the warehouses continued to be used for the storage of cargoes transported from vessels berthed at the deepwater section of the port.

The original dock, completed in 1796 and generally known as the 'Old Dock', fell into disuse and eventually it was closed off in 1927 and filled in. Part of the site lies under Memorial Road and the remainder lies within the re-aligned western boundary of the docks complex. Open areas adjoining George's Dock and the Inner Dock were used as coal banks for many years by the coal trade until 1975 when all coal ships were transferred to a new bulk discharge facility at South Bank Quay.

The term 'Banquet Hall' as applied to a warehouse might appear to be an ironic comment on a rather prosaic building but in fact the term is still used from time to time in reference to the warehouse known as Stack A and its day of glory on 22 October 1856. Following the return of Irish regiments from the Crimean War, the government decided to honour them with a banquet but it was found impossible to accomodate an attendance of over 3,000 people in any of the usual venues for public functions such as the Mansion House. An official of the Board of

Works suggested one of the dock warehouses and the work of transforming the bleak interior into a banqueting hall was commenced. Well-known city firms such as T. & C. Martin and Todd Burns offered to supply appropriate materials such as platforms, seating, table cloths and other furnishings; for a reason which is not apparent, an offer by Messrs. West to supply silver cutlery was not accepted but offers from other firms to provide foodstuffs, beer, wine and spirits were accepted with alacrity. Against a background of floral and other decorations the Lord Mayor presided and a contemporary newspaper account described a novel arrangement for giving notice of each toast, of which it appears there were many; four trumpeters were stationed behind the top table and they sounded a 'brilliant call' before each toast. The iron roof trusses were painted red, white and blue and remnants of the paint are still visible.

The act of 1866 authorising the purchase by the board of the Custom House Docks also provided that the board could acquire the Grand Canal Docks provided terms could be agreed with the Canal company. Negotiations were opened in July 1866 and continued in a fitful manner over many years but agreement could not be reached on the purchase price and the proposal was dropped.

The Late Victorian Period, 1868–98

THE first meeting of the newly constituted Dublin Port and Docks Board took place in the Ballast Office, Westmoreland Street, on 10 January 1868 when the following members took their seats:

The Lord Mayor Rt Hon. Sir William Carroll (ex officio)
Appointed by the Municipal Corporation
Ald. William Lane Joynt D.L.; Richard Joseph Devitt; Ald. Denis Moylan.
Nominated by the Commissioners of Irish Lights
Robert Callwell; Henry Thompson; Thomas Bewley; John Jameson Robertson; Richard Martin; James Chagneau Colvill; Thomas Weldon Adams.
Elected by Traders and Manufacturers
Edward Hudson Kinahan; Edward Barrington; Jonathan Pim MP; John Edmond Barry; John Lloyd Blood; Richard Wood Kelly.
Elected by Shipowners
Michael Murphy; William Watson; Sir John Ennis, Bart. D.L.; James Martin; James Stirling; James William Murland; Joseph Boyce. Andrew Bagot, a traders' representative, was ill and unable to attend.

The new board included seven members nominated by the members of the old board in their new rôle as the Commissioners of Irish Lights and consequently a fair degree of continuity and familiarity with the overall port situation was assured. At this first meeting a new Harbour Improvements Committee was appointed to examine and report on the measures required for the further improvement of the port. The report, which was produced in the following March, recommended works which should have priority, commencing with the re-building of 1,000 feet of the quay wall at Sir John Rogerson's Quay to give deepwater berthage with 22 feet at low water for foreign-going ships. The committee also recommended the provision of another graving dock but in referring to other projects the committee took the view that the board's financial situation would not warrant their commencement as

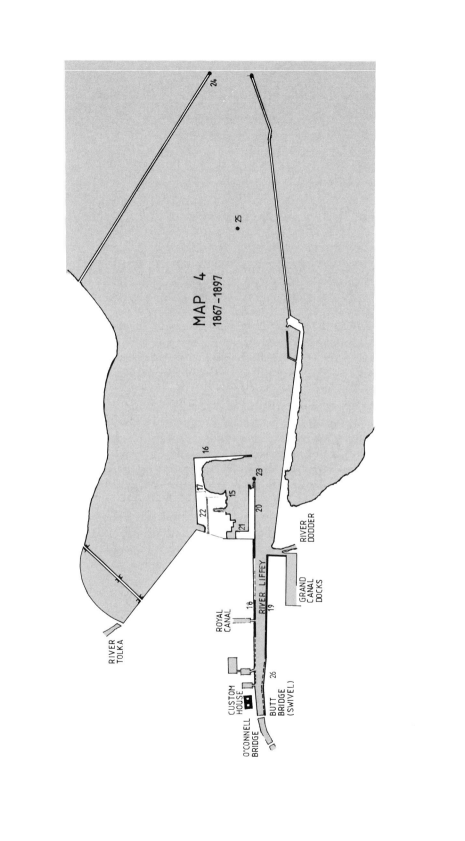

MAP 4
1867–1897

RIVER
TOLKA

RIVER LIFFEY

ROYAL
CANAL

RIVER
DODDER

GRAND
CANAL
DOCKS

CUSTOM
HOUSE

O'CONNELL
BRIDGE

BUTT
BRIDGE
(SWIVEL)

16

17

15

22

21

20

23

18

19

24

25

26

yet. The proposed extension to the North Wall suggested by the outgoing board was not seen as a priority.

One of the services for which the board was responsible gave particular cause for concern so far as finance was concerned. The act of 1786 which established the Corporation for Preserving and Improving the Port of Dublin, i.e. the old board, also provided that the authority was authorised to appoint pilots for the port and it obliged the masters of certain classes of vessels to employ such pilots when arriving or leaving the port. The authority was authorised to collect the charges for the pilots' services and to apply the revenue in paying the salaries of the pilots and the expenses of operating the services; powers were also given to make bye laws for the proper working of the service. By the mid-1860s, the pilotage service was incurring a substantial loss anually and in 1868 the new board decided that a bill should be promoted in parliament to authorise the revision of the pilotage charges and the reorganisation of certain administrative and operational matters. The board considered it advisable to take advantage of the bill to consolidate and arrange in one statute and in a classified form all the provisions of the previous statutes relating to the port, including pilotage, while deleting obsolete or inappropriate provisions. Certain new provisions were included for the amalgamation of the various existing borrowing powers and of the funds on the security of which borrowing powers would be exercised. The appointment of harbour constables was provided for and the constables were to have 'the same powers, protections and privileges within the limits of the docks, quays and river and shall be subject to the same liabilities as constables have or are subject to by the laws of the realm'. The bill proposed powers for the board to lay down tramways for the purposes of the port; in this context the term 'tramways' related to rails on which goods wagons could be moved, not for passenger tramcars. The tramway powers were subject to a curious restriction which provided that no method of propulsion could be used other than 'animal power'.

The bill passed into law in July 1869 under the title 'Dublin Port and Docks Act, 1869' (32/33 Vic., Cap 100) and it continued for many years to be the substantive statute relating to the port and to the powers and duties of the board; it was regarded as the port Bible by the board's officers.

So far as the general port finances were concerned, the board decided that the revenues which would be derived from new deepwater berthage would service a loan of £20,000 which was available from the bank, and in 1869 a contract was placed with the firm of W.J. Doherty for the re-building of the eastern section of Sir John Rogerson's Quay. By November 1871 a length of 850 feet of the quay had been rebuilt, enabling the barque *Peter Crerar* with a cargo of grain to berth and remain afloat at low water, her draught being $18\frac{1}{2}$ feet.

In the same year, 1871, the board decided to extend Doherty's contract to include the rebuilding of an oblique corner at the extreme eastern end of Sir John Rogerson's Quay and also to rebuild the quay wall at Great Britain Quay.

Further contracts with Doherty and other contractors were placed in succeeding years and in 1888 the port engineer reported that on completion of the contract then in hands, the whole of Sir John Rogerson's Quay would have been rebuilt from Creighton Street to the east end of the quay. Taken together with the rebuilding of Great Britain Quay a total of 4,000 feet of deep berthage had been created on the south side of the river.

The recommendation of the Harbour Improvements Committee regarding a new graving dock was deferred and indeed this project was not revived again until 1950.

To facilitate the berthing of colliers, where it had frequently been necessary to berth bow or stern on to the quay, new timber wharves were built in the 1880s between Butt Bridge and Creighton Street.

The Custom House Docks received considerable attention from theboard during this period and several proposals for major improvements were considered which would enable large vessels to enter and berth there but this project also was deferred because it would have involved closing the docks for a lengthy period thus transferring shipping which normally used these docks to berthage in the river which was already suffering extreme congestion. Over and above the operational difficulties involved, the costs of even a modest improvement scheme as against those for deepwater berthage downriver made the docks project unacceptable.

In 1869, attention was directed to the long standing proposal by Stoney for the extension of the North Wall Quay. The shear float and the diving bell ordered by the old board had been delivered in 1866 and in 1869 the engineer was ordered to commence this work. The preliminary task of building a new wharf east of the graving dock for the construction of the 350 ton blocks was carried out in 1870 and on 27 May 1871 the first block was laid. Progress continued apace and as each section of the new quay was completed it was made available for shipping. By 1882, over 2,000 feet of quay with a depth of 22 feet had been built on the river side of the works, and over 1,600 feet with 24 feet on the pond or 'basin' side. As work progressed on the quay walls on each side of the extension the area between was filled and paved and in 1882 a transit shed, later known as No. 1, was built on the river side.

The Prince and Princess of Wales visited Dublin in 1885 and on 11 April in that year they inspected the new extension, the Princess bestowing her own name, Alexandra, on the adjoining basin at the invitation of the board.

In the meantime the development of the western end of the new basin proceeded with the construction of a quay wall at right angles to the new quays and running parallel to East Wall, outside the line of the old steam packet wharf which was removed. This quay, 450 feet long, was known as the Crossberth. The area between the quay wall and East Wall, 200 feet wide, was already partly occupied by the offices of the port engineer and the harbour master, together with the No. 1 graving slip. The remainder was filled, paved and used for many years for the discharge of timber cargoes. Two further sheds were erected at the new extension but the remaining sections of quay wall were not commenced until 1931.

In February 1868, the firm of W.H.M. Goulding applied for a site of three acres on the lands then being reclaimed to the north of the graving dock. The site was required for a chemical manure works and the board agreed to the proposal and also to the construction of a jetty 150 feet in length at the eastern side of the graving dock. A tramway was built across the reclaimed land to connect the jetty with the new factory and the jetty was later extended to 180 feet. The jetty became known, naturally enough, as Goulding's jetty and although it was replaced in later years by Alexandra Quay, as late as the 1950s many port workers still referred to this quay as 'Goulding's jetty'.

Access from East Wall to the No. 2 graving slip, the graving dock, a shipyard operated by the firm of Walpole Bewley and Webb, and the new Goulding factory was by means of a somewhat devious road across the reclaimed lands. It was evident by the mid 1870s that development in this area was imminent but the foreshore owned by the board was limited as indeed were funds for new works. As a first step, the board sought in 1878 to open negotiations with the Vernon Estate for the acquisition of the foreshore extending from Clontarf to the river channel, bounded by the railway embankment and East Wall on the western side and on the east by the foreshore purchased by the board in 1819 for the building of the North Bull Wall.

The Vernon Estate refused to consider the proposal and the board thereupon promoted a bill in parliament to authorise the purchase of the foreshore and to increase its borrowing powers. The bill was modified in its passage through the House of Commons Committee by the exclusion from the area to be purchased of all foreshore within 1,000 feet of the Clontarf sea wall. Hitherto the audit of the board's accounts had been carried out by auditors appointed by the board itself but the new act which came into force in July 1879 (42/43 Vic., Cap. 170) provided that thereafter the audit should be conducted by auditors appointed by the Local Government Board.

The most immediate effect so far as the residents of Clontarf were concerned was the erection of seven stone pillars on the foreshore to mark the new boundary of the Vernon Estate property; only two of these pillars have survived.

The construction of a swivel bridge (Butt Bridge) opened in 1879 and the reconstruction of Carlisle Bridge, renamed O'Connell Bridge and opened in 1880, have been dealt with in Chapter 11.

The additional borrowing powers under the 1879 act enabled the board to place a contract with a Scottish shipyard for a new steam dredger and another contract with the Workman and Clark yard in Belfast for three hopper barges. The completion of the rebuilding of the south quays from the South Wall End to Butt Bridge, referred to earlier, was also made possible under the same powers, as was the rebuilding of the remainder of the North Quays which had commenced in 1864. By 1907 all the quays from Commons Street to the North Wall Extension had been rebuilt for the use of the cross-channel steamship companies and timber merchants.

To improve the access to the newly reclaimed lands north and east of the graving dock and to the graving dock itself a new road running eastwards from East Wall was commenced in 1881; it was later to be known as Alexandra Road and in 1887 a rail link was provided along this road from Gouldings to the Midland Great Western Railway company sidings at East Wall.

There had previously been no fence or boundary wall between East Wall and the old steam packet wharf but in 1892 a boundary wall was erected from the entrance to North Wall Extension as far as the present entrance to Tolka Quay Road, with gateways for access to the various premises, and the graving dock and slips; gates under the supervision of the harbour police were provided at the entrances to North Wall Extension and Alexandra Road.

In 1897 another application for a site on the reclaimed foreshore was received, this time from the Anglo-American Oil company who sought a lease of $8\frac{1}{2}$ acres for the storage of petroleum in tanks and for a barrel factory. The lease was granted and a new deepwater timber jetty was built at the company's expense to the east of Goulding's jetty with pipelines laid to the company's site. In February 1899 the first oil tanker, the *Potomac,* with a net tonnage of 2,468, arrived and discharged a cargo of petroleum into the new tanks.

The leasing of sites to Gouldings and the Anglo-American company, the erection of the two jetties, the commencement of Alexandra Road and the rail connection with the East Wall sidings taken together formed the nucleus of the modern port estate on the north side of the estuary.

A decline in the board's revenues between 1884 and 1888 was of major concern and it was the subject of representations to the Board of Trade as to the cause of this decline. The method of charging dues on the net tonnage of ships entering a port was laid down in the Merchant

Shipping Acts of 1854 and 1867; provision was made for the exclusion of certain spaces in steamships (engine room etc.) in calculating the net tonnage on which port dues were chargeable. The interpretation of these provisions gave rise to considerable controversy as between shipowners and harbour authorities; because of the methods used by shipbuilders in the construction of steamships and on the basis of a certain interpretation of the measurement rules, the theoretical net tonnage on which the dues were chargeable could be a negligible figure in comparison to the actual revenue earning capacity of the ship. The consequence for the harbour authorities was a sharp decline in revenue from tonnage dues. The interpretation issue was the subject of litigation ending with a House of Lords decision upholding the shipowners' view. The Board of Trade had endeavoured to bring in an amending bill but the influence of the shipowners was sufficient to block the progress of the bill.

The effect of the decline in the revenue of the port had been such that work on new projects had been stopped and the dredging programme severely curtailed. One of the proposals which the board considered in 1896 was the introduction of port dues on the cargoes as distinct from and in addition to the dues on the ships themselves. This proposal had been defeated by the trading interests when it had previously been proposed some twenty years previously and it was likely to meet the same opposition if included in a new bill. An alternative was proposed in an effort to remedy the effect of the tonnage measurement rules and increase the revenue; this was a proposal to charge tonnage dues on the gross tonnage instead of the theoretical net tonnage. The board decided to promote a bill to include this provision together with other urgent matters, including authority to reconstruct Butt Bridge which in its short existence had already proved to be inadequate for the traffic which required to use it. Powers to sell or lease the Custom House Docks and/ or the warehouses was also sought together with the inevitable enlargement of borrowing powers. For some years the Clyde Shipping Company had operated a towage service in the port which was mainly availed of by large sailing ships when arriving or departing; occasionally the board hired these tugs for towing dredging craft when its own tug was not available. It was decided to seek power in the bill to operate a public towing service. To meet constant complaints regarding the inadequate representation on the board of the trading and shipping interests it was proposed to amend the constitution to provide for eleven trader members instead of seven, eight shipping members instead of seven and six Corporation representatives including the Lord Mayor. The representation of the Commissioners of Irish Lights would be abolished.

The bill was withdrawn when it was discovered that in the event of its being defeated in parliament, the members of the board would be personally liable for the costs of promoting the bill which were likely to be substantial.

In 1898 the Chamber of Commerce, which had supported the proposal for reconstitution in the board's abortive bill, promoted a bill which provided for a board consisting of the Lord Mayor and six members of the Corporation, twelve trader members and nine shipping members. The bill also included financial proposals including the creation of stock and extension of borrowing powers but no provisions for charging tonnage dues on gross tonnage or any of the other revenue proposals in the board's bill. This bill became law in August 1898 and the new board came into office in the following January.

Before the old board went out of office it had considered reports from the engineer and the harbour master regarding the deterioration in the depth of water on the bar and in the river channel, resulting in a number of vessels going aground; these conditions had been due to the curtailment of dredging in previous years because of restricted revenue. The harbour master pointed out that the river buoys were unlighted in contrast to progressive ports elsewhere; as a result the unlit buoys could be more of a danger than an aid at night time. It was agreed that the more important buoys should be lit, and that dredging be resumed along the south side of the channel between Poolbeg and the Pidgeon House where groundings had taken place.

In December 1898 the engineer, Dr Stoney asked to be retired in view of his poor health. In agreeing to his request, the board paid tribute to him for the major contributions he had made to the development of the port throughout his service of almost forty-three years. The assistant engineer, John Purser Griffith (later Sir John Purser Griffith) was appointed as the new port engineer or 'engineer in chief' as the position was described.

Turbulent Times, 1899–1929

OF the twenty-eight members of the re-constituted board which came into office in January 1899, fourteen had been members of the outgoing board and the records indicate that they had been among the most dedicated and attentive members of that board. The new board held its first meeting on 12 January 1899, the membership being as follows:

The Lord Mayor Ald. Daniel Tallon (ex officio)
Nominated by the Municipal Corporation
Ald. the Rt Hon. J.M. Meade, LL.D., J.P.; Ald. T.C. Harrington; Councillors. E. Holohan; J. Hutchinson; J.P. Nannetti; D. Bergin.
Elected by Traders
J.E. Barry; George Jacob; M.E. Dockrell; Marcus Goodbody; Adam Findlater; Wm. Goulding; Wm. Wallace; Wm. Field, M.P.; John Mooney; L. Malone; Wm. Graham; James H. North.
Elected by Shipowners
Sir Richard Martin; John Weatherill; Robert Tedcastle; James Murphy; John Murphy; Michael Murphy; James O'Connor; Henry Burgess; George MacNie.

Names like Martin, Dockrell, Findlater, Goulding, Goodbody, Mooney, Murphy and Wallace were representative of major commercial and trading interests of the city in 1899 and for many years thereafter.

An innovation under the 1898 act was the annual election of a chairman and a vice-chairman, in contrast to the random arrangement which had been previously the custom. Sir Richard Martin became the first chairman under the new arrangement and Maurice E. Dockrell was the first vice-chairman. The new chairman had been a member of the board's predecessors, the Corporation for Preserving and Improving the Port of Dublin, and he had continued as a nominee of the sioners of Irish Lights since 1867. He died in 1901, having been a member continuously for over thirty-six years.

Following a survey by the Admiralty in 1899, the matter of the deterioration in the depth of water on the bar and in the river channel

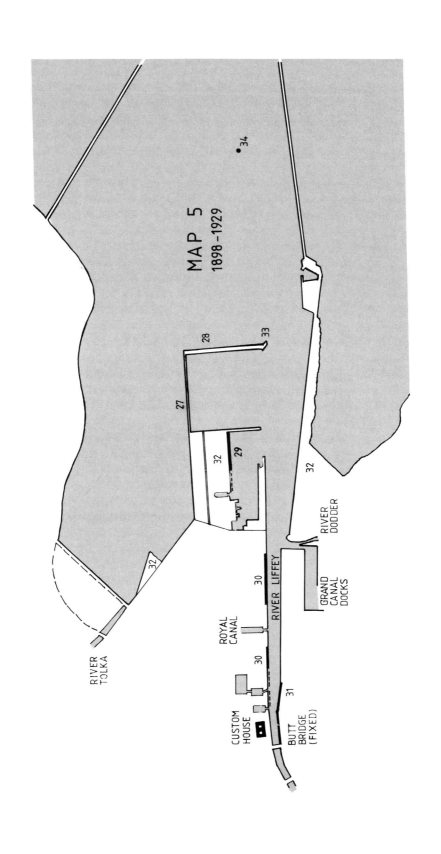

MAP 5
1898-1929

34

28

27

33

32

29

32

RIVER
DODDER

32

RIVER
TOLKA

32

ROYAL
CANAL

30

RIVER LIFFEY

GRAND
CANAL
DOCKS

30

CUSTOM
HOUSE

BUTT
BRIDGE
(FIXED)

31

became one of major concern to the new board and notwithstanding its straitened financial circumstances it decided to place a contract with the Dutch dredging firm of Kalis to dredge the bar; by 1903 the contract was completed, a total of 750,000 tons of sand having been removed from the bar by suction dredger and pumped ashore at the new reclaimed lands near the graving dock.

In the meantime, the board promoted a new bill in parliament designed primarily to remedy its financial situation by two important measures. The first was the assessment of dues on goods landed or loaded at the port, a proposal previously made by the old board without success. The second remedy was the removal of the anomaly arising from the existing system of measuring the net tonnage of ships; under a new arrangement the dues would be charged on the net tonnage or half the gross tonnage, whichever was the greater. The bill also empowered the board to erect an electricity generating station for the board's own purposes and the restriction on motive power other than 'animal power' for hauling wagons on tramways in the port was repealed. The board was authorised to operate a public towage service and to acquire by compulsory purchase portions of premises fronting the North Wall to enable that thoroughfare to be widened.

The bill also extended the board's borrowing powers, and following its enactment in 1902, the board was soon in a position to proceed with its continuous task of improving the port. In 1903 a contract was placed with the Dutch shipbuilder Smit and Zoon for a large suction dredger, specially designed for work on the bar and the vessel was delivered in the following year. Named *Sandpiper*, this vessel was responsible for the maintenance of the depth of water on the bar and the major portion of land reclamation undertaken by the board over the following half-century. A new tug, the *Anna Liffey* was built for the board by the Dublin Dockyard Company Ltd in 1904, to speed up the towage to sea of the floats loaded by the bucket dredgers.

New works undertaken by the board at this time included the extension of the timber jetties used by Gouldings and the Anglo-American Oil company to accommodate another oil company, the Asiatic Petroleum company, which had been granted a lease of two acres of the reclaimed lands. Additional berthage was required for timber cargoes at these jetties, and eventually almost 1,000 feet of deepwater berthage was provided at the jetties as extended.

The generating station provided for in the 1902 act was commenced and orders were placed for electric cranes, including the 100-ton crane which was erected in 1905 and was one of the most prominent landmarks in the port until dismantled in 1987. Ten other electric cranes of four tons capacity were ordered for the North Wall Extension and the Crossberth, duly installed and supplied with electric current from the generating station. Electric capstans were installed at the berths on the North Wall Extension for the haulage of wagons to and from ships, and public lighting was also provided on the quaysides and fed from the same source.

The work of rebuilding the South Quays from Great Britain Quay to Butt Bridge, begun in 1870, was completed early in 1913. Whereas the foreshore had been dry at low water for the full length of these quays before rebuilding, the new quays enabled vessels to berth and sail at all stages of the tide.

Work on the Eastern Breakwater progressed and portion of the earlier concrete wall, built in the 1850s to protect the Basin from easterly gales, was removed to facilitate vessels entering and leaving Alexandra Basin.

Labour disputes in the city culminated in a series of strikes in August 1913. A mass meeting addressed by James Larkin was batoned by police, resulting in the deaths of three people while scores were injured. A federation of employers organised by William Martin Murphy refused employment to any man who continued to be a member of the Irish Transport & General Workers' Union and a lockout followed. Sympathetic strikes throughout the city spread to the port and in October the cranemen, dredger crews and labourers employed by the board struck in sympathy with the men locked out by the city employers. Although the dredging plant had to be laid up, tradesmen and other employees did not become involved in the dispute and the work of the port was carried on, albeit with great difficulty. The strikes collapsed and the men returned to work in January 1914.

In the same year, a programme was initiated by the board to replace with electric cranes the existing steam cranes erected by various shipping and coal companies on the quays.

Because of the availability of accommodation at the deepwater berthage on the north side of the Alexandra Basin in 1913, the Merchants Warehousing Company applied for and were granted a lease of two acres adjoining the berthage, primarily for the erection of a grain silo, and 'tall ships' with grain from Australia became a regular feature at this berth when discharging into the Merchants' silo.

On 30 July 1914 the board received a telegram from the Admiralty which foreshadowed subsequent events; without preamble or explanation the board was ordered not to extinguish any harbour lights or remove any beacons or buoys until so instructed by the Admiralty.

The likelihood of war was no secret and on 3 August thirty-three employees of the board who were army or navy reservists had received mobilisation orders. On 4 August the British government declared war on Germany and on the following day the harbour master reported that military forces had taken over the North Wall Extension; two naval officers were installed in the harbour office, sentries and guards were posted and naval ratings and soldiers had been accommodated in the dockers' 'cookhouse'. In order to allow troop transports to berth, embark troops, horses and artillery commercial shipping was not permitted to use the North Wall Extension or Alexandra Quay. This restriction was later lifted and re-imposed only during the stay in port of the transports. The North Bull Wall and the Bull Island were taken over by the War Office and a military camp and rifle range were established.

The board was asked to store flour donated by the Canadian government for the relief of distress among the poor created by war conditions and the aftermath of the 1913 labour disputes. The reality of this distress was brought home by a letter addressed to the board in December 1914 by the Skerries branch of the Town Tenants League in which it was stated that the people of the town were in dire want because of lack of employment; the board was asked to send some of the flour as a matter of urgency since the people were 'on the verge of starvation'. The board had no function in the distribution of the flour stored in its warehouses and the request was forwarded to the Local Government Board.

One area in which plenty of work was available to skilled men was the Dublin Dockyard which carried out conversion work on merchant ships requisitioned by the government as troop transports. Steam fishing trawlers were also commandeered for conversion to armed patrol boats and minesweepers. Because of the need to have berths for troop transports available at short notice a standing regulation of the port at the time was strictly enforced, requiring every vessel, naval or otherwise, to shift berth to facilitate expeditious berthing and loading of troop ships. Some of the skippers of the trawlers under conversion were new to naval control and discipline to which they did not respond with any great enthusiasm; this attitude extended to instructions given by the harbour master from time to time to remove their vessels from berths required for troop transports. As a consequence the harbour master, Captain John Henry Webb, was obliged to complain to the naval officer commanding the area at the time, Rear Admiral Evelyn Marchant, who was based at Kingstown. The Admiral took exception to the harbour master's attitude which he described in a letter to the board as 'objectionable to an officer of my status'. Captain Webb, himself a former naval officer, was never a man to mince words and in his report on the matter he pointed out that the Admiral had chosen to ignore the attitude of the trawler skippers in impeding the troop transports; he went on to state that in order to carry out his statutory duties as harbour master he could make no distinction between any persons 'be they masters of schooners or Admirals of the Fleet'. The board backed the harbour master's stand and informed the Admiral accordingly. Subsequent communications from the Admiral on various matters were in a much more conciliatory tone.

In October 1914 the board enlisted assistance from an unusual source following the discovery of rat infestation in some of the transit sheds. By arrangement with the Society for the Prevention of Cruelty to Animals, ten cats were supplied by the society for a period of two months, the terms for the service being 'one shilling per cat, plus a sum of fifteen shillings and sixpence per week for wages for a part-time attendant and milk and food for the cats'. It seems that the cats performed their task efficiently since it was not found necessary to renew their contract.

A long-standing dispute between the port board and Dublin Corporation was resolved in 1916 when an agreement between the parties was made the subject of a High Court Order which acknowledged that the board was the owner in fee simple of the quays east of O'Connell Bridge from the water's edge to the frontage of the buildings along the quays but that the Corporation would pave and repair the roadway outside a distance of forty feet from the water's edge, the board being responsible for the remainder.

Following the occupation of the General Post Office on Easter Monday 24 April 1916 by members of the Irish Volunteers and the Irish Citizen Army under Padraig Pearse and James Connolly, the Ballast Office was taken over by British military forces on Wednesday in that week and on the same day Liberty Hall was shelled by the gunboat *Helga* which had been ordered up the river for the purpose. All works under construction by the engineer's department had been shut down on the Tuesday but the British authorities ordered that any personnel required to keep the port operational must remain on the premises; the staff concerned included the harbour master, harbour police, pilots, berthing staff, tug crews, generating station personnel and cranemen. Makeshift sleeping accomodation had to be improvised and food was obtained for all concerned by the harbour master who took a launch to the Clontarf seafront where he managed to collect enough groceries in local shops which were themselves in short supply. On Saturday 29 April, Padraig Pearse issued his order to surrender but normal work at the port did not resume until Tuesday 8 May. The port engineer reported that little damage had been suffered by the board's property except the Ballast Office where windows and roofs were damaged by rifle fire 'during the disturbances at Easter'.

The increased use of the North Wall Extension berths by the military authorities as the war progressed resulted in the enlargement of the two existing transit sheds by the War Department and the construction of another known as No. 3 or 'the Island' shed. Sections of the sheds were fitted out to accomodate troops awaiting embarkation and as billets for crews of naval vessels under repair. Following the heavy casualties suffered at the battlefront, other sections of the sheds were used as reception areas for wounded troops landed from hospital ships. In 1917 the War Department arranged for the construction of a rail connection from the North Wall (Point Depot) sidings to the Crossberth and thence to the berthage on the Alexandra Basin side of the North Wall Extension, to facilitate the movement of equipment, stores and horses.

By the end of the war in 1918, escalating wage rates and commodity prices obliged the board to seek an increase in the level of port charges; a bill was promoted in parliament and the relevant act was passed in 1919 but the effect of the increased revenue was not sufficient to meet the board's needs and a further act was successfully promoted and passed in 1920. In addition to providing for further increases in port rates, the act granted additional borrowing powers required in connection with an extensive scheme of improvements including improved and extended berthage, reconstruction of Custom House Quay, improvements to warehouses and the provision of additional cranes and equipment, and new dredging plant to replace worn out vessels.

The maintenance of the dredging plant had been greatly curtailed during the war because of 'difficult supply conditions and excessively high prices' as the engineer put it in his report for the year 1920. The improved financial situation enabled the board to replace two old bucket dredgers by a large dredger capable of an output greater than that of both of the replaced vessels. This was the *Deepworker* built for the board by Lobnitz & Company of Renfrew, Scotland; her main duty was the dredging of the river channel from Butt Bridge to the bar and also the Alexandra Basin, and she was soon as well-known as the *Sandpiper* not only to port workers but to the general public who had occasion to pass along the quays of the port.

Following the retirement of Sir John Purser Griffith in 1913 he was succeeded as engineer-in-chief by the assistant engineer who was his son, John W. Griffith. During his service with the board, Sir John had made no secret of his disapproval of its financial policy, particularly insofar as it related to port development; his subsequent involvement in the commercial life of the city qualified him to go forward for election to the board as a traders' representative and in due course he was elected to the board in January 1915. Throughout the next eighteen months his disagreement with policy developed into a major controversy and culminated in his resignation in July 1916. On the day following his resignation, his son tendered his resignation from the position of engineer-in-chief which, although couched in different terms from that of his father, was based on a similar conflict with the board's policy of seeking to achieve economies in the costs of port maintenance and development by reductions in staff.

A new engineer-in-chief, Joseph H. Mallagh, was appointed in 1917 and at an early stage he indicated his concern at the deteriorated condition of the timber jetties at the Alexandra Wharf used by Gouldings and the oil companies. In 1921 he submitted a proposal to the board for the replacement of the jetties by a masonry quay wall designed by himself on a principle which was later recognised internationally as a major development in the field of port engineering. The design provided for the construction of caissons which were essentially large rectangular re-inforced concrete boxes, each fifty feet long by thirty feet wide, about the size of a pair of semi-detached suburban houses, built on a slipway like a ship and launched in the same manner. Unlike Stoney's solid blocks, the caissons had open sections which enabled them to float and to be towed to a wharf where they were built up to the required height of forty-two feet; they were then towed into position and sunk on the site of the new quay. The caissons were then filled with spoil dredged by the *Sandpiper* and pumped ashore; a deck slab was constructed to form the new quay surface, and tracks for cranes and rail connections laid. The first caisson was launched on 16 March 1922 and Alexandra Quay, as the new quay was officially known, was completed in 1931.

Nicholas Proud, who had served under the Corporation for Preserving and Improving the Port of Dublin since 1862 and had been appointed the first secretary of the board following its re-consitution in 1867, died in 1921 and was succeeded by Edward H. Bailey.

The political and military situation in Ireland following the signing of the Treaty in December 1921 is well documented elsewhere as is the occupation of the Four Courts and the establishment of the building as the headquarters of the anti-Treaty forces in April 1922. What may not be so well-known is the fact that the Ballast Office, together with the Kildare Street Club, the Masonic Hall in Molesworth Street and other buildings, were also occupied. On 1 May the board's staff were unable to gain entry to the Ballast Office owing, in the words of the board's chairman, to its occupation by 'Armed Irregular Forces'. An emergency meeting of the board was convened and held in the offices of the Commissioners of Irish Lights in D'Olier Street; a deputation of three members of the board was appointed to seek a meeting at the Four Courts with Rory O'Connor, the commander of the occupying force. The deputation consisted of the Lord Mayor, Larry O'Neill; the chairman of the board, David Barry, and Alderman William O'Brien. They demanded the evacuation of the Ballast Office or at least the return of the board's books, ledgers and other records. Subsequently, the board received a letter from the Four Courts stating that the books etc. had to be used for the purpose of temporarily fortifying the offices

A replica of the Viking longship discovered at Gokstad in Norway, built as part of the Dublin Millennium celebrations. Named the *Dyflin*, the building of the craft was conceived by the East Wall Watersports Group and carried into effect with the co-operation of the port board and other sponsors. She is 76 ft long with a mast height of 42 ft and has 32 oars. The *Dyflin* is capable of a speed of 6 knots under oars and 12 knots under sail.

William Sadler's painting of Pidgeon House Harbour and fort, c.1820. In the foreground, soldiers can be seen on Pidgeon House Road. The building directly beyond the road is the officers' mess of the fort, formerly the hotel built by the port board to replace John Pidgeon's house. The building still stands and is used now by the ESB.

Edwin Hayes's painting, *The Emigrant Ship*, painted in the mid 19th century. The ship is moored to a buoy in Halpin's Pond.

An aerial view of the Custom House Docks complex, prior to its transfer to the Custom House Docks development authority in 1987. The carpark at the western end of the complex lies partly on the site of the original dock filled in in 1927. The two docks were known as Inner Dock (*left*) and George's Dock. Immediately beyond George's Dock lies Stack A warehouse, the venue for the great banquet for Crimean war veterans held in 1856.

A view of Clontarf Sheds made in 1785 by Francis Wheatley. It shows the shoreline at the junction of the present-day Vernon Avenue and Clontarf Road.

Prior to the construction of the present Baily lighthouse, completed in 1813, the Howth lighthouse, shown in this 1799 painting by F. Jukes, was situated further up the hill near the present carpark.

A view of the old Custom House near Essex Bridge in 1782 by John James Barralet. The old Custom House is shown in the extreme left background. The necessity for ships to moor in tiers is clearly shown: by law, Custom House Quay was the only permitted landing place for cargoes in Dublin before the present Custom House was built further down river and the port extended to the east. Note the rocky outcrops in the foreground which contributed to the difficult navigational conditions.

The City of Dublin mailsteamer *Connaught* in rough seas off Kingstown. The painting, by Richard Brydges Beechey, is dated 1868.

A model of the bell float also designed by Stoney for the preparation of the river bed to receive the concrete blocks.

A model of the sheer float designed by the port engineer Bindon Blood Stoney for lifting 350-ton concrete blocks for use in the construction of North Wall Extension.

A late nineteenth-century watercolour entitled *A View of the Custom House, Dublin.*

An aerial view of the modern port viewed from the north showing, in the centre, the terminal used by the B & I Line. The Sealink terminal is shown on the left. On the southside of the river (*top centre*) is the south bulk terminal used by CDL for its coal imports. Opposite the Sealink terminal, the present-day Pidgeon House Harbour can be seen.

The Bull Island, with the Bull Wall in the foreground and Ireland's Eye and Lambay Island in the background.

The new headquarters of the Dublin Port and Docks Board at Alexandra Road by night.

and asking if the board were prepared to supply filled sandbags in exchange! The board did not reply but issued a press statement, quoting the letter and stating that as it had been placed in an impossible position it had no alternative but to close down its operations; port dues could not be collected and staff would not be available to pay salaries and wages to upwards of 1,000 employees. Presumably the statement had the desired effect since the Ballast Office was evacuated on 8 May and the staff returned to their normal routine.

According to Dorothy Macardle, both the provisional government and the anti-Treaty forces appeared intent at this time on avoiding a major confrontation but the shooting of Sir Henry Wilson in London on 22 June brought matters to a head and the British government pressed the Provisional Government to take immediate action against the anti-Treaty forces. The occupation of the Four Courts had continued and it was the first target for the government's forces which had to borrow British field guns to bombard the building on Wednesday 28 June. By the following Friday the building had been reduced to a shell and what was left of the interior was in flames. The garrison surrendered but by then other anti-Treaty forces had established new headquarters in hotels in O'Connell Street and the government troops had occupied positions from which to attack; in addition the Ballast Office and other buildings were taken over by these troops following the example of their opponents two months previously. The subsequent bombardment destroyed most of the buildings on the east side of O'Connell Street; by Wednesday 5 July, resistance had ceased and the government were in control.

The record in the board's journals of the involvement of the Ballast Office in this second occupation is laconic in the extreme; at a meeting on 13 July the chairman referred to the cancellation of meetings scheduled for the previous week due to the military occupation of the offices, stating that the building had been returned to the board in the meantime, the offices being 'intact'. The occupation had not, however, been without tragic consequences for one of the military detachment in occupation and also for a civilian passer-by. The soldier was Daniel Brennan, one of two brothers in the detachment who had joined the pro-Treaty forces only one month before. He was killed while exchanging rifle fire with a sniper posted on the roof of the offices at Eden Quay formerly occupied by the City of Dublin Steam Packet Company and later by Palgrave Murphy Ltd. The civilian was a young girl who when walking along Westmoreland Street was killed by a stray bullet stated to have been accidentally discharged by the officer in charge of the detachment on the roof of the Ballast Office.

The new Irish Free State came into existence on 6 December 1922 and one of the immediate consequences for the port was the necessity for the provision of additional bonded transit sheds and warehouses since imports from Britain were no longer exempt from customs regulations and duties. The growth in demand for petroleum products for industrial purposes and also for the increased volume of private motor cars in the 1920s encouraged more oil companies to set up terminals in the port of Dublin; these included the the Shell Mex, British Petroleum, Irish American and Signal Galena companies.

In April 1923 a labour dispute regarding the wages of seamen and firemen on Irish registered ships spread to include dockers and other port workers; other Irish ports were similarly affected. Although Dublin port was not completely closed, trade was seriously affected throughout the duration of the strike which ended in November of that year. However, resumption of work by the dockers coincided with a ban on the import into Britain of Irish cattle, following an allegation that an outbreak of foot and mouth disease which was discovered in Leeds had originated in cattle shipped from Dublin.

The combined effect of the strike and the cattle ban was reflected in the small surplus of £917 from the board's operations in that year. A new shed was constructed at Great Britain Quay in 1924 for the reception of fruit cargoes. In the same year the board closed down its electricity generating station, thereafter taking current from the Dublin Corporation station at the Pidgeon House and converting it for port purposes by a rectifier station built beside the old generating station which was later converted into a transit shed.

A major controversy involving the Municipal Council followed a formal inquiry ordered by the Minister for Local Government in March 1924. The inspector conducting the inquiry acknowledged the excellent work done by many of the council's committees but his report was critical of the council as a whole and the Minister decided to dissolve the council and to replace it with three commissioners; however, the order for dissolution also provided that membership of public bodies by councillors in their capacity as representatives of the Corporation would not be affected. Accordingly, those councillors who were members of the port board were not required to resign; however, they ceased to attend meetings, presumably in protest at the dissolution. As they failed to attend the minimum number of meetings prescribed by statute, the board was obliged to declare their membership vacated and they were replaced in due course by the three commissioners, Seamus O'Murchadha, Dr W.C. Dwyer and P.J. Hernon.

The disputes between the British coal miners and the colliery owners, which led to the general strike in Britain in May 1926, dislocated the import of coal from the normal sources and although some coal was obtained elsewhere its inferior quality and high price added to the engineer's problems in maintaining his dredging programme.

The year 1929 saw the completion of a tunnel under the Liffey and it is likely that few citizens are aware of its existence. The tunnel was first proposed by Dublin Corporation in 1918 primarily as a service tunnel for electricity, water and sewage but provision was proposed for pedestrians also. Discussions involving the Corporation, the Pembroke Urban District Council and the port board were protracted, mainly on the grounds of costs. Eventually agreement was reached in 1926 for a smaller tunnel for water and electricity supplies only and work on the tunnel commenced in August of that year and was completed in 1929. The tunnel which is 830 feet long and 11 feet in diameter, is sunk at 100 feet below ground level at its northern end, close to the former offices of the harbour master at the North Wall Extension and it terminates at Thorncastle Street, Ringsend.

Disposal of domestic refuse had become a major problem for the Dublin Corporation in the 1920s and an agreement in 1931 between the port board and the Corporation paved the way for a mutually advantageous solution to the problem. The board, as owners of the foreshore adjoining East Wall Road, agreed to permit the Corporation to dump the refuse on the foreshore, covering it with top soil and thus effectively reclaiming land for port purposes. The area involved was triangular in shape, commencing near the railway bridge across East Wall Road, and to be bounded by a concrete retaining wall stretching in a south easterly direction, to meet the base line of the triangle extending from the entrance to Tolka Quay. Work on the concrete retaining wall commenced in 1929 and as each section of the wall was completed a further area became available to the Corporation for reclamation. Later agreements provided for the extension of the works to form most of the land between Promenade Road and Tolka Quay.

The thirty years since the re-constitution of the board in 1898 had seen many fundamental changes in the character of the port and of the shipping it served. Perhaps the most notable was the gradual increase in the overseas trade, facilitated by the new deepwater berthage and the provision of modern cargo handling equipment. However, there was still a long way to go to bring the port and its services to the stage where vessels would not have to spend from ten to fourteen days in the discharge of their timber or grain cargoes because of outmoded systems of discharge, both human and mechanical, aggravated by the fact that Alexandra Quay, the board's most modern deepwater berthage, was frequently congested when oil tankers vied with timber, grain and general cargo ships for berths.

18

The Thirties and the 'Emergency', 1930–46

IN the years following the establishment of the Irish Free State, the new government was faced with major tasks, not least in drafting bills to correct what would otherwise have been serious anomalies in central and local government. Although the need to review the administration and operation of the ports of the state was recognised, there were other priorities and it was not until 1926 that government attention was turned to ports. In May of that year a tribunal was established by the Minister for Industry and Commerce to enquire into and report upon the position of ports and harbours, in particular regarding the constitution, powers and administration of the respective authorities, and their finances and facilities; it was directed also to report on the existing statute law relating to ports and as to any changes which appeared necessary or desirable. The tribunal's brief included an examination of the extent to which the trade of the ports was carried in ships owned in the state.

Twenty-six ports and harbours were named in the Minister's order, state-controlled ports such as Dun Laoghaire being excluded, and local sittings at which evidence was taken were held by the tribunal in practically all the ports named in the order.

The report of the tribunal, published in 1930, referred to the inconsistencies as between ports, even those of similar size, in almost every facet of their administration and operation, due mainly to lack of uniformity as between the statutes applicable to the various ports, and to inconsistencies between general acts and local acts. Consequently there was a wide divergency in constitutions, membership, powers and functions and an absence of uniformity in financial matters. Abundant evidence had been noted of inefficient, uneconomic and extravagant management which could not be checked under the existing law. Six different government departments had functions of varying degrees of importance in relation to ports but while the general oversight of port matters was the responsibility of the Minister for Industry and Commerce, he did not possess in relation to port authorities the powers that

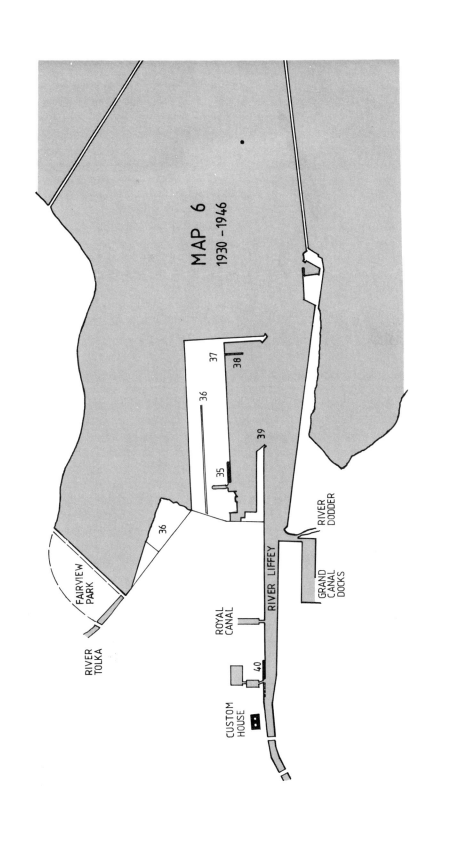

MAP 6
1930 - 1946

RIVER
TOLKA

FAIRVIEW
PARK

36

35

36

37

38

39

RIVER LIFFEY

RIVER
DODDER

GRAND
CANAL
DOCKS

ROYAL
CANAL

40

CUSTOM
HOUSE

the Minister for Local Government had in relation to local authorities, and such powers as he had were derived from isolated provisions in local acts, limited in scope and of relatively minor significance.

The tribunal's main recommendation was that the various existing statutes relating to the ports, with the exception of the Pilotage Act 1913, should be replaced by a General Consolidated Act, embodying such of the existing statutory provisions as experience had shown to be valuable and desirable, together with such provisions as might be necessary to give effect to other recommendations and suggestions contained in the report. The other major recommendation was that the Department of Industry and Commerce should be placed as regards ports and harbours in much the same position as the Department of Local Government and Public Health occupied in relation to local authorities.

The ministerial order setting up the tribunal stated that it was 'expedient that a tribunal be established for inquiring into a definite matter of urgent public importance, that is to say, the present position of the several ports and harbours in Saorstat Eireann specified in the Schedule to this Resolution'. In the preliminary observations of its report, the tribunal stated that 'the public generally do not, we fear, appreciate the importance of our harbours as a vital part of the country's economic structure and are prone to forget that the external trade of the Saorstat is, with the exception of trade with Northern Ireland, entirely waterborne and that inefficient harbour administration inevitably reacts on that trade, handicaps exporters and raises prices of commodities imported'. One might be forgiven for suggesting that a further factor extended responsibility for this situation to the government, namely its tardiness in dealing with the recommendations of the tribunal, since a bill such as proposed did not come before the Oireachtas for another fifteen years. However, it must be acknowledged that the change of government in 1932 and the 'Emergency' of 1939–45 provided some excuse for the delay. The bill was eventually enacted as the Harbours Act 1946; it marked a watershed in harbour administration in the Republic and is dealt with in Chapter 19.

The tribunal had noted that, according to *Lloyd's Register*, the average size of steamships throughout the world had increased by almost 60 per cent between 1900 and 1928 and that facilities to accomodate larger ships were so expensive as to set an immediate limit to the number of ports which could hope to handle them in any country; in this regard, the tribunal noted also that Dublin was 'best situated to serve the needs of the Saorstat as a whole' and that it was 'the best equipped of the ports'.

Following the passing of the Local Government (Dublin) Act 1930, a new Municipal Council was elected and their representatives once more appeared at meetings of the port board, led by the Lord Mayor, the famous 'Alfie' Byrne; the other councillors nominated by the council to the board were Sean T. O'Kelly, TD (later Minister for Local Government and Minister for Finance, stages in a career which culminated in his election as President of Ireland in 1945), James Larkin, Patrick Belton, John Ryan, David Coyle and George Gillespie.

Work on the construction of the North Wall Extension had been suspended in 1881 until a decision should be made on the future development of Alexandra Basin. In 1931, sixty years after Stoney had supervised the placing of the first 350 ton concrete block for the Extension, work on its completion commenced. This last section of the Extension was built with caissons and the final stage of its construction was the re-positioning of the North Wall Lighthouse at its extremity in 1937.

The port of Dublin was faced with a major challenge when it became known that the Eucharistic Congress would be held in Dublin in June 1932. The berthing of seven large ocean liners was unprecedented and created problems for the harbour master and his staff, as did the scheduling of pilots and tugs to attend the liners. Five other liners anchored in the bay, the passengers being ferried ashore by tenders. Extra cross-channel passenger services from Liverpool and Glasgow were arranged by the Congress organisers; the LMS diverted one of their mail ships, *Scotia*, to Dublin while maintaining their usual Holyhead/Dun Laoghaire services.

As is customary, all the liners had facilities on board for holding religious services, but because of the numbers of passengers wishing to attend Mass each day, a transit shed at the Crossberth at the North Wall Extension, which had formerly housed the board's electricity generating station, was given a new rôle during the Congress. Renovations were carried out, the shed was suitably decorated and temporary altars were installed to enable Masses to be celebrated each morning.

The five tenders which ferried the passengers from the liners anchored in the bay included three vessels well known to Dubliners as excursion ships in Dublin Bay—*Royal Iris* and *An Saorstat*, both former Mersey ferries, and *Cynthia*, a more graceful vessel which was formerly a tender serving liners of the Anchor Line at Derry; the latter ended her career in Dun Laoghaire harbour in the following year when she broke away from her moorings in a gale and became a total wreck. Fifty-eight ships berthed at the quays during the Congress, in addition to the five which anchored in the bay. Of a total of sixty-three vessels, twelve were ocean liners, thirteen were cross-channel passenger ships, nine were foreign cargo ships, twenty-four were cross-channel cargo ships and colliers, the remaining five being the tenders.

The service provided to the 'Congress' shipping while maintaining normal port operations with minimal disruption evoked tributes from all the shipping interests concerned and the experience of the port gained by the ocean liner operators led to its use for pilgrims travelling by sea to Lourdes and Rome. Those bound for Lourdes disembarked at Bordeaux and those for Rome at Civitta Vecchia at the mouth of the Tiber. In 1934 four pilgrim liners berthed at Alexandra Quay, the White Star Line *Laurentic*, the Cunard Line *Lancastria* and the Pacific Steam Navigation Company's *Orduna* and *Royal Star*; the programme was repeated and extended in 1935. In January 1936, the Anchor Line notified the board of its intention to include Dublin in their regular North Atlantic schedule operating between Glasgow and Boston/New York, making calls en route at Belfast and Derry. The board agreed to provide a new passenger facility at Alexandra Quay; the building included waiting rooms, customs examination hall, immigration office, baggage room and the usual cloakroom facilities. The service opened on 9 May 1936 with the arrival of the company's *California* 20,000 tons gross; four other liners berthed at Alexandra Quay in that year and a further twenty-three anchored in the bay and transferred their passengers by tender to the Liner Hall, as it became known. In 1937 the figures were five liners at Alexandra Quay and fifty-four in the bay; in 1938 only two liners berthed while fifty-six anchored in the bay. Early in 1939 the Anchor Line management decided that the demand for a service to Dublin did not justify a continuation of their calls and they were abandoned.

In June 1936 approaches were made to the board on behalf of the London and Thameshaven Oil Wharves, with whom was associated the shipping firm of Andrew Weir and Company, who sought a site of seventy acres at the port on which an oil refinery would be built. The proposal had already been broached to the government who had agreed to grant the necessary operating licence for the refinery. Land reclaimed or substantially reclaimed, totalling fifty-three acres, was then available and the board agreed to lease this land to the company and to reclaim a further seventeen acres. In addition two jetties were to be built to accomodate tankers of 15,000 tons deadweight and oil pipes were to be laid connecting the jetties to a tank farm where the crude oil would be stored pending refining. It was intended that most of the country's oil requirements would eventually be met by the refinery.

A new company, Irish National Refineries Limited, was formed and the directors included Lord Inverforth and Lord Glenavy. Since the board's dredging plant was not in a position to carry out all the reclamation and filling within the required period, the Dutch dredging firm of Bos and Kalis was engaged for the purpose.

By the end of 1938, reclamation work was well advanced and construction of the first of the two jetties had commenced. Seven new oil tankers were commissioned by the associated firm of Andrew Weir to carry the crude oil to the refinery; the last of these vessels was launched late in 1938 and all seven ships were registered in Dublin.

Early in 1939 it became evident that although the boiler house and other buildings required for the refinery were practically complete, the parent company was slowing down on the project. In March 1939 the company informed the board that they could not proceed with the project at that time because of financial and other difficulties. Various schemes for re-structuring the parent company were proposed and eventually it was taken over by the associated firm of Andrew Weir. Hopes that the project might be carried on or taken over by other parties persisted until June 1940 when, following the Dunkirk evacuation, it became clear that it could not continue, at least for some years. The board agreed to its suspension until after the war.

For older members of the board's staff, memories of the call-up of reservists in July 1914 were revived in July 1939 when employees who were reservists in the British navy were called up. Following the outbreak of war on 3 September 1939, an Emergency Powers Order placed restrictions on the movement of persons, imposed censorship on newspapers, radio broadcasts and news films, placed restrictions on ships, aircraft and lighthouses and put all communications, supplies and services under government control. In 1940 an examination service was set up by the Department of Defence at each of the major ports, under the control of a naval officer known as the Competent Port Authority. A request was made to the board to provide accomodation in the harbour master's office for a CPA, as he was known, to be appointed for the port of Dublin. No accomodation was available but the impasse was solved when it transpired that the assistant harbour master, Captain A.J. O'Brien-Twohig, a former naval officer in British submarines, was to be the new CPA with the Irish naval rank of Lieutenant Commander. The Liner Hall was handed over to the Department of Defence as the headquarters of the port control service, in charge of Lieutenant George McGuirk acting under the CPA. The latter was fond of describing himself as a 'veritable Pooh Bah' since, following his later appointment as harbour master, he had to communicate regularly by letter with himself as CPA. The pilot steamer was requisitioned temporarily for use as an examination boarding vessel and she, like the harbour master, acted in a dual capacity for some time. Later the Department of Defence hired a small tug named *Noray* which was normally used by the engineer's department for towing dredging plant, and she took over the duties of examination vessel from the pilot steamer. A chief petty officer in the examination service at that time later achieved fame in a somewhat different milieu, that of television. He was the Honorable Patrick Campbell, son of Lord Glenavy, and the speech impediment which added to his personal charm on television never appeared to interfere with the due performance of his naval duties insofar as could be judged in the course of his frequent calls to the harbour master's office.

The outbreak of war underlined the extent to which the state had been dependent on foreign shipping for the import of such commodities as grain, oil, timber, coal, steel and fertilisers, a fact that had been noted by the Ports & Harbours Tribunal in its report. Few Irish registered vessels were capable of deepsea work; in any event, most of them were already committed to their existing task of maintaining supply lines to cross-channel and near continental ports. The loss of bases in the Republic in 1938 did not encourage the British government to view the Republic's supply problems or its shortage of ships as a high priority, and the lack of an adequate Irish merchant shipping fleet was brought home in no uncertain manner to both government and people. Eventually in March 1941 a national shipping company, Irish Shipping Limited, was established, the majority (51 per cent) shareholder being the Minister of Finance while $43\frac{3}{4}$ per cent was held by Grain Importers Ltd, the balance being held by Limerick Steamship Co. Ltd, Palgrave Murphy Ltd, and Wexford Steamship Co. Ltd. By the end of 1941, the new company had acquired ten ships, eight by purchase and two by charter. The condition and previous history of the ships were as varied as the nationality of their previous owners. Once more, the dockyard in Alexandra Basin resounded to riveters and other trades repairing and refitting many of the new fleet when they made their first call to the port. The ships were managed by the three shipping companies who were named as shareholders in the new company. Five more ships were acquired, two by purchase and three by charter before the war ended in 1945. To the crews of these ships all of whom were regular visitors to Dublin, and those owned by other Irish shipowners, including the Dublin Gas company colliers, Dublin trawlers and Arklow schooners, the country's survival was largely due. In his book *The Long Watch* Captain Frank Forde gives a vivid and comprehensive account of Irish ships and their crews, their losses and their achievements in what was officially known as the 'Emergency'.

A bill promoted by the board in 1939 became law in 1940 and was principally concerned with the reallocation to port works of funds specified in the board's act of 1920 to be used for certain purposes; these had included a new graving dock which was not regarded as a priority in 1939. As a consequence, the board was in a position in 1940 to commence the Ocean Pier which was in effect a continuation of Alexandra Quay in a south-easterly direction.

Because of the possibility of an invasion, preceded by air attack, the board established air raid precautions teams, fire fighting squads, first aid teams and, under the aegis of the Local Security Force, a demolition squad was set up under the command of the assistant chief engineer, F.W. Bond. In conjunction with the City Corporation's scheme for building air raid shelters throughout the entire city, the board arranged for the provision of both overground and underground shelters in the port area, including the Custom House Docks.

Because of a substantial drop in revenue between September 1939 and June 1940, due mainly to the fall off in shipping arriving from overseas, the board found it necessary to introduce economy measures, including a shorter working week for employees in June 1940. None the less, within its limited resources, the board continued with its projected works, which included the replacement of the old timber jetties east and west of the entrance to George's Dock in the Custom House Docks complex, by modern masonry quay walls. Progress was understandably slow, because of lack of funds and the general problem of obtaining materials and spare parts throughout the war years and continuing for some time afterwards; it was occasionally necessary to suspend work altogether.

During the 'Emergency', strange occurrences and curious cargoes were by no means infrequent at the port but a most unusual item arrived from Holyhead in October 1941, aboard the LMS cargo ship *Slieve Bawn*. It was one of three packing cases from London, labelled as containing paintings by an artist named de Loubezac, intended for exhibition at a Dublin art gallery. After the three cases had been unloaded, an LMS employee heard a sound as though someone within one of the cases was knocking. On the instructions of his supervisor he prised open the case to find a man inside in an exhausted condition and almost totally enclosed in a plaster cast. He was taken to hospital and was later interrogated by the Gardai. It transpired that he was the artist de Loubezac, a Frenchman who gave his address as Le Bourget, near Paris which, considering that France had been over-run by German forces in 1940, was to say the least odd. Neither the Gardai nor the Department of External Affairs, who intervened in the matter, would give any information or offer any explanation as to M. de Loubezac's curious choice of conveyance.

The engineer's department displayed considerable ingenuity in devising alternatives when standard spares for machinery could not be obtained and because of the difficulty of obtaining supplies of suitable coal for the dredging plant, pilot steamers and tugs, a briquette manufacturing plant was set up in the Crossberth transit shed which had started life as an electricity generating station and in 1932 had been used for the celebration of Mass during the Eucharistic Congress. Because of the curtailment in petrol supplies, the board's motor lorries were adapted for running on gas, a practice widespread among commercial transport owners. Some native timber was available but little could be done to eke out the board's stocks of iron, steel, wire ropes and lubricating oil.

To assist in the general efforts to provide fuel for both domestic and industrial purposes, the board agreed to the storage of turf and coal on a section of Alexandra Quay and on the adjoining reclaimed lands, by Fuel Importers (Eire) Ltd, the ESB and Irish Shipping Ltd.

Following the retirement in 1941 of Mr Mallagh, chief engineer and Captain Webb, the harbour master, their assistants, Mr F. W. Bond and Captain A.J. O'Brien-Twohig were appointed acting chief engineer and acting harbour master respectively. In December 1942 their appointments as chief engineer and harbour master were confirmed and in the same month the board found it possible to restore the full working week for all employees.

In the report of the Ports and Harbours Tribunal it had been recommended that as in the case of Cork and Waterford, the ports of Dublin and Limerick should have general managers and in May 1944 the Chairman of the Dublin Port and Docks Board, Mr Thomas O'Connor, suggested to the board that they should proceed with the appointment of a general manager through the medium of the Local Appointments Commission without waiting for the proposed new harbours legislation. The board agreed and the matter was put in train.

In the same year, following the establishment of Coras Iompair Eireann, the board agreed to convey to the new organisation a portion of the Custom House Docks premises adjoining Store Street for the erection of a central bus station and agreement was also reached with Dublin Corporation for the transfer to them of a further portion of the ground for the purpose of a new road connecting Amiens Street with Beresford Place, later to be known as Memorial Road.

Following the end of the war in 1945, the port control and examination service at Dublin and other ports was withdrawn. A gradual improvement in overseas shipping was evident by the end of the year and the lifting of wartime restrictions enabled more and larger cargoes to be shipped from Canada and the United States, including wheat, timber, newsprint, agricultural and other machinery, steel and foodstuffs, together with timber from Sweden, steel, fruit and coffee from Brazil, fruit and wine from Spain and bananas from the Canary Islands. For some people the arrival of the first post-war consignment of Hennessy brandy from France signified the real end of the war in Europe.

In April 1944 the British naval authorities had suspended the issue of navicerts to Irish ships which were necessary to enable them to sail to and from Lisbon; the reason became clear two months later when the allied invasion of Normandy commenced. In June 1945 this restriction was lifted and sailings resumed to Lisbon where 70,000 tons of various commodities consigned to the Republic had accumulated over the preceding twelve months; some of these goods had originated in the USA, Canada and the Mediterranean but the majority were from South America.

In September 1945 the first of many small fishing vessels and yachts arrived in Dublin carrying refugees from European countries, principally from the Baltic states, on the first stage of what was intended to be a transatlantic crossing to a new life in the New World. The aftermath of war in Europe and the consequent distress and hardship for so many was brought home to the Irish people by these unfortunate travellers but relief schemes had already been set up by the Irish government, the Irish Red Cross and other agencies. In the same month that saw the arrival of the first boatload of refugees, the port welcomed the Dutch motorship *Orestes*, 7,500 tons gross, to load cattle, foodstuffs and other goods for Rotterdam, to assist in the relief of distress. The *Orestes* was soon joined in regular trips between Rotterdam and Dublin by the *Prins Willem van Oranje* which on its first return trip back to Dublin carried a thank-you gift to Dublin Corporation of 100,000 Dutch flower bulbs for the city's parks.

The fall in port revenue during the war years, together with the difficulty of obtaining materials, had necessitated the deferment of major port improvement works with the exception of the re-building of the quay walls at Custom House Quay, east and west of the entrance to George's Dock. The board had, however, considered and approved recommendations from the engineer-in-chief, harbour master and warehouse manager in 1944 for the formulation of a programme of major works to be undertaken as soon as circumstances permitted. The programme included the completion of the Ocean Pier, new two storey transit sheds at North Wall Extension and at Alexandra Quay, a new warehouse at No. 2 Branch Road adjoining Alexandra Quay, a new graving dock and a new central office at Custom House Docks to house the board's administrative, technical and clerical staff.

Following the cessation of hostilities, the improvement in the trade of the port and the consequent improvement in the board's financial position, together with the gradual easing of the supplies difficulty, enabled the board to proceed with these works. By the end of 1946 considerable progress had been made on the construction of Ocean Pier and a new transit shed had been completed at the North Wall Extension. Plans for the new transit shed at Alexandra Quay and the new warehouse were well advanced and arrangements were in train for the recruitment of technical staff for the design of the new graving dock.

The new warehouse, later to be known as Stack D, was designed so that part of the building could be used as a transit shed thus giving it a dual rôle; here, perhaps a brief summary of the differences between a transit shed and a warehouse would be appropriate. As its name may indicate, a transit shed is intended to shelter goods, usually described as break-bulk cargo, awaiting custom clearance while in transit through the port. Break bulk cargo refers to goods such as those packed in crates, boxes, barrels, sacks etc. in contrast to bulk cargoes such as oil, coal, grain and ore or goods packed in containers. A transit shed requires to be located at or adjacent to a shipping berth to enable the break-bulk cargo to be landed therein with the minimum of delay and effort, and therefore of cost, and the sheds are always under customs supervision. Goods lying in a transit shed are deemed to be in the custody of the shipping company or shipping agent to whom the shed has been allocated for the time being and pressure is exerted on the owners of such goods, through the application of special bye-laws, to remove their goods as soon as possible, thus freeing the shed to receive another cargo. A warehouse, on the other hand, is intended to provide long-term storage and a range of warehousing services which will be dealt with in Chapter 21.

The board's policy in relation to its new works was based on the assumption of an increase in the number and size of the types of vessels which had been trading to the port in previous years. Accordingly priority was given to the provision of larger, better and more modern facilities of the kind which had been standard equipment in most ports for many years, and these facilities were welcomed and availed of in the immediate port-war years by shipping arriving at the port. However, the need was already apparent for a new appraisal of the nature of the future demands which would be made in view of changes in methods of transporting goods and in shipbuilding technology. This dichotomy was well illustrated in the contrast between two contracts placed by the board in 1946. The first was for the supply of twenty-six new electric cranes partly to replace old and wornout cranes, partly to provide additional facilities at existing berths and partly to equip the new quays coming on stream. Later in the same year, a contract was placed for the supply of six fork-lift trucks, a commonplace sight nowadays not only at ports but at factories and elsewhere. The trucks ordered by the board, however, were the first to be seen in this country and they were an indication of things to come in regard to the mechanisation of dockers' work. Coinciding with these intimations of technological changes, the passing of the Harbours Act 1946 brought about a new concept in port administration in the Republic which is dealt with in the next chapter.

19

Post-War Reconstruction

THE Harbours Act 1946, which became law on 2 April 1946, gave statutory effect to the majority of the recommendations of the Ports and Harbours Tribunal as set out in its report of 1930. The act gave to the Minister for Industry and Commerce powers of general oversight of those harbour authorities to which the act referred, as set out in the first schedule to the act, and provision was made for their re-constitution. The authorities were divided into two groups, the first group consisting of Dublin, Cork, Limerick and Waterford, and the remaining twenty-one harbours to which the act related were listed in the second group. In the case of the first group, the act provided that each authority should consist of twenty-three members, as follows:

5 local authority members
4 Chamber of Commerce members
2 'livestock' members
2 manufacturer members
2 labour members
4 elected members (usually described as shipping members)
4 members nominated by the Minister

In the case of Dublin, the appointing authorities and organisations were Dublin Corporation, Dublin Chamber of Commerce, Irish Livestock Traders, Federation of Irish Manufacturers and the Dublin Council of Trades Unions. The shipping members are elected by Irish shipowners who have paid a prescribed minimum amount of port dues to the harbour authority.

The general powers and duties of harbour authorities are set out in part V of the act and consist of two mandatory and many enabling provisions. Section 47 provides that 'a harbour authority *shall* take all proper measures for the management, control and operation of their harbour and *shall* provide reasonable facilities and accommodation therein for vessels, goods and passengers [and] the maintenance of all works, bridges, equipment and facilities under their control'. Section 48

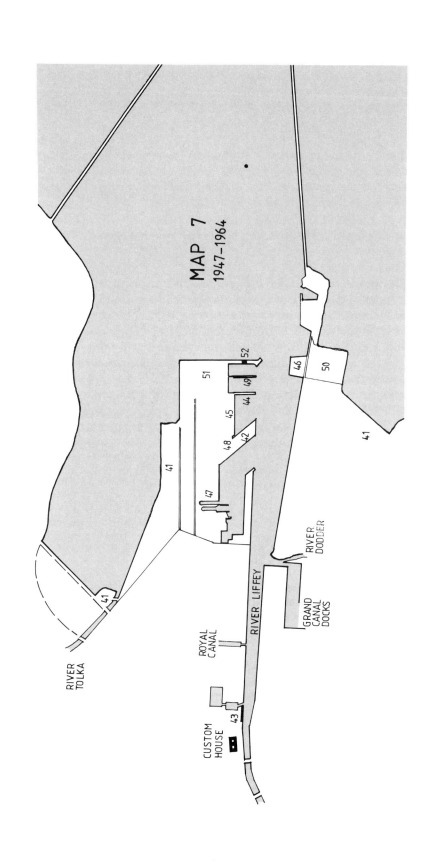

MAP 7
1947-1964

RIVER TOLKA

RIVER LIFFEY

ROYAL CANAL

CUSTOM HOUSE

RIVER DODDER

GRAND CANAL DOCKS

41

41

41

41

43

44

45

46

47

48

49

50

51

52

provides that 'a harbour authority *shall* take all proper measures for cleaning, scouring, deepening, improving and dredging their harbour and the approaches thereto and, subject to any direction which the Minister may give, *shall* dispose of dredged material either by depositing it at sea or in such other way as they think proper.' The two mandatory sections apply to all harbour authorities covered by the act, irrespective of size, and a harbour authority could be held to be in breach of its statutory duty if by act or omission it failed to comply with these provisions. The enabling sections, on the other hand, relate to the provision of tenders, dredgers, lifeboats, lighters, tug boats, cranes, tools, plant, machinery, sheds, warehouses, warehousing services and other facilities; because of the variation in the size of the harbours, the nature and extent of their trade and therefore the wide variety of services which might be required in some ports but not in others, such provisions could not be made generally mandatory.

Apart from procedural matters in relation to their constitution harbour authorities are obliged to seek ministerial approval for variations in harbour rates, borrowings and bye-laws, and othewise as noted hereunder, the day-to-day operations of harbours are carried out without ministerial involvement.

The finance and accounts of harbour authorities are regulated on a uniform basis under part VII of the act and all harbour authority accounts require to be audited by an auditor appointed by the Minister.

The Minister's sanction to major port construction projects such as docks, graving docks, quays, roads or embankments is conveyed by means of a statutory instrument known as a Harbour Works Order and such orders may also be invoked to fix or vary the limits of a harbour or to transfer to a local authority a harbour or part of a harbour, or transfer to a harbour authority a specified port or pier.

A similar instrument known as a Harbour Rates Order is used to signify ministerial approval for any variation in harbour rates or charges.

A curious feature of the new act was its title since, as we shall see, a harbour might form only part of a port, and in the case of Dublin the definitions of the port of Dublin and of the harbour of Dublin under the 1869 act make this quite clear (see Chapter 22). Although the attention of the government was drawn to this matter in the course of the board's observations on the bill, no action was taken on the issue of the title to the bill; however, a special provision was added to the definitions in Section 2 of the act which states in effect that any reference in the act to the limits of Dublin harbour shall be construed as a reference to the limits of the port of Dublin as defined in the 1869 act (see Chapter 22).

The first meeting of the Dublin Port and Docks Board, as reconstituted under the 1946 act, took place on 10 October, 1946, the

membership being as follows:
Local Authority (Dublin Corporation) members
Ald. Martin O'Sullivan, TD, PC; Ald. Senator A.S. Clarkin, PC;
Ald. John McCann, TD, Lord Mayor; Councillor James Larkin;
Councillor Maurice E. Dockrell, TD.
Dublin Chamber of Commerce members
Mr C.M. O'Kelly; Mr Percy McGrath; Mr John McEvoy, PC;
Mr Stephen MacKenzie.
Livestock (National Executive of the Irish Livestock Trade) members
Mr John Bruton; Mr Michael Bermingham.
Manufacturer (Federation of Irish Manufacturers Ltd) members
Mr P.L. McEvoy; Senator F.M. Summerfield.
Labour (Dublin Council of Irish Unions) members
Mr Sean O'Moore; Mr Frank Robbins.
Elected (by shipping interests) members
Mr E.J. Betson; Mr L.S. Furlong; Mr J.P. Reihill; Mr R.W. Sinnott.
Nominated (by the Minister for Industry and Commerce) members
Mr D. Figgis; Capt. Alan S. Gordon; Mr N.P. McEvoy; Mr D.J.
Twohig.

Alderman Martin O'Sullivan was elected chairman of the new board
and Mr John Bruton was elected vice-chairman. Mr Sean O'Moore,
Labour member, should not be confused with Mr Sean Moore TD (later
Lord Mayor and a Minister of State) who served the board in later years
as a Dublin Corporation representative.

Only eight members were new to the board, Councillor Conway,
Messrs. Dockrell, Summerfield, O'Moore, Robbins, Furlong, P.L.
McEvoy and N.P. McEvoy; the remaining fifteen had been members of
the old board and were therefore conversant with the existing proposals
for port development. Appropriately enough, within two months of the
board's first meeting, its first general manager, Mr Denis A. Hegarty,
took up duty, having been recommended for the position by the Local
Appointments Commission. Mr Hegarty had previously been in the
local government service as city manager of Waterford and also as
county manager for Sligo/Leitrim.

In addition to the major projects of new berthage, transit sheds,
cranes, warehouse, graving dock and dredging, a great deal of the
board's plant and equipment had to be replaced, having had its normal
life span extended throughout the Emergency by various shifts and
stratagems. The growth in the actual area of port operations involved
minor building projects to house harbour police, berthing staff, cranemen and other sections of the work force and included temporary
buildings for employees working away from base on the reclaimed
lands. Reclamation was followed by road extensions, surfacing of areas
adjoining berthage, provision of main services such as electrical,

drainage, water, sewage and public lighting not only for the board's own purposes but also for tenants to whom sites were leased on the new lands. All these services were provided by the board.

The volume of work necessitated the recruitment of temporary technical staff for design work, and skilled and unskilled labour for those works carried out by direct labour, particularly the building of caissons.

As a consequence, the following seventeen years saw an unprecedented expansion in port facilities and associated activities, including those of port users and tenants of the board, and these developments and events are outlined hereunder.

1947. The Irish National Refineries company notified the board in 1947 that it was obliged to abandon its plans for an oil refinery at Dublin on the reclaimed lands leased from the board in 1936. The company asked to be relieved of its obligations to continue with the project, the board to be re-imbursed for its outlay in the matter. The release of the reclaimed lands tied up in the refinery project suited the board in view of other demands for land and it assented to the proposal. At this time the ESB was in some difficulty in securing coal supplies for its generating station at the Pidgeon House and although it had plans afoot for a new oil burning station at Ringsend, the need was urgent for a station to help to maintain electricity supplies in the interim. The boilerhouse constructed for the aborted oil refinery project offered a solution and with the agreement of the board the ESB bought the building from the refinery company together with some ancillary sheds. The board agreed also to lease to the ESB seven acres of the lands reclaimed for the refinery, for the purposes of the new station. The necessary plant was installed in the boilerhouse and the new station came on stream in 1949 under the name of the 'North Wall Generating Station' although its association with the North Wall remains unclear.

The increasing number of vessels from overseas carrying general cargo, grain, timber or oil and all seeking deepwater berths at Alexandra Quay continued to create problems at that berthage, particularly having regard to the special precautions required by bye-law to be observed during the discharge of oil tankers although the congestion was somewhat eased as berthage at Ocean Pier became progressively available. It was considered that a radical change was necessary in respect of the discharge and storage of oil and in 1947 the harbour master and the engineer recommended the creation of an oil zone within the port where the discharge and storage of oil products would be concentrated as far as possible, and which would be served by two new oil jetties with two berths on each jetty. The project involved a major upheaval in the existing installations of the oil companies which were strung out along Alexandra Road and connected with Alexandra Quay by underground pipelines but it had been obvious for some time that the companies would have to enlarge their terminals because of the continued growth in oil imports. The oil zone scheme proposed that the jetties would have a system of common oil pipelines carried on overhead supports so arranged that by means of appropriate valve systems the cargo for any particular company could be directed into its terminal; provision was also made for private lines for companies who so desired. The advantages to be derived from berthage exclusively reserved for tankers, obviating delay in securing a discharging berth, were substantial and eventually all the oil companies joined in the scheme. The Irish Shell company took an initiative early in 1948 by bringing to Dublin a storage hulk, the *Shelfoil,* formerly a tanker that had been severely damaged during the war and was in fact now only half a tanker. The board gave permission for her to be moored at the original oil jetty built for the refinery project near the eastern breakwater, where she provided additional storage for the company pending the completion of the new installations. The jetty was subsequently enlarged and improved to become the first (or eastern) oil jetty under the new scheme; a second (western) jetty was completed in 1952 and the common pipeline scheme was substantially finished in 1953.

Reclamation of foreshore adjoining berthage was usually carried out by deposit of suitable filling from the spoil dredged by the board's dredgers or those of dredging contractors. Reclamation at East Wall had continued throughout the Emergency, the board constructing the retaining wall and Dublin Corporation using the area thus enclosed for the dumping of domestic refuse which was compacted and covered with topsoil. Sites were leased to various interests and when the ESB commenced its rural electrification scheme the board agreed to lease a site at East Wall containing seven acres for the storage of poles imported for the scheme; in subsequent years further sites were leased to the ESB at East Wall. As the reclamation progressed the board decided as a matter of policy that its lands would in future be leased only to companies the nature of whose business required a location in the port area.

1948.   Supplies of coal improved to the extent that it was found possible to close down the briquette plant at the Crossberth and return the building to its former function as transit shed. An oil bunkering barge was purchased by the board enabling ships to be re-fuelled at their berth more quickly than was possible by the existing method of using a number of road tankers. A new survey launch for the hydrographic service was required and the design was entrusted to Mr John B. Kearney, formerly the board's superintendent of works, who was well known in yachting circles as the designer of the famous 'Mermaid' class of centre-board dinghies.

Side by side with the need to develop new deepwater berthage was the need to deepen the bar so as to enable vessels drawing thirty feet to enter the port on any high water, spring or neaps. The Nash Dredging and Reclamation company was employed for this work and, using their dredger *Port of Spain*, the task was completed in 1951.

In his annual report for 1948 the engineer noted that the demand for ballast had practically ceased; most modern vessels do not use solid material for ballast, as they are equipped with self-ballasting tanks using seawater. Thus was terminated one of the primary functions of successive port authorities since the establishment of the original Ballast Office in 1707.

1949. Concurrently with its conversion of the refinery boilerhouse to a generating station, the ESB proceeded with its plans for a new station at Ringsend to replace the Pidgeon House station and the board agreed to reclaim foreshore to the south of the Pidgeon House Road for the station itself, and to construct a new wharf 550 feet long on the river front with associated reclamation for storage of coal adjoining the wharf. The station was designed to operate either on oil or pulverised coal and a mechanical overhead conveyor was installed to take the coal from the wharf across the road to the station, the oil being conveyed in the normal way by pipeline. The new station, known as 'Ringsend No. 2', came into operation in 1955 and the new wharf enabled tankers drawing up to twenty-seven feet to discharge oil into the station's storage tanks.

1950. The continuing demand for additional transit sheds was partly met by the completion of a new two-storey transit shed (No. 6) at the west end of Alexandra Quay. At the North Wall Extension, the old 'Island' shed known as No. 3, which had been built by the War Office during the First World War, was demolished to make way for the widening of the new No. 3 North two-storey shed built in 1946/47, and the commencement of its twin, No. 3 South Transit Shed, on the river side of the Extension. A second contract with the firm of Sir William Arroll for seven more four-ton cranes was put in hands. The four-ton crane had been the workhorse of the port for many years, capable of lifting most items of break bulk cargo. However, items over four tons had to be unloaded at the 100-ton crane and this caused considerable expense in shifting vessels to the crane, possibly for only one lift. The need for cranes with a somewhat larger capacity than four tons was evident and the board ordered three 6-ton and two 10-ton cranes from another crane maker, Stothert & Pitt, who specialised in this type of crane. When delivered these 6- and 10-ton cranes were strategically sited so as to minimise the shifting of ships and thus leave the 100-ton crane free for heavy machinery, boilers, generators etc.

Following the decision of the Department of Posts and Telegraphs to establish a new Central Sorting Office for Dublin, agreement was reached between the Department and the board for the sale of portion of the lands lying at the northern end of the Custom House Docks, adjoining Sheriff Street.

1951. The board had had under consideration for some years the provision of a second and larger graving dock, the existing dock being too small for the large modern ships using the port. Financial considerations had deterred the board from a positive decision on such an expensive facility; the existing graving dock had accumulated a deficit on its operations between 1932 and 1940 of £5,000, a considerable sum in those days and one which had to be recouped from the general port revenues and therefore paid for by the users of the port as a whole. Admittedly the increase in ship repair work during the Emergency had improved the situation somewhat but the estimated cost of servicing capital and working expenditure on a new graving dock was estimated to result in an annual deficit of £2,500, notwithstanding the anticipated demand for the facility. The board came to the conclusion that the provision of such a dock was a national rather than a local issue and, following protracted discussions with the Department of Industry and Commerce, the Minister (Mr Sean Lemass) acknowledged that it was essential to have ship repair facilities for large Irish ships at Dublin including adequate dry dock accommodation particularly to ensure the maintenance of essential supplies in the event of another emergency.

For this reason, the government agreed to contribute £500,000 or two-thirds of the actual cost, whichever was the lesser, of a new graving dock. The board agreed to proceed on that basis and a consultant engineer, Mr Nicholas O'Dwyer, was appointed to design and supervise the construction of the dock. The design and tender stages were protracted but eventually a contract was placed with a consortium of three well-known Irish firms for the work, T.J. Moran Ltd, R.J. Campbell Ltd, and the South of Ireland Asphalt Co. Ltd. Work commenced in 1951 but exceptional difficulties were encountered in the excavation and preparation of the site of the new dock, which adjoined the old dock on its eastern side, on land formerly leased by the board to Gouldings Ltd and the Irish American Oil Company. As a consequence, the dock took six years to build instead of the estimated three, the final cost being almost £1.5 million instead of the estimated £900,000, the board's share of the cost being £1 million. A new deepwater berth was approved by the board, extending from Ocean

Pier to the western oil jetty and the work of dredging and placing caissons was put in hands. Although intended originally for the reception of timber cargoes, it became evident that it would be required for diverse cargoes; the berth was later known as Alexandra Quay East.

1952. Mr Robert F. Lowe, who had succeeded Mr Bailey as secretary to the board in 1938, retired in December 1952 and was succeeded by Mr Joseph P. Murphy.

1953. Following the death of the engineer-in-chief, Mr F.W. Bond, his principal assistant, Mr C.J. Buckley was appointed to the position. The port hailing station had for many years been sited at the east end of the North Wall Extension from where the arrival and departure of ships could be observed and the details recorded by one of the board's staff of berthing masters. The name 'hailing station' derives from the nineteenth century when advance information of vessels expected at the port was seldom available and arriving masters would hail the station, giving details of the vessel, her cargo and port of loading; conversely, the hailing station man would inform the master of the berth he was to take, except, of course, in the case of the regular cross-channel ships which usually occupied the same berth on each arrival. With the development of Ocean Pier, Alexandra Quay East and the oil jetties it was difficult for the hailing station staff to see all the ships down river of the station and thus a new station was built at the Eastern Breakwater.

1954. Coal and oil had long been established as the main fuels imported at Dublin and the requirements for the accommodation of colliers and tankers were well known but the board was faced with a new problem when facilities were sought for the import of a fuel previously unknown at Dublin. This was liquefied petroleum gas which was proposed to be imported from Denmark by the firm of Tholstrup with whom were associated the local firm of McMullan Brothers who had long been involved in the distribution of oil from Dublin port. Intensive investigations were made as to the arrangements at other European ports where LPG, as it was usually described, was imported and stored, particularly in regard to safety precautions. As existing bye-laws were inadequate to deal with the special risks involved, the board, in agreeing to grant a site to the new company, known as McMullan Kosangas, for the import and storage of the gas, imposed a set of very stringent conditions pending the drafting for ministerial approval of special new bye-laws.

The quay superstructure of Ocean Pier was completed and the work of surfacing, laying crane and tramrails and services proceeded.

1955. The innovations in sea transport developed for military purposes during the Second World War included landing ships with opening bow doors and ramps, enabling troops, motor transport, tanks and other mobile equipment to be landed on the invasion beaches without the need for piers or jetties. The concept was adapted for peacetime purposes so that converted landing ships could be accommodated at special port installations designed to take the vessels' ramps. The idea was developed further by the building of special ships on the same principle of opening doors in bows and sterns enabling lorries or trailers to be loaded or unloaded with very little delay. These ships are well-known nowadays as roll-on/roll-off (or 'ro-ro') ships. The shore installation consists of a ramp which can be raised or lowered according to tidal conditions to accommodate the ship's ramp, thus forming a continuous gangway from ship to shore. A company known as Transport Ferry Services had established ro/ro services between ports in Southern England and the Continent, and also between Larne and Stranraer, and they proposed to establish a similar service between Dublin and Preston. Negotiations with the board were followed by approval for the installation at Dublin to be carried out at the company's expense, and one more development project was added to the long list already being carried out by the board's engineering department. The installation was completed in May 1956 but its implementation was frustrated by the opposition of the Dublin dockers who naturally enough feared a potential threat to their employment and as a result the completed installation lay unused for many years.

A new hopper for the board's dredging fleet, named *Number Ten* was launched from the Liffey Dockyard's building slip in June 1955, the last steam hopper to be commissioned by the board.

The board was a founder member of the Dock and Harbour Authorities Association which had been established in London in 1913, and it continues to be represented on the executive council and the technical committees of the association, an involvement which facilitates the exchange of administrative and technical information on common port problems. However, the constitutional and legislative changes since 1922 meant the activities of the association in relation to legislation in the UK was of less value to Irish ports and in the 1950s it had become evident that an Irish forum was required not only to exchange information on port problems but to act as a watchdog on behalf of Irish ports in relation to prospective legislation or other measures which might affect the interests of the ports. Following a number of exploratory meetings between some ports, instigated by Mr D.A. Hegarty, general manager of Dublin Port, the Irish Port Authorities Association was formed in September 1955. Mr Stephen MacKenzie, chairman of the Dublin Port Board was appointed the first chairman of the association; Mr Hegarty was appointed as honorary secretary and he was the moving spirit behind the association's activities over the following nineteen years until his retirement in 1974.

1956. As reclamation at East Wall extended into the area opposite Tolka Quay, a new roadway was commenced leading from East Wall along the line of the old wall to provide additional access to sites lying between Alexandra Road and Tolka Quay, and later to provide access to sites on the new reclaimed areas.

Prior to 1930 the Revenue Commissioners had accepted, for the purpose of assessment of duty, weights of tobacco arrived at in Great Britain before being exported to this country, but in that year the Commissioners discontinued this arrangement and ordered that all tobacco be nett weighed on arrival. To accomodate the additional business a new warehouse, Stack G, had been built in the Custom House Docks; but by the 1950s it had become inadequate to cope with the current demands. Accordingly, in 1956 the board decided to build a new warehouse for the purpose; completed in 1959, it was known as Stack L.

Since the establishment of the board in 1867 the port board's legal work had been carried out by a law agent who was invariably a member of a firm of solicitors and was not therefore occupied full-time on the board's legal business. Following the retirement of Mr Edward Fitzgerald, the then law agent, the board decided in 1955 that it required the services of a full time law agent who would be a member of the management team and have his office in the board's head office. On the recommendation of the Local Appointments Commission, Mr Henry Murray was appointed to the position in June 1956.

1957. The new (No. 2) graving dock was completed in March 1957 and the first vessel to enter for repairs was the B & I company's *Kilkenny*; a coaster, *River Fisher,* was docked at the same time, the dimensions of the dock being more than adequate to accomodate two vessels of this size together. Several other vessels underwent overhaul in the new dock in succeeding months, including the 12,000 ton tanker *North King.* The official opening ceremony, however, did not take place until 27 June, ninety-seven years after the opening of No. 1 Dock. The formal opening was performed by the President of Ireland, Sean T. O'Kelly, on board the Shell tanker *Narica*, 8,000 tons, a ribbon across the dock entrance being cut by the ship's bows as she entered the dock.

The depths of water in the shipping channels and berths within the limits of the port had been monitored continuously by the board's hydrographic survey service since its inception, and up to 1922 responsibility for surveying the bay outside the limits of the port (roughly a line from Sutton to Dalkey) lay with the British Admiralty. Following the establishment of the state in 1922, the Admiralty withdrew the survey service from Irish waters. The continued growth in the size of vessels trading to the port made the lack of such a survey a serious matter and in the absence of a state hydrographic survey the board decided that, as and when circumstances permitted, a survey of the outer approaches to the port should be carried out over a period of years. The survey was completed in 1962 and the results were transmitted to the British Admiralty for inclusion in their charts, which are the charts generally used by international shipping.

1958.   Dockers employed by the shipping companies engaged in the regular cross-channel services are usually employed on a permanent basis but those required for the discharge of foreign ships and also of all coal ships were traditionally employed ad hoc for each ship. Dockers seeking work attended at the North Wall Extension at specified hours when the foremen of the various shipping companies or stevedores would pick out the men they required. This procedure, known as a 'read', took place in the open air in all weather conditions and it was a long-standing source of grievance between the dockers and the shipping interests represented by the Association of Dublin Stevedores. In 1958 the board indicated that it was prepared to build premises at East Wall at the expense of the stevedores where the dockers could assemble for the 'reads'. When completed the 'read room', as it was called, was regarded by the dockers as inadequate and they refused to use it, reverting to the old arrangement. In 1962 the board agreed to allow No. 5 transit shed at the Crossberth to be used for 'reads', adding one more function to the list of diverse activities for which the building had been used since first built as a generating station in 1904.

1959.   With the completion of services for Ocean Pier, it was necessary to consider the type and position of transit sheds for the pier. Two disused aircraft hangars were purchased in Northern Ireland and the steel framework was used, together with new profiled aluminium cladding, for the erection of four transit sheds. This innovation had advantages of economy of cost and speed with which the sheds could be erected in contrast to traditional types of brick and concrete sheds. The first two sheds (Nos 9 and 10) were completed in 1960 and the remaining two (Nos 13 and 15) in 1961.

1960.   Another innovation was the introduction in 1960 of a port fire alarm system, the first in any port in Ireland or Great Britain, by means of which a fire in any part of the port estate to the east of East Wall Road could be notified to the fire brigade and also to the harbour police merely by pressing an alarm button. These press buttons were located at various points through the port estate and in the premises of the oil companies and other tenants of the board.

1961. Notwithstanding the additional transit shed accomodation provided in the port since 1946, sheds were frequently congested because some consignees delayed the removal of their goods. In some cases, the reason for delay was to economise on storage costs elsewhere. To curb this abuse, the board introduced a system of compulsory removal of such goods from the shed, the goods being transported to a special shed at Alexandra Quay, known as the 'removals' shed; while lying in this shed the goods incurred substantial charges to deter the consignees concerned from repeating the abuse.

1962. A major change in the pattern of coal imports assumed significance in the early 1960s when an increasing proportion of coal was carried to Dublin from American and Polish ports in ships from 10,000 tons to 20,000 tons capacity. The traditional method of discharging coal by dockers shovelling it into tubs of one ton capacity in the ship's holds, to be lifted one at a time by one of the board's four-ton cranes was clearly outdated, as had already been discovered in 1947 when American coal first arrived in Liberty ships. Following discussions between the Stevedores Association and the union representing the dockers the board purchased automatic grabs for use on such ships. The new trend caused a major problem in that the large coal vessels had to be berthed at deepwater berths at Ocean Pier which were designed for general cargo ships, and thus these vessels were sterilising not only the general cargo berthage during their prolonged discharge but also the transit sheds.

Twelve new four-ton cranes of a new design, described as 'electro-hydraulic', were ordered in 1962 as part of the continuous programme of modernisation of equipment.

1963. The board had agreed in 1937 to a proposal by Dublin Corporation to dump domestic refuse at Ringsend, on an area of about twenty acres of the foreshore adjoining Ringsend Park. There was an important distinction between the dumping at Ringsend and that at East Wall: the board was the owner of the foreshore at East Wall, it being part of the area acquired from the Vernon Estate under the 1879 act. Ownership of the foreshore at Ringsend and, indeed, of all the South strand was, however, claimed by the Pembroke Estate which had given the Corporation permission to carry out the dumping. As port authority, the board's consent was necessary in view of its statutory rights and obligations (as distinct from ownership) in respect of all foreshore within the port, under its private statutes, principally the act of 1869; consequently its consent was also required for the dumping. The dumping continued throughout the 1940s and 1950s and by 1959 it became clear that it had exceeded the area permitted in 1937. The board was less concerned by the excessive dumping than the purposes to which the reclaimed land might be put by the Pembroke Estate or by any person (in the legal sense) to whom portion of the land might be sold or leased, particularly in the vicinity of Pidgeon House Road or the Great South Wall. Since a trial of strength as between the board's rights and obligations and those of such a purchaser or tenant was undesirable, the board opened what proved to be protracted negotations with the Pembroke Estate, culminating in the purchase by the board in 1963 of 650 acres of foreshore lying to the south of the Pidgeon House Road and the Great South Wall. The ESB and Dublin Corporation had in earlier years purchased areas of foreshore for their respective purposes in this locality and eventually the board joined in a tripartite agreement with these two bodies, involving the exchange of lands as between the parties, in order to rationalise each party's holdings in view of future developments.

A new pilot shore station was opened in July of this year, as a base from which pilots could be taken by fast motor pilot cutters to vessels requiring pilots in the bay, thus eliminating the maintenance of a pilot steamer cruising in the bay (see Chapter 23). A new transit shed was completed at Alexandra Quay East using the system which was now standard in the port, i.e. steel framing with aluminium sheet cladding; with a floor area of 62,000 square feet and a clear internal height of 30 feet, this shed, known as No. 20, serves the deepwater berthage at Alexandra Quay East which is 1,200 feet long and has a depth at low water of thirty-two feet.

The year saw the end of an old established ship-repairing firm, Ringsend Dockyard Ltd, which paid off its employees early in the year because of lack of work and subsequently put its premises up for sale.

1964.   Additional transit shed accomodation at Ocean Pier was provided by joining two existing sheds, Nos. 13 and 15. Otherwise, development work continued on new roadways, services, minor buildings.

By 1964 all major projects undertaken by the board since 1947 had been completed, but long before this stage was reached the board's management had under consideration the nature and extent of port installations required to meet changing conditions in sea transport which had become apparent in the late 1950s. Their investigations and recommendations as submitted to the board contained a programme of development covering the period up to 1971. Justification of the need for further development was evident from the growth of the trade of the

Sir John Purser Griffith, chief engineer to the port board from 1898 to 1913.

The *Clare Castle*, one of the colliers purchased by Guinness from Kelly of Belfast and converted for the transportation of stout in barrels.

The foreground shows the final completed section of the North Wall extension in 1937. The background shows dredgers working on the proposed reclamation for the abortive oil refinery project.

The view from the big gasometer at Sir John Rogerson's Quay shows the Isle of Man passenger steamer in mid stream, an LMS cargo ship, and a Burns & Laird passenger/ cargo ship berthed at North Wall, c.1938.

Nicholas Proud, secretary to the port board from 1867 to 1921.

The port board's steam tugs, *Ben Eadar* and *Coliemore* towing the collier *Kylecastle* into Dublin port.

The *Melida*, one of the Liberty ships which brought American coal to Dublin in 1947.

The hulk *Shelfoil*, which was used as a temporary oil storage ship pending the completion in 1954 of the new oil jetties.

The four gas company colliers, *Glenbride*, *Glencree*, *Glenageary* and *Glencolm* in Ringsend dock.

A general view of shipping at Alexandra Quay showing Liberty ships and a Texaco oil tanker, 1947.

An aerial view of Alexandra Basin, 1949.

One of the Blue Funnel Line ships engaged in the Far East trade in Number 2 graving dock.

port since the establishment of the state in 1922, which, with the exception of the fall-off in imports during the Second World War, showed a continuous rise. The total throughput (tonnage of imports plus exports) of the port in 1938 was 2.7 million tons; in 1947 the figure was 2.8 million tons and in 1964 the figure was 4 million tons. An apparent paradox lies in the fall in the number of ships which arrived at the port in the years referred to: 1938–5,537; 1947–3,366; 1964–3,818. The explanation lies in the fact that a greater proportion of the trade was arriving in larger vessels from overseas as already mentioned. For example, whereas the average collier bringing English or Welsh coal to the port in 1938 carried about 700 tons, the American Liberty ships carrying coal in 1947 averaged 10,000 tons, the equivalent of fourteen of the traditional smaller colliers. By the early 1970s, Polish and American coal was arriving in cargoes of up to 20,000 tons, equal to the capacity of twenty-eight of the smaller vessels.

A recurrent complaint from the general public over the years regarding the state of the bed of the Liffey, and in particular its smell, was the subject of many newspaper editorials and gossip columns which frequently ascribed the problem to a disagreement between the board and Dublin Corporation regarding ownership of the bed of the river. It is true that as far back as the mid 1800s questions of ownership, rights and obligations in respect of the bed of the river were the subject of litigation, the decision being in favour of the board on the grounds that it was not the owner of the bed of the river (which had not been claimed on its behalf) and that it was not the party by whom nuisances complained of were caused. A case was stated on behalf of the Corporation and when it came on for hearing the decision was again in favour of the board. Over the past thirty years the relationship between the two bodies has been characterised by consultation and co-operation at all levels and on all matters, and when the matter of cleaning rubbish from the River Liffey along the western quays arises it is carried out usually by the Corporation, the board contributing half the cost. Another aspect of this problem is the discharge of offensive effluent into the waters of the Liffey. Where this occurs within the limits of the board's jurisdiction, the offensive matter is removed as soon as possible and the culpable parties are prosecuted; in the case of some oil spillage which extended as far as the foreshore at Clontarf, the offending parties were duly dealt with by the courts. The board can do little about discharges outside the port limits, and in particular into the River Camac or the River Dodder. Most of the nuisance complained of derives from decayed vegetable matter, branches, leaves, twigs etc., which are carried down from the upper reaches; these become water-logged and sink to the bottom. In warm weather fermentation can take place as a result of which the material rises to the surface in ugly and smelly patches. This is particularly noticeable when berth dredging is carried out near Memorial Bridge. The problem of unsightliness is not assisted by those citizens who think nothing of throwing household rubbish and debris of all kinds into the Liffey, ranging from ordinary domestic rubbish to bedsteads; on one occasion a piano was found in the river. One wonders about the pianist—was it a case of 'Don't shoot the pianist, drown him'?

20

Dublin Port Since the Mid Sixties

WITH the completion in 1964 of Alexandra Quay East and its associated transit shed and open storage areas, the main quay construction programme, which had commenced in 1946 with a direct labour force, came to an end. However, the further development of the port had been the subject of intensive examination by the board's management in the early 1960s, including a searching investigation of modern port installations abroad. The trends in the transport of goods by sea which had been foreshadowed in the late 1940s had developed into three clear patterns which had practically universal application. The first was the widespread use of unit loads (containers and flats) for what otherwise would have been regarded as break-bulk cargo; second, the increasing number of ro-ro ships in operation, and third the increase in the size of ships, particularly those designed to carry bulk cargoes such as oil, coal, grain, timber etc. and the consequent need for specialised installations in specific zones in a port.

The results of the study carried out by the management team was a five year development programme for the years 1966–71 which was approved by the board in 1965. The programme was focused mainly on the development of the foreshore on the river side of the Pidgeon House Road which had been acquired from the Fitzwilliam (now Pembroke) Estate in the early nineteenth century. The programme proposed the construction of 2,500 feet of new medium depth quays for continental and cross-channel traffic with twenty-three acres of reclamation between the new quays and Pidgeon House Road, to be provided with cranes, a transit shed and the usual services. Provision was also made for a new 1,200 feet deepwater quay for bulk cargoes such as coal, together with thirteen acres of reclamation on which the appropriate installations and services would be provided. The development of additional support areas on foreshore to be reclaimed or developed south of Pidgeon House Road was also included. In addition to its own project the board had agreed with the ESB to include in its reclamation programme an area of thirty-six acres of foreshore east of the old Pidgeon House

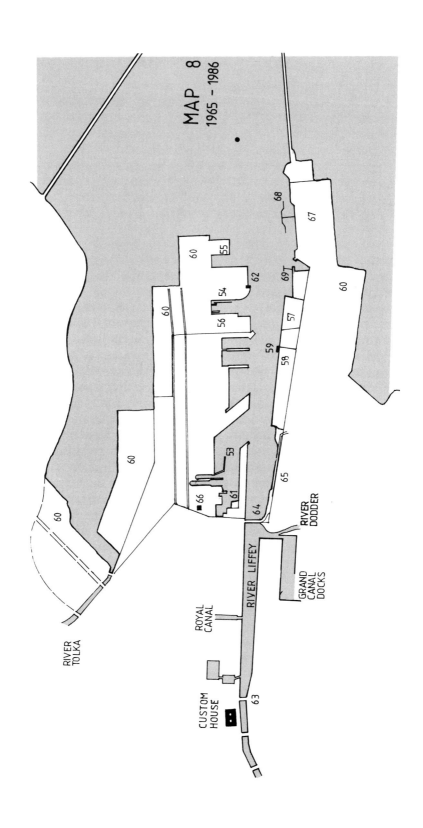

MAP 8
1965 – 1986

RIVER TOLKA

CUSTOM HOUSE

ROYAL CANAL

RIVER LIFFEY

GRAND CANAL DOCKS

RIVER DODDER

60

60

60

53

61

66

60

54

56

55

62

57

59

58

65

64

63

68

69

67

60

generating station for a new generating station (later to be known as the Poolbeg station). Subsequently the board decided to develop part of the new medium berth quay as a container terminal and also to provide a ro-ro installation.

On the north side of the river the development programme envisaged the reclamation of almost 100 acres north of the existing port estate opposite Clontarf, to provide sites for port users requiring storage areas and installations. Reclamation was to be associated with a contract for deepening the bar by three feet and improving the depths in the river channel accordingly. Two canteens for dockers were planned—one at North Wall Extension, and one at Alexandra Quay. Plans for the latter were later extended to include accommodation on upper floors for customs staff and shipping companies. Improved accommodation for the staffs of the chief engineer and the harbour master, new workshops and equipment, and a new tug to assist with the larger vessels which were arriving at the port, were all included in the programme.

Zoning of grain and oil posed little problem for the board since grain ships had traditionally discharged at Alexandra Quay, using the Merchants Warehousing company's specialised discharge facilities, and the establishment of the oil zone had solved the difficulty so far as oil imports were concerned. New open storage areas for timber cargoes were available adjoining the new berthage at Alexandra Quay East and Ocean Pier, to supplement the space at Alexandra Quay which had been traditionally used for timber cargoes for many years. The zoning of dry bulk cargoes such as coal and the raw materials for fertilisers had been decided upon in February 1964 when the board had approved in principle of two new bulk discharge berths; one was a new jetty in Alexandra Basin intended primarily for the use of bulk cargoes for Goulding's fertiliser factory, and the other a new deepwater quay for bulk cargoes, including coal; the latter was included in the five year development programme and described as a 1,200 feet deepwater quay with associated reclamation of thirteen acres of foreshore.

In the meantime shipping companies in the cross-channel trades were adapting to the new patterns, particularly in the matter of unit loads. The concept of a container for transport of goods is, of course, not new; one has merely to look at the furniture removal container which has been in existence since Victorian days. In the 1930s the LMS railway company had developed small containers with a capacity of four tons. These containers and other larger items were usually loaded on the after deck of the LMS ships and discharged by the company's twenty-ton steam crane near the entrance to Spencer Dock at the North Wall; later this crane was replaced by a thirty-ton crane when standard twenty-ton and thirty-ton containers were in use. What was novel was the concept of a ship's total cargo being carried in standard containers, a concept which had been taken up and developed in the 1950s and 1960s worldwide. This change from break-bulk general cargo to containerised cargo has frequently and validly been described as being as revolutionary as the change from sail to steam. The consequence for dock labour was profound since the number of dockers required for a container ship was only a fraction of that required for an equivalent break-bulk cargo, whether on cross-channel or overseas routes. The same considerations applied to the discharge of a large coal ship by automatic grabs.

On the retirement of the chief engineer, Mr C.J. Buckley, and the harbour master, Commander O'Brien-Twohig in 1965, they were succeeded by Mr Paul O'Sullivan and Captain Peter Leighton respectively.

In 1960 the B&I company had received permission to erect a twenty-five-ton derrick crane for unit loads on the open quay beside the former Burns & Laird berthage and the development of the company's unit load traffic was such that a second derrick crane was erected in the same location in 1967. In 1966 the Bristol Seaway company moved its operations from George's Quay to Custom House Quay in order to open a unit load service to Bristol. In each case the quay space for landing unit loads was restricted and it was understood by all parties that when new berthage with better facilities for unit load traffic became available, the board would facilitate the companies concerned.

In the continental trade, Palgrave Murphy inaugurated a container service to the continent in 1965 when they were permitted to place a seventeen-ton derrick crane on the east side of Ocean Pier; subsequently the operation was moved to the south end of Ocean Pier and a thirty-two-ton crane replaced the earlier unit; in 1969 the board erected a thirty-five-ton derrick crane for container traffic on the west side of Ocean Pier.

The tendency for the best laid schemes to be overtaken by subsequent events was noted many years ago by Robert Burns and in this respect the five-year development programme was no exception. Although the first caissons for the new south quays were placed in position early in 1966, the timetable had to be recast when in March 1967 the B&I announced its intention of replacing the existing conventional passenger ships on the Liverpool route with ro-ro car ferries. In the negotiations with the board which followed, the company indicated its hopes to commence the service in May 1968. One of the board's assistant engineers, Mr M.F. Ennis (now chief engineer) was given the task of designing and supervising the construction of the new car ferry terminal which was to be located east of the Eastern Breakwater. To meet the deadline proposed it was necessary to transfer the operations of the contractor for the new south quays, Collen Bros. and also the dredging contractor, Britannia Dredging Co., to the new development which involved the reclamation of ten acres of foreshore. Work commenced in

April 1967 and the terminal was ready within fourteen months of the board's approval for the project, in time for the company's inauguration of the service in May 1968.

In the same year Captain Hubert Walsh succeeded Captain Leighton as harbour master and pilot superintendent.

Concurrently with its proposals for the new car ferry service, the B&I had had in prospect the matter of a new freight terminal and, following the opening of the ferry service, the company asked the board to provide a unit load terminal to be located adjoining the new ferry terminal. Hard on the heels of the B&I decision came a proposal by British Rail (now Sealink) to transfer its operations to a similar new freight terminal downriver. This terminal sited on eight and a half acres of reclaimed land was opened in 1970; the B&I freight terminal was a larger development on twenty-five acres (later extended to twenty-eight acres) and it came into operation in 1972.

The consequence for the South Quay development was a delay of four years beyond the period envisaged for the completion of the programme. The first section of the new medium depth quays was completed in 1969 enabling Bristol Seaway to transfer its operations from Custom House Quay to the west end of the new development, where a new transit shed and container crane had been erected by the company. The original ro-ro installation which had lain unused at Ocean Pier since its completion in 1956 was put into operation for the first time in March 1973 with the arrival of the *Seaspeed Ferry* operated by Morland Navigation Co. Ltd to inaugurate a ro-ro service between Dublin and Barry; by 1975 the company found the Ocean Pier installation inadequate and as the board's new ro-ro ramp at the South Quay development was almost complete the company was permitted to transfer its operation to the new terminal in March 1975. The service did not, however, prosper and in November 1975 it was terminated.

The remaining section of the new medium depth quay, which had been designated as a common user container terminal (i.e. not allocated to a particular company) was completed early in 1974; pending the completion of the erection of a new thirty-ton Liebherr container crane for the board, the terminal was used for the discharge of break-bulk cargo. Following the commissioning of the new container crane, the terminal was brought into operation in 1975 with the commencement of a container service between Dublin and Russian ports.

Following the decision in principle by the board in 1964 that there be two dry bulk terminals in the port, negotiations were opened with Gouldings Fertilisers Ltd, as a result of which a jetty 760 feet long with a depth of thirty-one feet of water alongside was built in Alexandra Basin extending from the west end of Alexandra Quay. It was equipped with two 10-ton grabbing cranes and an overhead conveyor for the discharge and transport to Goulding's factory of phosphate rock; pipelines were laid between the jetty and the facory for the conveyance of liquid sulphur and other liquid cargoes. The jetty was commenced in 1965 and completed in 1967.

The board had decided that the second bulk terminal should be located at the south side of the river, between the quay serving the Ringsend generating station and the Dublin Corporation settlement tanks which had been constructed in the old Pidgeon House harbour. Preparatory dredging for the caisson walls commenced in 1967 but progress was delayed due to the diversion of contractors to the new car ferry terminal and freight terminals referred to above. The new quay with a depth alongside of thirty-seven feet, together with the associated reclamation behind it was completed in 1972. In the meantime lengthy discussions had taken place between representatives of the board and of the main coal importing firms. The board was concerned to convince the coal firms of the advantages to be derived from a unified bulk coal discharge installation at the new quay, and of the necessity for the coal firms to merge in a new company to import the coal and provide the discharging, storage and distribution plant. It was made clear on behalf of the board that the discharge of coal at various berths throughout the port, cheek by jowl with general cargoes, particularly in the case of Ocean Pier, could not continue. Eventually the coal firms formed a new company, Coal Distributors Ltd, to carry out the project envisaged by the board. By the end of 1973 part of the new installation was sufficiently advanced to enable operations to commence. Equipped with two 10-ton grabbing cranes and a conveyor system between the quay and the storage area, the terminal was fully in operation in 1974.

Concurrent with the development of the new quays and the reclamation on the north side of the Liffey, investigation of wave action, current flows and siltation in the bay and in the harbour proceeded under the guidance of the Wallingford Research Station, and surveys of road traffic flows on the approaches to the port were also undertaken. In 1970 the board agreed to join with Dublin Corporation and the ESB in an extensive study of water pollution in the Liffey estuary and Dublin Bay.

In 1971 the new ESB Poolbeg generating station came into operation and its 680 feet high chimney became the most prominent landmark in the port, the 100-ton crane at the North Wall and the large gasometer at Sir John Rogerson's Quay having shared pride of place in this regard for many years. Subsequently the Poolbeg station was extended and a second high chimney was erected.

Mr Edgar Hanrahan, who had been the board's warehousing manager since 1938, retired in 1971 and Mr J.F. Furlong was appointed warehousing and commercial manager.

Before their contract was completed, the Britannia Dredging Company went out of business and their contract was taken over by the Westminster Dredging Company. Compared with the modern dredging equipment used by dredging contractors, the board's dredging units, *Deepworker* and the steam hoppers, were uneconomic and it became clear that maintenance dredging of the bar and main shipping channels could be more efficiently and economically carried out under a maintenance contract with one of the major dredging contractors. Accordingly a five-year contract was entered into with the Westminster company covering the period 1972–6. The *Deepworker* and *Number Nine* hopper were sold and a new grab dredging pontoon was ordered from Verolme Dockyard for berth dredging. The work of deepening (as distinct from maintenance) of the bar had been completed, and to complement this work a limited width of the river channel was deepened likewise from Poolbeg Lighthouse to the oil jetties under the new maintenance contract with the Westminster company.

In 1972 the board recognised that the increase in the traffic handled by Atlantic Steam Navigation company justified additional facilities and the company were permitted to move their operation to Alexandra Quay East, where they had erected a new thirty-two-ton transporter container crane.

Two major issues relating to the port attracted considerable public interest to the point of controversy in 1972. The first was a proposal submitted to the board by a firm of Dublin solicitors on behalf of certain oil interests who proposed the construction of an oil refinery on foreshore to be reclaimed south of the Pidgeon House. When the project was announced, strong opposition was voiced on behalf of local residents living near the shores of the bay, particularly those in the Ringsend and Sandymount areas, and criticism of the board for entertaining the proposal was loud and trenchant. Many meetings with interested parties and opponents of the project were held to explain the board's stand in the matter. Briefly, this was that the board was not the planning authority and could not therefore make a decision on the project in relation to planning and environmental aspects; further the project required a Harbour Works Order to be made by the Minister for Transport on behalf of the government. Unless both the planning authority (Dublin Corporation) and the Minister approved of the scheme, it could not be carried out. However, in order that both the Corporation and the Minister could examine the matter fully, it was necessary in the first instance, under the provisions of the Planning Acts, for the board to give its provisional approval so that the necessary formal procedures could be followed. Critics of the board took the view that the board should never have considered the proposal in the first place; the board's response was that the matter was not simply a local issue but one of national importance and having regard to all these circumstances the board could not arrogate to itself the functions of a final arbiter in the matter. In the event, an application by the promoters for planning permission was refused, and an appeal against the decision was also unsuccessful. Subsequently the Minister refused to make the necessary Harbour Works Order and the board thereupon withdrew its approval, in accordance with the conditions on which it had been originally granted.

As the five-year plan drawn up in 1965 drew to a close in 1972, the board published documents described as 'Studies in long term development of the Port of Dublin'. The studies had been undertaken in the first instance by the board's chief officers and an outline sketch of their projections was published in 1965; it was subsequently decided to expand the team so as to secure expertise in the wider fields of economic and social planning, including the directors of town planning and economic and transportation planning for the city of Rotterdam, together with a traffic adviser to the British government, an Irish economist and an Irish landscape architect. In the introduction to the studies it was stated that they should not be regarded as a plan in the rigid sense of the planning legislation but as a projection of how the port might develop in the long term, having regard to the demands which were likely to be made upon it not only in terms of shipping facilities but also in regard to port-orientated industries, with associated requirements for housing and amenities for those expected to seek employment and homes in the hinterland to the working area of the port.

Because of the pace and nature of changes in sea transport forward planning had hitherto been based on relatively short term projections of facilities envisaged as being required and the long term studies were intended, *inter alia*, to guide such planning in order that short-term development would not inhibit the possible ultimate development of the port envisaged in the studies. Since one of the objectives of the studies was to stimulate public awareness of how the port might develop it was emphasised that public comment and criticism would be welcomed so that the views of all interested parties could be taken into account and as far as possible reconciled with the future planning. The publication of the studies was accompanied by a public exhibition illustrating features of the studies which was intended to last for two weeks but, because of the public interest, had to be extended for a further two weeks. The comments received by the board indicated that the studies had succeeded in arousing a greater awareness of the importance of the port and of the manner of its development and gradually the controversy died down.

While the development of the port was proceeding, two important events occurred. In 1967 the board celebrated the centenary of its reconstitution in 1867 as the Dublin Port and Docks Board. In 1969, following the failure of the City Council to strike the municipal rate, the Minister for Local Government dissolved the council and appointed Mr John Garvin as City Commissioner. Mr Garvin represented the Corporation on the board until 1973 when the Corporation membership was resumed by public representatives.

An unusual feature in the port in 1973 was the construction by Ascon Ltd of concrete caissons which on completion were towed to Liverpool where they were used in the replacement of the old floating landing stage. The landing stage was well known to passengers on the Dublin/ Liverpool service for many years.

On the retirement of Captain Walsh in 1973, Captain Colm Lawless was appointed harbour master and pilot superintendent.

According as new tenants leased sites on the newly reclaimed lands the board's programme of new roads and services continued on both sides of the river to serve the new sites.

The sudden death of the board's chief engineer, Mr Paul O'Sullivan, in January 1974 came as a great shock to all who knew him not only in this country but in many ports abroad. Mr O'Sullivan was succeeded by the deputy chief engineer, Mr M.C. Smyth. In July of the same year, Mr Denis Hegarty, who had been the board's general manager since 1946, retired and Mr J.P. Murphy, secretary to the board was appointed as acting general manager.

From 1974 increasing costs of materials made accurate estimating of contract costs very difficult and in the case of contracts in progress little could be done to keep the final cost from exceeding the contract price because of standard price variation clauses. The consequences were naturally reflected in the reduced surplus on the board's accounts in succeeding years from which port development is normally financed.

Landscaping in the port area and along its perimeter had been undertaken by the board in 1972. One of the areas which had been given special attention was in the vicinity of Beach Road, Sandymount but this area received attention of another and unwelcome kind during 1974. At least 300 young trees and shrubs were stolen or destroyed and the vandalism continued over a period of years.

The main development envisaged for the five years from 1975 to 1980 was the construction of additional quays and back-up storage areas in the vicinity of the B&I car ferry and freight terminals, and the British Rail terminal. A Harbour Works Order had been made in respect of the proposed development by the Minister for Transport and work commenced in 1975 on reclamation, using material from demolition and construction sites, an economical method and one which was mutually advantageous to contractors wishing to dispose of such material and to the board. Subsequently work commenced on a new deepwater quay and ro-ro berth south of the car ferry terminal.

Regular consultations took place during 1975 between technical officers of the board and of Dublin Corporation on matters such as the cleansing of the River Liffey, the revision of the city development, access to the port for road traffic and other matters of mutual concern.

Mr Robert N. Hayes, formerly county manager of Tipperary South Riding, was appointed as the board's new general manager on the recommendation of the Local Appointments Commission; he took up duty in November 1975.

Because of a severe trade recession in 1975 the scope of some contracts in progress was reduced and only essential work was carried out. However, a contract was placed for the extension of No. 9 Transit Shed which would double its floor area. New grain discharging equipment was provided by Merchants Warehousing Company at Alexandra Quay, giving a significant improvement in the grain handling facilities at this berth.

Although port trade was somewhat slow to recover in 1976, the overall throughput for the year was up by 9 per cent on the previous year. The new container terminal at the South Quay development was brought fully into use with the transfer of the operations of Port Services Ltd from Ocean Pier to the new terminal.

A connection with the port dating from 1868 was broken in 1976 when the firm of Gouldings announced that it was ceasing operations at its factory in the port. However, an announcement by Tara Mines Ltd that they had chosen Dublin port for the export of zinc and lead concentrates brought a note of optimism. The board had agreed with Gouldings that it would facilitate the company in the event that it was found possible to resume operations; in the meantime an arrangement was reached as between Gouldings, Tara Mines and the board whereby Tara would use the jetty in Alexandra Basin formerly used by Gouldings and a new conveyor system would link the jetty with a storage terminal in a site to be leased to Tara Mines near No. 2 graving dock. Another new port user in 1976 was Asahi Ltd, a Japanese company which had set up a factory in Co. Mayo for the production of synthetic textiles. The raw material used was a chemical known as acrylonitrile and a new terminal was built at Alexandra Road Extension which was linked by pipeline with the Eastern Oil Jetty where tankers carrying the chemical could berth. From the storage terminal at Dublin the acrylonitrile was to be transported by rail, using demountable tanks on rail wagons, to Ballina from where the tanks were to be conveyed by road to the factory at Killala. Public unease at the possible hazards involved in the storage and transport of the material was understandable but in the event the disquiet has not been justified.

A related concern was expressed at the possible hazards involved in the handling of lead concentrates for export by Tara Mines and monitoring stations were set up to establish the levels of lead in the air. Monitoring of SO_2 levels had been in operation for some years following complaints about emissions from the Gouldings factory and the ESB generating stations. The closing down of the Goulding operation brought about a significant improvement in this regard. The absence of a national standard enforceable at law for SO_2 was a major obstacle to proper supervision and representations were made by the board to the Department of Transport and Power (as it was now described). The monitoring of the lead levels showed that there was no hazard and no cause for concern. The maintenance of a high standard of fire precautions was always in the forefront of the board's developments and agreement was reached with Dublin Corporation for the laying of a duplicate 24 inch diameter water main to supply the port area in the event of a break in the existing trunk main. With the ever-increasing number of premises storing and distributing hazardous materials, the board decided to appoint a special inspector whose duties consisted mainly in the regular inspection of the premises concerned to ensure that the terms of licences and leases granted by the board were being strictly complied with, particularly in regard to safety and environmental considerations.

The five-year dredging contract for maintenance dredging on the bar and the river channels, placed with the Westminster Dredging Company in 1975, was completed in 1976 and was highly successful inasmuch as dredging was found to be necessary in only three of the five years covered by the contract.

Following the retirement of Mr J.P. Murphy, the present writer was appointed to succeed him as secretary to the board in April 1976. A reorganisation programme for the clerical and administrative staff was approved by the board and a new personnel department was established with Mr H.W. McGuinness as personnel manager. Having regard to the number of categories of employees in skilled, semi-skilled and unskilled grades, in addition to the clerical and technical grades, involving regular meetings and negotiations with thirteen trade unions the new department was welcomed generally as a measure long overdue for the maintenance of staff/board relations. Because of the financial implications of the continued expansion of the port and of the board's operations and services, the board decided, on the retirement of Mr W.F. Dwyer, accountant and collector of port dues, to appoint a financial controller. On the recommendation of the Local Appointments Commission Mr Brian O'Hegarty was appointed to the position in 1976.

The terminals established by Tara Mines and Asahi were fully in operation in 1977 and despite the close down of the Atlantic Steam

Navigation Company's operations, the total trade for the year showed a slight increase over the previous year. In the same year the board joined with Ocean Inchcape (Ireland) Ltd in a short-lived venture servicing an exploration rig established on the Kish Bank.

Five years had become the accepted span of the board's development programmes and in 1977 a new development plan was presented by the management to the board with a new flexibility built in. The plan was intended to be revived annually on a rolling basis, so as to take account of new priorities but always with a five-year horizon.

The first stage of the plan envisaged an additional ro-ro ramp for the B&I freight services. Otherwise, development in 1977 consisted in consolidating the works carried out in previous years; this included the removal of the thirty-two-ton container crane formerly owned by Palgrave Murphy Ltd from Ocean Pier to Port Services terminal at the new South Quays and a ten-ton crane was transferred to the terminal from Sir John Rogerson's Quay. A new Harbour Works Order was made by the Minister for Transport and Power covering the reclamation of foreshore north and south of the British Rail terminal. A noticeable trend was the drop in the usage of the board's four-, six- and ten-ton cranes and an increase in the use of container cranes.

The building which had served at various times as the board's electricity generating station, as a temporary chapel during the Eucharistic Congress in 1932, as a dockers' read room in the late 1950s and 1960s and in between times as No. 5 transit shed, was demolished in 1977.

The work of consolidating and improving the works carried out since 1965 included major improvements in public lighting throughout the port estate, improved signposting particularly for tourists arriving by car ferry, and re-paving of the older roads. A new compound for the storage of empty containers was opened on the south side of Pidgeon House Road.

The increasing competition in the motor trade from Japanese manufacturers was manifest in the arrival of large car carriers from Japan in 1977. These ships had their own ramps on which cars could be driven off whatever the state of the tide; it was possible for a car carrier with a capacity of 5,000 cars to unload consignments of cars at various British, continental and other ports (including Dublin) with only a short stay in each port.

The maintenance dredging contract for the period 1978–82 was placed with the Irish Dredging Company which was a subsidiary of the Westminster Company.

Consultations with local residents associations, yacht clubs, rowing clubs and other organisations regarding port development continued to be a feature of the board's public relations policy and it culminated in the decision of the board to transfer to Dublin Corporation for amenity purposes land at Ringsend with a total area of seventeen acres, close to the new Corporation housing development built on what was formerly known as the Shelbourne stadium.

The board was represented on the special development team set up by Dublin Corporation, the aim of which was the creation of employment in the inner city, and in this connection the board agreed to convey to the North Wall Community Association for use as a workshop, sections of transit sheds at North Wall formerly used by the B&I conventional freight services. The board was also represented on the Eastern Regional Development Organisation and technical data was furnished during the year to a special sub-committee charged with the task of preparing guidelines for a regional plan.

A new record for throughput was achieved in 1979 with a total of 7.9 million tons, a figure which would have been higher except for a number of industrial disputes in the port itself, in the country generally and also in the UK.

One of the most important decisions in the board's history was made in 1979 when it decided to become directly involved in stevedoring i.e. the actual operation of unloading and loading ships and the employment of dock labour for the purpose. The management was directed to negotiate with the parties concerned.

On the basis of the first annual review of the current five-year development plan, the board decided to apply for a Harbour Works Order to authorise the construction of a new deepwater quay 1,300 feet long south of the British Rail terminal and associated reclamation of ninty-four acres of foreshore; part of the proposed reclamation was earmarked as an extension to the oil zone to meet the demand for additional facilities sought by a number of the existing oil companies and also for a site for the new National Petroleum Corporation.

Following the installation of a new ro-ro ramp at the B&I freight terminal in 1979 the company replaced its lo-lo cross-channel service to Liverpool with a more intensive ro-ro service to Fleetwood, in association with Pandoro, and a new ship, m.v. *Tipperary*, was placed on the route.

As demand for the new south quay container terminal increased, the board decided to order a second container crane from Liebherr of Killarney.

The four-acre site adjoining South Bank Quay, formerly used by the ESB for storage of coal for the Ringsend generating station, was handed back to the board and arrangements were made for its re-surfacing to accommodate new cars landed from car-carriers.

The trade returns for the port for the year 1980 showed a very slight drop in the total throughput as against 1979; a drop in imports of

200,000 tonnes reflected the general recession which was also a factor in the closure of the Dublin/Bristol service operated by Bristol Seaway and its predecessors for over 140 years. However, a very heartening feature was the record figure of over 2 million tonnes of exports, an all-time record.

Two proposals for the storage of LPG were submitted to the board in 1980. The first involved a system of underground storage caverns; the second involved the mooring of a large LPG tanker outside Dublin Bay from which the gas would be transhipped in smaller tankers.

Proposals were approved for the re-development of the ESB North Wall generating station to enable natural gas to be used.

A new traffic in bulk cargoes in 1980 was facilitated by the granting of sites to Agrivest Ltd and Hibernian Molasses Ltd for the storage in large tanks of molasses. Arrangements were made for the discharge of Agrivest cargoes at the jetty used by Tara Mines in Alexandra Basin, from which the molasses was conveyed by pipeline to tanks on a site formerly leased to Gouldings. Hibernian Molasses were granted a site south of Pidgeon House Road, close to the bulk discharge jetty used by Coal Distributors Ltd, the molasses being similarly conveyed from the bulk jetty by overhead pipeline.

The board's intention to become involved in stevedoring was re-affirmed in 1980 and for this purpose a new company—Dublin Cargo Handling Ltd—was formed. The board appointed three of its members and the general manager as directors of the company with instructions to continue the negotiations with the existing stevedores.

The board decided to apply for outline planning permission for the re-development of the Custom House Docks premises in accordance with plans drawn up for the purpose by the firm of Scott, Tallon & Walker, architects, who also designed the board's new offices, Port Centre, at Alexandra Road. This decision, taken together with the decision to form a new stevedoring company, represented two of the most important enterprises undertaken by the board for many years. The re-development envisaged the transfer of warehousing operations from the Custom House Docks to a site on the board's lands at East Wall, and the erection of offices, shops, showrooms, light industry buildings, a trade exhibition hall, a hotel and port-related buildings.

A major road development by the board in conjunction with Dublin Corporation in 1980 was the construction of a new link road connecting Pidgeon House Road with Beach Road, Sandymount.

The main features of the port's trade for the year 1981 were a drop in the throughput from 7.9 million tonnes in 1980 to 7.4 million tonnes in 1981, due mainly to a reduced volume of oil imports, and an industrial dispute at Tara Mines which resulted in a substantial reduction in exports. The new head offices of the board at Alexandra Road were opened in August 1981 and with the exception of the warehousing department and engineering stores all the board's administrative, clerical and technical staff were transferred to the new Port Centre. Work commenced on the new deepwater quay south of the car ferry terminal; it had been decided that it should have a dual function and a new ro-ro ramp for the quay was included. Land reclamation continued north of Tolka Quay and near the British Rail terminal, and other works included the widening of Tolka Quay to accommodate the heavy traffic to and from the various installations served by the road. A new addition to the fire precautions scheme was the introduction of a fire main using saltwater, a third line of defence, so to speak, in the event of a breakdown in either of the two water mains serving the port estate. The Whiddy oil jetty disaster provided lessons for every port involved in oil discharge and storage operations, and the board decided to provide new 'escape capsules' at the oil jetties; these were essentially lifeboats capable of being launched by one man, but with a capacity for twenty-two people. The term 'capsule' derives from the construction of the craft which gave total protection from fire to the occupants.

Although the board's traditional policy in relation to its lands was that they would be allocated only on lease to port users, the board retaining the fee simple interest, a departure from this policy was made in 1981 when it was decided to sell two ten-acre plots to the IDA for general industrial development. The location of the plots, one at East Wall and the other at Ringsend, meant that the sale would not interfere with the normal policy of retaining ownership of quays and directly associated storage areas and installations.

The application by the board for planning permission for the re-development of the Custom House Docks was successful but the consent was accompanied by what the board regarded as very restrictive conditions and an appeal against these conditions was duly lodged.

A further drop in throughput to 7.1 million tonnes in 1982 reflected the continuing general recession. Although Dublin Corporation consented to the proposed LPG cavern storage system the decision caused considerable controversy; a number of parties objected to the planning permission and an application was made to An Bord Pleanala for an oral hearing of the objections. The appeal by the board to An Bord Pleanala against the restrictive conditions in the planning permission granted by Dublin Corporation in respect of the Custom House Docks was successful, subject to certain amendments of the conditions attached to the original consent. The matter became a subject of much public and political debate culminating in a proposal in 1982 by the government of the day to introduce the Urban Areas Development Bill. The bill provided, *inter alia*, for the establishment of an authority to be known as the Custom House Dock Development Authority to whom the

Custom House Docks premises would be compulsorily transferred at a price to be determined by the Minister for the Environment with the consent of the Minister for Communications and the Minister for Finance. However, the bill fell with the dissolution of the Dail later in 1982.

As Gouldings had indicated to the board that they could not resume operations at Dublin, the company's leases were surrendered to the board, which agreed to lease the premises to the Development Capital Corporation. DCC, as it was known, set up a subsidiary, National Coal Company, to operate a bulk coal terminal on portion of the former Gouldings site at Alexandra Road, adapting the old Gouldings' ore conveyor to take coal from the jetty in Alexandra Basin. Arrangements were made whereby Tara Mines continued to use the north side of the jetty on which their loading out plant was situated while the new coal company used the south side of the jetty, using the ten-tonne grabbing cranes formerly used by Gouldings.

Following the completion of the natural gas main between Cork and Dublin, permission was granted to An Bord Gais to lay pipelines through the board's properties to serve the ESB generating stations at North Wall, Ringsend and Poolbeg.

The 200-year old Great South Wall was extensively damaged by storms in 1982. Repairs were made and arrangements approved for the placing of protective rock armouring on the south face of the wall and also at the base of the Poolbeg lighthouse.

Mr Henry Murray, the board's law agent, retired in 1982 and was succeeded by Mr William S. Barrett.

The new stevedoring company, Dublin Cargo Handling, were granted a lease of the offices at East Wall formerly occupied by the staffs of the chief engineer and the harbour master. The new company commenced operations in July 1982, although negotiations with a small group of the stevedoring companies and with the dock labour force had not been completed, and were still ongoing at the end of the year.

The year 1983 brought a further decline in the trade of the port with a total throughput of 6.59 million tonnes, a drop in oil imports accounting for almost 0.5 million tonnes of the decline. Lengthy strikes in the dock labour force and unofficial stoppages also affected the throughput although the impact was mainly felt on the imports side; exports were 50,000 tonnes up on the 1982 figure.

As a result of the decline in crane usage a progressive programme of scrapping the older four-ton cranes and 'mothballing' the remainder was put into effect. The 100-ton crane also began to show its age and it became necessary to de-rate its capacity to fifty tons.

Following the retirement in February 1983 of Mr H.W. McGuinness, the board's personnel manager, and also of the present writer, Mr Noel Shanley was appointed as secretary to the board and Mr Gabriel Agnew was appointed as personnel manager.

A further decline in oil imports in 1984 was offset to some extent by an increase in exports to a record high of 2.15 million tonnes, resulting in a marginal overall drop in throughput for the year of .01 million tonnes. Industrial relations difficulties involving the new stevedoring company, Dublin Cargo Handling, and the dock labour force in the deepsea sector, together with financial difficulties arising as a consequence, dominated the board's affairs during the year. Following the intervention by the Minister for Labour, Mr John Horgan of the Labour Court was appointed chairman of a review group whose terms of reference and recommendations are dealt with in the next chapter, together with the problems encountered by Dublin Cargo Handling.

The board's own operations were affected by a strike of craftsmen which continued for six weeks in the autumn of 1984 and most of the board's staff were affected by the dispute. The board's tenants, including the cross channel, ore and oil trades, were not affected. The completion of the new East Link Toll Bridge in 1984 together with the opening of the new Fairview by-pass was welcomed by many interests, including port users. However, the great increase of traffic on the East Wall Road resulting from the new facilities created considerable difficulties for traffic using the entrances and exits of the port and were the subject of discussions with Dublin Corporation.

The decline in the demand for the older transit shed and berthage accommodation at the North Wall Extension and the Crossberth influenced the board in deciding to fill in portion of the Alexandra Basin at the Crossberth, to provide a large open area which could be adapted for various traffics if and when the need arises. A Harbour Works Order was made by the Minister to authorise the work and reclamation commenced in 1984.

An Bord Pleanala's long awaited decision on the appeal against the proposed storage of LPG in caverns was announced, upholding the objections.

A disappointing feature of the year was the closing down of the National Coal Company's coal terminal at Alexandra Road. A bright feature in an otherwise gloomy year was the continuing favourable results of the monitoring of air pollution in the port.

Further disputes involving the deepsea dock labour force did not assist the maintenance of the port's throughput for 1985 which fell to 6.4 million tonnes, notwithstanding an increase in coal imports and in ro-ro traffic. Following settlement of the long standing dispute with the deepsea dockers, a return to work was followed by a big improvement in the turnround time of shipping using the deepsea sector and brought favourable comment from shipping interests and renewed interest in the use of Dublin port.

An extension to the bulk discharge quay at the south side enabled two large vessels to use the quay at the same time.

The new ro-ro ramp and associated reclamation south of the B&I car ferry terminal was completed.

The year saw the sale of the last of the board's steam hoppers *Number Ten* which had played its part with the remainder of the old dredging fleet in the removal of about 300,000 tonnes of spoil annually from the river and bar down the years.

The favourable reactions of shipping interests to the 'new look' deepsea sector became evident in the increase in container traffic through the new South Quay container terminal. This return of confidence by port users in the port and in the deepsea docker force was manifest in the upswing in the port's throughput for 1986. At 7.6 million tonnes, it was 20 per cent over the 1985 figure and had been exceeded only in the record years of 1979 and 1980. An additional factor in the improvement was the increase in oil imports.

An announcement by the B&I Line that it was considering transferring its operations to Dun Laoghaire was regarded with some surprise, having regard to the limited space available there in contrast to the forty acres occupied by the company at Dublin. In view of the fact that the Dun Laoghaire terminal would have to be shared with British Rail (or Sealink as it had now become) the board approved of the drafting of a scheme for a unified terminal for both companies at Dublin. This was prepared with two options, the first being based on the North Wall Extension together with the additional space available at the Crossberth and the new reclamation adjoining. The second option proposed the use of the new ro-ro installation at the new deepwater quay south of the car ferry terminal. The proposals were submitted to consultant economists and planners who expressed their conviction that Dublin was the only viable location for the unified terminal having regard to the existing and projected demands of the two companies concerned. Because of the difficult situation which has confronted B&I in recent years, the matter of a unified terminal is not an immediate priority.

The financial difficulties encountered by the board as a result of its involvement in stevedoring are dealt with in the next chapter. The consequence of these difficulties in 1984 and 1985 was a postponement of major development works and of dredging on the bar and the river channel. The improved situation in 1986 enabled the board to enter into a new contract for maintenance dredging with the existing contractors, Irish Dredging, and in a short time the full depths on the bar and in the channel were restored.

21

Dublin Cargo Handling and the Custom House Docks

THE financial difficulties experienced by Dublin Cargo Handling since its establishment were the consequence of the general recession in trade, the problems associated with a new deal with the dock labour force involving permanent employment for a smaller number of dockers and the cost of the consequent redundancies. As the company is a wholly owned subsidiary of the Dublin Port and Docks Board which guarantees the company's financial commitments the consequences for the board were severe but not totally unexpected since the board had from the outset recognised that the fundamental change involved in the new stevedoring arrangements would have far-reaching and expensive effects. The board provided and controlled all the infrastructure of the port from the lighthouses to the quays and transit sheds and practically all the ancillary services involved in putting a vessel in a position to discharge or load its cargo economically and efficiently; however the major gap in the board's control of port operations was that hitherto it had had no control over the stevedoring companies which managed the dock labour force.

The process of the daily 'reads' for employing dock labour has already been explained but what is not so easily recognised by those outside the port scene is the frustration of men working under this arrangement who had no permanent employer and whose employer for the time being saw his obligations to the docker as fulfilled by the payment of wages for the period of the discharge of the particular ship. It is true that the trade unions representing dock labour had agitated for many years for a new deal, generally known as 'decasualisation', and some advance had been made in this direction in the 1970s. The pace of change was slow, although a scheme introduced in 1971 provided for a reduction to 550 of the labour force with compensation to be paid to an agreed list of dockers who would have no further hope of employment. With the continuing swing away from break bulk cargo to unitised loads, even this arrangement could not provide employment for the remaining men on the register, and the scheme provided for a daily payment known as 'fall back' pay to those men who attended for work but were not employed. The system of 'reads' was replaced by a rota system which was intended to spread the available work over all those on the register. However, negotiations opened by the stevedores in 1974 through their Association of Dublin Stevedores sought further reductions in the manning scales, i.e. the agreed number of dockers required to work a particular type of ship or cargo, and greater flexibility in working arrangements, and offered an improved bonus scheme in return. Agreement was reached on the proposals but its implementation coincided with a general recession in 1974-5 involving large numbers of men on the daily 'fall back' pay and a new arrangement was made whereby each man attended for work for only two weeks in every three, receiving no pay for the week off; and only 'fall back' pay for days in attendance on which he got no work.

With an improvement in port trade in 1976 it was possible to withdraw the 'one week off in three' arrangement but full employment for all dockers seemed as far away as ever with the continuing rise in unitised cargo. To assist in resolving the general difficulty, the board agreed to guarantee two loans arranged by the Association of Dublin Stevedores and these loans were duly repaid. The loans financed a voluntary severance scheme as a result of which the docker force was reduced to 452 with 96 checkers. So far as the employers were concerned the continuing burden of 'fall back' pay was unacceptable bearing in mind that in other industries men in the same position would qualify for unemployment benefit from the state. The increase in costs to the users of the port made it unattractive to continue using the port when other alternatives were available. It was admitted by many importers and exporters that Dublin was best equipped to give a good shipping service and quick turn round but increasing labour charges and continual disputes with consequent stoppages were a major deterrent to using Dublin port. So far as the stevedores were concerned an average of 147 men on fall back pay had to be paid for in addition to standard overheads, insurance, social welfare contributions, pensions and repayment of loans, which worked out at a total labour cost almost double the wages paid to the dockers.

From the board's point of view Dublin stevedores had enjoyed decades of good trading results at the port with substantial profits none of which had been re-invested to the port's long-term advantage. A typical example was the arrangement under which the board provided the dockers' canteens which were used primarily by the dock labour force but partly by other port workers. A substantial share of the costs of building, maintaining and operating the canteens was met by the board. Other major employers in the port area provided such facilities for their staffs without any involvement by the port board. Another example was the reluctance of the stevedores to provide mechanical plant for their operations. There were examples in the past of companies making profits in Dublin but investing their capital in other ports. It was, however, recognised that the Association of Dublin Stevedores had made genuine efforts to improve the difficult situation of dock labour but with less success than these efforts merited. Internal difficulties as between the members of the association did little to advance an agreed solution to the problem.

It is against this background that the subsequent decisions of the board regarding stevedoring have to be considered. Various proposals were put forward to the stevedores in an effort to achieve progress, but without success, and eventually the board decided that there should be a single stevedoring company in the port with substantial port board participation. Clearly the stevedores would not be willing to relinquish their interests voluntarily and the arrangement proposed by the board involved compensation to be paid to each stevedore related to his proportion of the total business. Negotiations dragged on and were not facilitated by a number of labour disputes. The creation of a stevedoring company, Dublin Cargo Handling, by the port board and its designation as the only authorised stevedoring organisation spurred a settlement with the stevedores, and the final terms provided for compensation to four companies who agreed not to engage in stevedoring at any east coast port for seven years. Two companies, Merchants Warehousing Ltd and Coal Distributors Ltd who employed labour only for their own ships, ceased stevedoring operations without compensation and entered into service contracts with DCH. The remaining group, consisting of George Bell, Irish Shipping and R.A. Burke Ltd, had already joined in a new company entitled Associated Port Terminals Ltd which in turn was owned by Wahner Investments. Wahner agreed to join the new stevedoring company on the basis of being granted a 50 per cent stake in lieu of compensation for their component businesses, the board holding the other 50 per cent.

Because of the mounting financial difficulties of Dublin Cargo Handling, Wahner decided in 1983 to opt out of the business and sold its 50 per cent share to the port board for a nominal sum. Wahner's assets and goodwill had been lost at this stage but they had been relieved of their obligations in the matter of guarantees given by themselves and the board in respect of borrowings by DCH. The board thus became ultimately responsible for the financial affairs of DCH.

Following a strike by the deepsea dockers in August 1984 the Dublin Docks Review Group was set up by the Minister for Labour to report on the reasons for the difficulties in the deepsea section of the port and to examine the organisation necessary for the efficient operation of the port and to make recommendations thereon.

Under the chairmanship of Mr John Horgan of the Labour Court, the group consisted of three representatives of the dock labour force, two from Dublin Cargo Handling and the general manager of the port board. The group was assisted by two advisers, one from the Marine Port & General Workers Union and one from the Federated Union of Employers.

The report of the group, published in October 1984, was highly critical of the financial projections on which the decision to form DCH was based, although it acknowledged that if the port board had not acted when it did an uncontrolled collapse of stevedoring would have occurred, in which event the extent of government involvement would have been greater than envisaged in the report. The conclusions of the report were that the problems of the port were to a considerable degree a result of the port's declining commercial fortunes; further, Dublin had seen its natural monopoly position eroded through technological change which had increased competition between ports and business had been lost because of cost competitiveness and unreliability. The conclusions also included a critical analysis of the finances of the board in relation to DCH. The fact that DCH had to carry excessive numbers of employees was recognised as contributing to the financial crisis and the report recommended that the dock labour force be reduced to 120 by means of voluntary redundancy. The cost of this redundancy programme was to be funded by the board through the sale of surplus assets, principally the Custom House Docks site.

The major recommendation of the report was that the port board should be replaced by a new authority which would be a commercial semi-state company with not more than eight (board) members appointed by the Minister for Communications and paid in line with rates for directors of other semi-state boards. (It might be noted here that members of harbour authorities in the Republic including the Dublin port board receive no remuneration whatever for the considerable time and effort they put into the work of administering Irish ports and the report was emphatic that there was no implication that present or past members of the Dublin port board had failed to act responsibly in the performance of their duties.) The report included a number of other recommendations related to procedures as to labour requirements, industrial relations and the suggested re-organisation of the port board.

As stated above, the board had recognised that to bring about the desired improvement in the stevedoring situation, there would be expensive consequences but it had made its decision in the knowledge (or more correctly, in the belief) that it had a major saleable asset in the Cutsom House Docks site in respect of which it had received many enquiries from prospective purchasers, some of which crystallised into serious consideration following the granting of planning permission for the re-development of the twenty-four acre site in 1982. The intervention of the government by bringing forward the Urban Development Areas Bill in 1982 had resulted in the collapse of the potential market for the sale of the premises at the valuation recommended to the board by its property advisers, the proceeds of which would have obviated the need for substantial borrowings and the very heavy interest which had accumulated thereon in the subsequent years. The fall of the government resulted in the fall of the bill but so far as the board was concerned the market for the Custom House Docks had vanished almost overnight since the possibility of the bill's being resurrected in one form or another could hardly entice a prospective purchaser to pay what would otherwise have been an open market price if the government of the day were to take up the running and acquire the site compulsorily. Furthermore, under the Harbours Act, the board is precluded from disposing of property without the consent of the Minister. The matter lay dormant until 1986 and in the meantime the board was labouring under the burden of heavy interest repayments on its borrowings, partly for port development works, but mainly to maintain DCH in business.

Following the next change of government the bill made a reappearance, with some variations, under the title of the Urban Renewal Bill 1986 which was enacted as the Urban Renewal Act in June 1986 and the authority foreshadowed in the earlier bill was established by Ministerial Order in November 1986 under the title of Custom House Docks Development Authority. In January 1987 a further Ministerial Order transferred ownership of the Custom House Docks site to the new authority with effect from 1 March, almost 118 years since the ownership of the premises had been vested in the port authority in 1867.

The question of compensation had dragged on and was to some extent bedevilled by the fact that the government had recognised the board's financial crisis in the intervening years and had granted repayable loans totalling £9 million. Eventually the board was awarded a total of £10.55 million, less the amount of the loans already granted, leaving the board with a net £1.55 million with which to organise the transfer of its operations to a site in the port area, but nothing wherewith to reduce its outstanding borrowings.

In the midst of these traumatic events, the board celebrated the bicentenary of the establishment of the Corporation for Preserving and Improving the Port of Dublin as the port authority for Dublin in May 1786. The celebration was marked by a formal dinner in the historic Royal Hospital at Kilmainham at which state departments, local authorities and other organisations with which the board has close relations were represented. In the course of the function, the Minister for Transport, Mr Jim Mitchell who was the guest of honour, announced his intention to implement the recommendation of the Horgan Working Group relating to the abolition of the port board as constituted under the Harbours Act 1946, and to replace it with a smaller board to be appointed by the Minister. The Coalition government fell in February 1987 and with it the Minister's proposal.

Arrangements were duly put in hands for the transfer of warehousing operations from the Custom House Docks to the port estate at East Wall. These operations had undergone many changes since the board took over the warehouses in 1869 when the main commodities stored were grain, whiskey, wines, timber and slates. Grain continued to be stored until the Merchants Warehousing Company set up its grain silos at the port in 1914. One of the major operations in the board's warehouses since the late 1920s and early 1930s has been the warehousing of tobacco under bond, together with associated services such as sampling, nett weighing etc. As the trade grew it became necessary to build four successive warehouses over the years for this trade alone (Stacks F, G, H and L). Tea has also been an important component of the warehousing operations. Prior to the Second World War, Irish tea merchants bought their requirements on the London tea market but when, following the outbreak of war, this was no longer possible the government established Tea Importers Ltd in 1941 as a purchasing agency to organise the purchase of tea from various sources overseas and to arrange its shipment to Ireland by a variety of routes throughout the war years. As the board was the largest warehousekeeper in the country it was natural that it should be asked to undertake the task of warehousing whole cargoes and providing services such as blending for particular merchants. This involved the renting of additional storage at Chapelizod and Bonham Street in premises formerly used as distilleries. In 1947 the government decided that in future tea must be shipped direct from the countries of origin and the arrival of shipments of up to 31,000 chests at a time created additional pressure which was eased following the completion of the Stack D Warehouse at Alexandra Quay. With six acres of floor space, Stack D was capable of providing all the necessary space for storage and operations, to deal with up to 200,000 chests of tea per annum.

The extensive range of vaults which were constructed under the old warehouses in Custom House Docks clearly indicates the importance at that time of the storage of wines and spirits in casks, but in modern times the main demand in this area has been for storage of cases, rather than casks, of 'wet goods' as wines and spirits are usually described in warehousing parlance.

All goods warehoused other than tobacco, tea and 'wet goods' are described as 'general' and cover a wide range of commodities.

Groupage is the name given to the assembly for transport in one container of small consignments which individually do not justify a container each. Importation of groupage containers requires that they be unloaded (or 'stripped') under customs supervision at a groupage depôt and the board has operated such a depôt for over twenty-five years.

The removal of goods left in transit sheds or on the quays beyond the permitted time is carried out by the warehousing department and the goods are stored in the removals shed which is located beside Stack D.

With this chapter we close our review of the growth and development of the port of Dublin using that term in its narrow sense of the quays, piers and facilities for shipping in the estuary of the Liffey. In its strict legal sense, however, the port of Dublin encompasses other harbours and these are dealt with in the next chapter.

Dublin Port Trade

TABLE SHOWING TOTAL CARGO TONNES AND NUMBER OF SHIP ARRIVALS 1939-86

Year	Imports (m. tonnes)	Exports	Total	Arrivals
1939	2.65	.30	2.95	5450
1949	2.55	.39	2.94	4429
1959	2.75	.52	3.27	4892
1969	4.42	.93	5.35	6418
1979	6.13	1.81	7.94	4835
1985	4.30	2.13	6.43	3343
1986	5.36	2.33	7.69	3966

22

Outports

THE statutory responsibility of the Dublin Port and Docks Board as a harbour authority extends to the harbours of Balbriggan, Skerries, Bullock and Sandycove. While the inclusion of Bullock and Sandycove under the board's statutory wing, situated as they are in Dublin Bay, might seem logical, the board's involvement with Balbriggan and Skerries has always been something of an anomaly, the harbours being at a distance of twenty miles and eighteen miles respectively from Dublin. The fact that the intervening harbours of Rush and the inlets of Malahide and Rogerstown are not within the board's jurisdiction makes the situation all the more confusing.

The historical relationship between the harbours of Howth and Kingstown/Dun Laoghaire on the one hand and the port of Dublin on the other has been reviewed in Chapter 13 and calls for no further comment but some explanation is necessary in regard to the first-named four harbours.

The development of Balbriggan in the eighteenth century from a small fishing village to a thriving town was due mainly to the Hamilton family whose Holmpatrick estate included much of the land in the Balbriggan/Skerries district. In 1763 Baron George Hamilton built a pier with the aid of a parliamentary grant and in 1780 he established two cotton factories which, with associated dye-works, employed over 300 local people. A salt works and a tanning yard were started by local merchants, bringing further employment to the town. Following the death of Hamilton in 1793, his son Rev. George Hamilton administered the estate and both he and his son, George Alexander Hamilton, were involved in further improvements for the town's benefit, including a second pier built in the 1820s and financed partly by the Hamiltons and partly by the Fisheries Board. As the town developed so did the trade of the harbour; in 1833 a total of 163 ships arrived including 134 colliers and twenty-nine coasters loading out corn for cross-channel ports.

The Dublin port authority's first association with Balbriggan dates from 1790 when a general statute relating to the development of ports and harbours in the United Kingdom was passed; the act provided that if any outport within the 'district of the Port' required repair or improvement, it should be lawful for the authority of the principal port to collect from shipping using such outport the same rates and duties as applied to the principal harbour, such revenue to be used on the repair and improvement of the outport. The term 'district of the Port' is somewhat confusing so far as the port of Dublin is concerned, since the statutory limits of the port were not defined until 1811, and those of the pilotage district until 1869; the only reasonable explanation is that the reference was to the customs port which in the case of Dublin extended from the Nanny river, which enters the sea at Laytown, to Arklow. Balbriggan was therefore an outport for which the Dublin authority had certain responsibilities but in fact the day-to-day management remained with the Hamilton estate, Dublin acting more or less in an advisory and supervisory capacity.

Siltation at the mouth of Balbriggan harbour has always been a major problem, particularly after easterly or north-easterly gales and the Dublin authority frequently sent barges and other equipment to assist in dredging the harbour. In June 1866, Baron Hamilton asked the board to consent to an application which he proposed to make to the government requesting that the harbour be transferred totally to the Dublin authority. The consent was forthcoming and the harbour was duly vested in the Dublin Port and Docks Board under the Balbriggan Pier and Harbour Order 1867.

The continuous dredging drained the revenue of the harbour and between 1869 and 1871 the Commissioners of Public Works advanced £1,700 by way of loans but the revenue was insufficient to provide for the repayment of capital and interest and in 1928 the sum of £1,250 was still due to the Commissioners. In later years many methods were tried in an effort to solve the siltation problem including the use of dredgers owned by the Office of Public Works but none could cure the basic problem which was the situation of the harbour itself. The costs of maintenance of Balbriggan Harbour, particularly the dredging, and also those in respect of Skerries Harbour, continued to grow, resulting in substantial deficits and in the course of its observations to the government on the bill which became the Harbours Act 1946, the board sought to limit its responsibility for further expenditure on these harbours to an amount equal to the revenue derived therefrom. These representations were unsuccessful.

With the fall-off in shipping other than fishing vessels in the 1950s a temporary expedient was adopted with moderate success. Shortly before the arrival of each collier or coaster, high pressure water jets were used to clear the entrance for long enough to enable the vessel to enter. Having discharged her cargo, she would, of course, have less difficulty negotiating the mouth of the harbour when leaving, but with the total cessation of commercial shipping, other than fishing, in the 1960s, no further dredging was carried out.

The revenue from the fishing vessels at 50p each for an annual licence to use the harbour was negligible and although a portion of the harbour was leased for a marina in 1973, the rent received made little difference to the annual deficit which was of the order of £2,000. In 1977 the board made a policy decision that further expenditure on Balbriggan and Skerries harbours could not be justified since a heavy burden was falling on the general funds of the board which were provided by the shipowners using Dublin port; having regard to the funds expended by the state on other fishing harbours such as Howth, Dunmore East and Killybegs, the position in regard to the finances of Balbriggan harbour was totally anomalous.

Following a severe gale in December 1979, portion of the south pier subsided and further damage was sustained in 1982. The cost of repairing the damage totalled almost £90,000 which the board agreed to bear but the government departments concerned, Dublin County Council and local representatives were put on notice that no further expenditure would be made on Balbriggan harbour beyond that which was necessary for the protection of life and limb. Many meetings were held with all the parties concerned in the course of which the board's representatives emphasised the fundamental changes in conditions since the transfer of Balbriggan to the board in 1867 and suggested that the Minister for Transport might consider exercising his powers under Section 134 of the Harbours Act for the purpose of transferring all the outports of Dublin to the appropriate local authorities. The board's arguments were accepted by the government and in a Green Paper on transport published in 1985, the government of the day outlined proposals for, *inter alia*, the transfer of the outports to local authorities; to date, however (1988), no further action has been taken in the matter.

In addition to the three islands (Shenick, Colt and St Patrick's) which lie off the shore at Skerries, the headland known as Red Island was at one period an island separated from the mainland but siltation gradually transformed the intervening channel into a sandy isthmus on the north-western side of which a causeway developed; this causeway later became the present Harbour Road. Although Skerries appears to have been used as a landing place from the second century A.D. the earliest record of a pier occurs towards the end of the fifteenth century. In the recitals to a lease made in 1605 it was stated that 'when the said port [i.e. Skerries] was built many boats from England, France, Spain and Scotland came there annually to fish....' In 1689 a Williamite naval officer reported landing with 200 men at Skerries where they stove in or burnt 'all the small vessels and fishing boats'.

The US aircraft carrier *Saipan* arriving at the port of Dublin in July 1952.

The launching of the B & I's cargo livestock ship *Meath* from the Liffey Dockyard in 1960.

The car carrier *Hoegh Trader* discharging cars at the south quays.

The Bull Wall, a favourite promenade for Dubliners.

The *Memmon* discharging cargo from West African ports at Ocean Pier.

The *Miranda Guinness*, the world's first specially commissioned bulk liquid carrier, arriving at the port of Dublin.

The early Dublin pilot cutters were similar to this Bristol Channel pilot cutter photographed around 1890. The photograph (*below*) shows the *Dodder*, one of the modern diesel engine pilot cutters operating from the pilot shore station at the Eastern Breakwater.

The method of discharging coal cargo remained unchanged for many years. The photograph shows dockers filling tubs in the hold of the collier and a filled tub being tipped into a railway wagon for CIE.

The modern method of discharging coal by grab at the South Bulk Terminal.

Aerial view of the port in the mid 1960s. In the left foreground, the quay serving the ESB Ringsend station is visible; on the right, the Eastern Breakwater is in the foreground, and immediately behind it lie the two oil jetties, Ocean Pier and Alexandra Quay East.

Past and present in the modern port. The photograph (*above*) shows the Argentinian sail training vessel *Libertad* and the Norwegian liner *Royal Viking Sea*. The photograph (*below*) shows the Italian sail training ship *Amerigo Vespucci*.

Shipping at Alexandra Quay and Ocean Pier.

The Chairman, Mr. E.W. Beck, addressing the last meeting of the Dublin Port and Docks Board to be held in the Ballast Office, Westmoreland Street, February 1976.

The town of Skerries with its harbour was purchased by the Hamilton family in 1721 but by 1755 the estate found it necessary to apply for government aid to repair and extend the pier. Although the petition was ultimately successful, the proposed improvements were not effected for another ten years by which time another petition emphsised the need for a further extension of the pier to give a depth of 10 feet at low water alongside which, in the words of the petition, would make the harbour 'safe and commodious at all times'. In its report the examining committee of the House of Commons stated that in the year 1756-7 almost 1,200 ships and vessels employed in the trade of the port of Dublin, including packets, had been forced by contrary winds to take shelter at Skerries. The petition was unsuccessful as was a later one in 1769 and repairs to the pier continued to be carried out by the Holmpatrick estate.

Following a public meeting at Drogheda in 1854 a memorial was submitted to the Admiralty suggesting that, in view of the great number of ships wrecked off the east coast, particularly between Howth and St John's Point in Co. Down, a survey should be carried out for the purpose of providing a harbour of refuge at Skerries. In reply, the Admiralty stated that they did not consider that another harbour of refuge (in addition to Kingstown) was necessary. In a statement accompanying a later petition in 1858 it was stated that there were fifty vessels of over fifty tons belonging to Skerries with another thirty under fifty tons but that the pier was not capable of sheltering more than forty vessels; in addition to the locally-owned craft, up to twenty coasters had sheltered in Skerries Roads in severe gales and fishing vessels based in Dublin, Howth, Baldoyle and Rush also sought shelter at Skerries in winter months. This petition met with no more success than its predecessors.

In the late eighteenth century Skerries had been regarded as the most important fishing harbour in Ireland, the local fleet being engaged mainly in herring fishing. By the mid nineteenth century the herring fishing had greatly declined at Skerries although sporadic attempts were made to engage in deepsea fishing for cod off Iceland.

On the basis, no doubt, of his success in having responsibility for Balbriggan harbour transferred to the port board in 1867, Baron Hamilton approached the board in March 1876 seeking consent to a similar transfer of Skerries harbour. After some deliberation the board eventually agreed but insisted on an indemnity from the Holmpatrick estate whereby the estate would be liable for any deficiency in working the harbour, calculated on a three years' average. In due course the harbour was transferred to the board under the terms of the Skerries Harbour Order 1877.

The connection with the Holmpatrick estate was not completely broken since the board appointed a committee to supervise the undertaking at Skerries, under the chairmanship of Baron Hamilton. The harbour was formally taken over on 17 November 1877 and George Carter was appointed harbour master. The first work undertaken by the board on the recommendation of the committee was the erection of a lantern at the end of the pier which showed a red light visible for five miles in clear weather. Local efforts to press the government to fund improvements at the harbour were revived in the years immediately preceding the First World War without success.

Apart from the fishing industry, the trade of Skerries harbour between 1880 and 1914 consisted mainly of coal imports and exports of local limestone, potatoes and herrings but over the following decade the exports practically disappeared while coal imports declined over the ensuing years, the last coal cargoes being unloaded in 1961. However, the fishing industry had improved sufficiently to convince the government that the harbour should be improved and in 1968 work commenced on an extension to the pier of 180 feet. The original wooden lantern house had been destroyed by fire in 1925 and replaced by a concrete structure; with the extension of the pier in 1968 a new lighthouse was provided at the seaward end together with a shelter, lighting, water and fuelling facilities for the fishing vessels. The cost of these works was borne by the state and Dublin County Council on a 50/50 basis and the Dublin port board undertook to maintain the harbour as extended.

The small inlet of Dublin Bay near Dalkey, known as Bullock harbour, formed part of a grant of lands to the Cistercian monks of St Mary's Abbey, Dublin, in the fourteeenth century. The monks built a castle and a primitive pier at the inlet and they levied tolls in kind from fishing vessels using the inlet, one of the few landing places for small craft in this part of Dublin Bay. In the eighteenth century the inlet was the scene of bloody confrontations between revenue officers and smugglers but in the early nineteenth century a more peaceful activity characterised the inlet and the village which had grown up beside it. In 1804 the Carysfort Estate granted leases to the Dublin port authority of lands at Bullock, including the castle and the harbour pier, and also lands and a small harbour at Sandycove; the board's object was primarily to acquire the granite quarrries which formed part of the castle lands, and from which stone could be quarried and transported by barge across the bay for use in building and repairing the quay walls, including at a later stage the North Bull Wall. George Smith, a local builder, was employed to quarry the stone and he was also given a contract to improve and extend the medieval pier still used by fishermen. The harbour at Bullock was for a period used as a base for the Dublin pilot vessels and in 1806 Smith was given a further contract for building a number of cottages to house the pilots at £10 per cottage.

Although small coasters occasionally used Bullock harbour up to the early 1920s, since then it has been used mainly by yacht and boat owners and fishermen from whom the board derives no income; the only revenue produced from the harbour is that from small rents of portions of the quayside.

The lease of the lands at Bullock and Sandycove expired in 1903, although the use of the quarries had been discontinued many years previously but as the two harbours were within the port of Dublin as defined by the Dublin Port and Docks Board Act 1869, the board had a continuing statutory obligation to maintain them for the purposes of commercial navigation which for many years has been nil. Indeed there is no record of Sandycove harbour ever having been used commercially and it is difficult to see how even the smallest coaster could have used it. For many years the harbour has been used solely for amenity purposes by local residents and visitors. Frequent requests are made to the port board to improve the amenities but since the board's powers in regard to expenditure are limited by statute to purposes directly or indirectly related to navigation, and as no revenue is derived from the harbour, such improvements as have been carried out have been the work of the Dun Laoghaire Borough Corporation by agreement with the board.

Coliemore Harbour (which should not be confused with Dalkey harbour referred to in the port statutes—see Chapter 23) lies within the statutory limits of the port of Dublin and the board has statutory jurisdiction over all matters relating to navigation and pilotage insofar as they may arise in connection with the harbour. However, the piers at Coliemore were built by the Dalkey Town Commissioners in accordance with powers conferred by the Dalkey Township Improvement Act 1867 which also authorised the commissioners to make regulations for the harbour and for the control of boatmen and others using the harbour. Unlike Balbriggan and Skerries, the Coliemore piers were never transferred to the port board, and Dun Laoghaire Borough Corporation, as successors to the Dalkey Commissioners, own and are responsible for the maintenance of these piers.

23

Pilots, Tugs and Navigational Aids

THE earliest statutory definition of the term 'pilot' was contained in the Merchant Shipping Act 1854 and repeated in later pilotage legislation. It reads 'any person not belonging to a ship who has the conduct therof'. Simple as this statement may appear, it contains many pitfalls even when interpreted by legal experts for the purposes of litigation or otherwise. The view of a pilot's function which prevailed for many years was that he was employed by the shipmaster in an advisory capacity, but this interpretation was regarded as too narrow in several judicial decisions. Nowadays a pilot is generally taken to be a person who is not an officer or member of the crew of a ship but is entrusted with the navigation of that ship usually when entering, leaving or moving within a port, the shipmaster intervening only if he is satisfied that the pilot is incompetent, a relatively rare occurence.

By the sixteenth century the need was recognised for the control of pilotage to prevent incompetent persons from acting as pilots or from charging exorbitant fees and also in the general interests of the safety of shipping in a particular district. The first statute relating to pilots at Dublin was an act of 1763 (3 Geo. III, Cap. 15) which followed a petition by the City Council seeking powers to regulate haven masters, pilots and lightermen (see Chapter 3). The duties of the haven masters as set out in the act were to 'take care that buoys and floating perches be placed and constantly kept up on the north and south ends of the bank called the Kish and on other banks in the bay and harbour' and they were also obliged to direct the anchoring or berthing of ships within the harbour. Pilotage was compulsory for every ship arriving at or departing from the port except those trading coastwise with coal or grain and the rates to be charged for the pilots' services were set out in the act. The City Council was empowered to appoint such pilots as might be required not excceding fifty and to pay them each the sum of forty shillings yearly together with the appropriate charge in respect of each pilotage service provided by the pilot concerned.

Although the act required that only duly qualified persons be licensed as pilots, it placed no restriction on other persons acting as unlicensed pilots. These were usually local fishermen who apart from offering their services as pilots usually performed the function of boatmen, attending to the mooring of the vessel upon arrival in port. Operating as they did from small open rowing boats, their occupation was a hazardous one and they were usually known as 'hobblers'. Later the term 'hobbler' came to refer solely to boatmen who vied with each other in Dublin Bay for employment in mooring vessels after arrival in port, the successful contender being towed up the river by the ship. 'Hobbling' died out partly as a result of the introduction of a contract system between ship agents and boatmen, and partly following a tragedy in December 1934 when three young hobblers were drowned during a gale in Dublin Bay.

When the City Council acting through its Ballast Committee was replaced as port authority by the Corporation for Preserving and Improving the Port of Dublin, the act of 1786 setting up the new body contained similar provisions to those of the 1763 act relating to the licensing of pilots, and provided in addition for the appointment of a pilot master to examine candidates for pilots' licences and to collect and distribute their fees. Prior to 1786 each pilot usually provided his own boat but later the practice grew whereby the pilots as a group hired boats and paid the owners 20 per cent of the earnings of the boats. The seaworthiness and general condition of some of these hired boats frequently left a lot to be desired and under new regulations made in 1823 provision was made for the building of pilot boats by the authority, a deduction being made from the pilotage fees, similar to that paid previously for hire, to cover the cost of the new boats. By 1835 there were four boats under forty tons and three between forty and fifty tons. Each boat (or cutter as they were known because of their cutter rig) had a master, eight pilots and two apprentices. There were also nine river pilots who attended to outgoing vessels or vessels shifting within the pilotage district.

Early in the nineteenth century, the owners of ships engaged in regular trading to particular ports became dissatisfied with the obligation placed on the masters of the vessels to employ pilots, on the grounds that masters making frequent calls were as familar with the navigational hazards of that particular port as were the pilots; further, the masters were more familar with the distinctive characteristics and idiosyncrasies of their own ships. Eventually by the act of 1854 (17/18 Vic. Cap. 104) which dealt generally with merchant shipping, a number of general provisions relating to pilotage were included and provision was made for the exemption from compulsory pilotage of ships whose masters had satisfied the local pilotage authority of their local knowledge and had been issued with an appropriate certificate.

A later Merchant Shipping Act (1894) repealed the 1854 act and purported to consolidate all existing legislation relating to pilotage but no real effort was made to consolidate and rationalise acts applicable only in particular pilotage districts, and variances and inconsistencies between general and local acts continued to pose problems.

From 1869 the Dublin pilotage service operated under the Dublin Port and Docks Act passed in that year, which had originally been intended to reorganise the finances and administration of the pilotage service but which in the event was extended to consolidate and update all existing legislation relating to the general administration and operation of the port of Dublin. The 1869 act defined the limits of the harbour, the port and the pilotage district. In simple terms, the harbour of Dublin is any place between Carlisle (now O'Connell) Bridge and the space of one mile east of the Poolbeg Lighthouse in which a ship can lie and obtain shelter, or ship or unship goods or passengers, in effect the water area within the prescribed limits in which a ship can anchor, moor or berth. The port consists of the river Liffey and the quays and walls bounding it, including the 'north, south and east walls' together with the bridges, piers, jetties and tidal basins belonging to the board and the strands, bays and creeks, between Barrack (now Rory O'More) Bridge, the 'harbour' of Sutton on the north side of the bay and the 'harbour' of Dalkey on the south, but excluding Kingstown (Dun Laoghaire) harbour and the Royal Canal Docks. The term 'harbour' in relation to Sutton and Dalkey sometimes creates confusion but in this context it derives from the fact that up to the eighteenth century small ships took shelter in Sutton Creek and in Dalkey Sound; at the latter anchorage ships frequently discharged cargoes into small boats to be landed in adjacent coves. As indicated in the statutory definition of the 'harbour' of Dublin, the term 'harbour' does not necessarily connote piers, jetties etc.

The area or 'pilotage district' within which the port board exercised jurisdiction in pilotage matters was bounded on the seaward side by a line from Rockabill Lighthouse, near Skerries, to the lightship (now a buoy) at the south end of the Arklow Bank. Within the pilotage district, three divisions were defined in the act: outer, inner and bay. The bay division consisted in effect of Dublin Bay west of a line joining Baily Lighthouse on Howth Head with a point at Dalkey now called Sorrento Point. The inner division consisted of the area lying outside the bay division but within a line from Ireland's Eye to the Kish Lightship and thence to Bray Head. The outer division consisted of so much of the pilotage district as was not included in the other two divisions.

Pilot boats were deployed as required in the three divisons and those on the outer division required to be sturdy, seaworthy craft operating as they were in open sea conditions for almost 60 miles from the Rockabill to the Arklow Bank. Unfortunately, very little detailed information is available on the pilot boats, but they are believed to have been similar to the famous Bristol Channel pilot cutters which sometimes sailed as far as Land's End to meet incoming vessels. Pilots were transferred from the cutters to ships in rowing boats which were normally secured in davits on the cutters or towed behind.

The first steam pilot vessel to be introduced on the Dublin pilot service was the *Energy* which was chartered in 1899 as an experiment to reduce operating costs; later it was decided to buy the vessel. The experiment was a success both from the point of view of the pilots and of the economies effected and a second steamer, the *Dolores*, was acquired in 1902, by which time all the sailing pilot boats had become worn out. The *Energy* and the *Dolores* operated the service until 1923 when the *Dolores* was replaced by a converted fishing drifter, the *Lady Fry*. The *Energy* was withdrawn in 1932 following the purchase and conversion of another drifter, the *Kent County* which was renamed *Inis Fail* when she was put into service. The *Lady Fry* was retained as a standby vessel, the new vessel being capable of maintaining the service using motor launches to put the pilots aboard ships.

In 1909 a departmental committee of the Board of Trade was set up to enquire into the state of pilotage law and administration and as to what changes, if any, were desirable. In its report published in 1911 the committee referred to the problems created by the inconsistencies between general and local pilotage acts, and it recommended a new general act to repeal all local acts which would also provide for the constitution and limits of jurisdiction of each pilotage authority, with powers to draw up schemes of re-organisation and new bye-laws for its own district. On the basis of the recommendations in the report, a new general pilotage bill was introduced in parliament and passed in 1913. Although substantial changes have been made in recent years in the law of pilotage in the United Kingdom, the Dublin pilotage service continues to operate under the 1913 act together with ministerial orders, confirmed by acts of the Oireachtas, relating to Dublin, and bye-laws drawn up and revised from time to time by the pilotage authority (i.e. the port board) with the approval of the appropriate Minister. The major changes at Dublin effected by pilotage orders related to alterations in the limits of the pilotage district and the substitution of a shore-based pilot station at the Eastern Breakwater in place of the cruising pilot steamers. The limits of the Dublin pilotage district were reduced by the Pilotage Order Confirmation Act 1926, whereby the district thenceforth consisted of the areas formerly covered by the bay and inner divisions, these divisions being abolished. In 1963 the district was further reduced to the area formerly known as the bay division, and the relevant order also provided for the establishment of the pilot shore station to replace the pilot steamers. The universal use of VHF radio by modern shipping means that the pilot can be put aboard incoming vessels from a fast diesel-engined pilot boat on receiving a radio call at the pilot station from the vessel, advising her expected time of arrival in the bay. Advance notice of vessels expected to arrive and depart is also supplied to the pilot station by the harbour master's office.

The first tugs acquired by the board were used for the towage of the dredging plant, towage of ships being provided by independent operators. Competition between the towage companies was so keen that the tugs used their maximum speed to get out to the bay when a large sailing ship was reported. The 'races' caused problems for other vessels whether proceeding on the river or berthed at the quays because of the wash raised by the tugs. The 1902 act empowered the board to operate a public towage service but this right was invoked only when the tugs were not engaged in towing the board's own vessels. The private operators eventually withdrew and, following the purchase in 1916 of a small tug capable of handling the dredging plant in normal conditions, the tugs *Anna Liffey* and *Majestic* were put on public towage full time. The *Anna Liffey* was withdrawn in 1927 and replaced by the *Coliemore*, formerly the *Foremost 42*, and the *Majestic* was replaced in 1932 by the *Ben Eadar*, formerly the *Foremost 84*.

In addition to their primary duty of harbour towage, the *Coliemore* and *Ben Eadar* featured in a number of salvage and rescue cases during their thirty plus years of service and the increased number and size of steamships arriving at the port provided plenty of work since large vessels, sailing or otherwise, need the assistance of tugs when navigating in confined waters such as river channels and harbours. The tugs were also used for a time as passenger tenders serving liners anchoring in the bay, but perhaps their busiest time was in 1947 when American coal was shipped to Dublin in Liberty ships. It was not uncommon to see six to eight Liberty ships discharging while three or four more anchored in the bay, awaiting berths. The board was under pressure to facilitate quick discharge and accordingly the vessels discharged from 8 a.m. to 10 p.m. with intervals for meals. At each break, a movement of the ships took place, the amount of coal discharged in each period lightening the ship's draught and enabling her to move to a shallower berth. Sometimes this movement would be merely a 'quay' shift which could be effected by the vessel hauling herself along the quay with her own capstans; however the tugs would be required to move vessels from a 28-foot berth at Alexandra Quay to a 26-foot berth in Alexandra Basin, and thence to a 22-foot berth at the North Wall extension; later she would move to the South Quays. As each ship moved, her berth was taken by another and when a vessel was down to 17 feet draught she was ready to be moved to City Quay where she finished discharge; the Liberty coal ships were the largest ever to berth in that section of the port. In addition to the coal ships, the tugs had to attend on large general cargo vessels and oil tankers; in one notable week, they were working almost continuously for fifty-six hours.

In the early 1960s it became obvious that the *Coliemore* was nearing the end of her useful life and the board ordered a new diesel tug to be built by Richard Dunston of Hessle on the Humber, a shipyard specialising in tugs and similar craft. The new tug was delivered in December 1963 and named *Cluain Tarbh*, and the *Coliemore* was withdrawn and sold for scrapping. Ten years later the *Coliemore*'s stable companion for so many years, the *Ben Eadar*, had likewise to be replaced. Her replacement was bought second-hand, but as she was practically a sister ship to the *Cluain Tarbh* and built by the same builders in the same year, she was a suitable and economic purchase. The tug rejoiced in the curious name *Applesider* which was changed to *Coliemore* after her arrival in Dublin in April 1972, following a stormy passage from the Tyne in Force 9 gales before reaching the comparative shelter of the Caledonian Canal, under the command of the deputy harbour master, Captain Paddy Greevy.

The need for a third tug to enable one to be retained as a stand-by, or to assist with the larger vessels using the port, was met by a further order to the Dunston shipyard for a new tug but one with a difference. The new vessel was delivered in March 1973 and given the name *Ben Eadar*, maintaining the tradition of naming the tugs after the prominent headland on the north side of the bay and the well-known small harbour on the south. The difference in the new tug was in the method of propulsion known as Voith Schneider in which the traditional propeller and rudder were replaced by a vertical rotor installed in the hull about one-third of the tug's length from the bow. The tug design was one of a new category described as tractor tugs and the manouevrability achieved was far beyond that available by the standard type of propeller and rudder, a highly desirable feature particularly in a tug.

In 1936 two-way radio was installed on the tugs, pilot steamer and harbour office, to facilitate the passing of information as to ship movements, and following the establishment of the shore station it also was equipped with radio.

The importance of lighthouses to seamen requires no proof and the effect on the port of Dublin of the building of the Poolbeg Lighthouse has been described in Chapter 3. The lighthouse was later increased in height and the original gallery, which appears in contemporary pictures was removed in 1813. Other lighthouses provided by the port board are the North Bull Light, the North Bank Light, the Eastern Breakwater Light, and the North Wall Light. A lighthouse at the end of the North Bull Wall was proposed by Stoney, the port engineer, in 1868 but its erection was not finally approved until 1871, despite repeated representations from ship masters. It is, however, true to say that considerable difficulties were experienced in placing foundations for it but it was eventually completed and lit for the first time in 1880.

In July 1908 a new lighthouse was completed at the North Bank, about midway between the Eastern Breakwater and the North Bull Light. It replaced an older light, known as the Beacon light which was situated close to the site of the new light but somewhat to the south where it formed something of an obstruction in the river channel. It had been intended to remove the Beacon light after the North Bank light became operational, but its removal was precipitated when it was struck and shattered by a steam collier, the *Marquis*, in February 1908. The new light did not escape damage by impact from ships in later years, and eventually it also was replaced by a new reinforced concrete tower easily recognisable by its being constructed on 'stilts', with an automatic (unwatched) light which came into operation in May 1940.

The Eastern Breakwater lighthouse was built in the early 1900s and was first lit in August 1904.

The first North Wall light was built in 1820 at the eastern end of the North Wall Quay roughly where the East Link Toll Bridge joins the North Wall. When the construction of the North Wall Extension was suspended in 1881, a new lighthouse was built at its then eastern extremity. On the completion of the extension in 1937, the lighthouse was moved to its present location at the eastern end of the extension.

The river buoys indicating the north and south limits of the dredged channel were replaced by illuminated buoys in 1899.

On completion in 1950 of the new South Bank Quay to serve the new generating station at Ringsend for the ESB, an automatic flashing red light was established at the eastern end of the quay.

In 1964 automatic apparatus was installed in the Poolbeg Lighthouse which had been tended by lightkeepers since it came into operation in 1767. Although far removed from the bustling activity of the unloading and loading operations at the shipping quays, the lightkeepers at the Poolbeg down the years must have had many stories to tell of the ships which came and went past their lighthouse, and indeed of the tragedies in the bay, particularly in the nineteenth century, many of which would have been visible from the Poolbeg. The Poolbeg lighthouse was the last to be automated and an era in the history of the lighthouses and indeed of the port ended with the withdrawal of the Poolbeg lightkeepers.

To complete the picture of the services and navigational aids provided to ensure the safe navigation of ships within the port, it is necessary to look at the method whereby the extent of dredging required in the port approaches, the river channel and the berths is ascertained. Up to the late nineteenth century depths were ascertained by the age old lead line and later by a mechanical variation of the lead line known as the

Sutcliffe machine. By the 1930s the necessity for greater depths to accomodate larger ships called for precise information to enable dredging plant to be operated in an efficient and economical manner. The science of hydrographic survey was advanced immeasurably with the introduction of the echo sounding machine which generates sound waves; reflected by the river bed, the echoes are picked up by a receiver which translates the continuously recorded echoes on to a calibrated roll of special paper from which the recorded depths can be ascertained. The board's first echo sounder was purchased in 1934 and installed in a specially designed motor launch named, appropriately, *Depthfinder*. With the new apparatus greater depths could be accurately recorded and every variation in the level of the river bed noted. Wrecks of small craft, lost anchors and other items which could be misssed by the older methods were relatively easy to find with the echo sounder which could operate in conditions where even a slight sea could hold up sounding with a lead line or Sutcliffe machine. Relating the depths recorded to the relevant position on the harbour charts was made possible by a system of cross fixes, which was improved and developed by the board's first hydrographic surveyor, the late William F. Staveley.

This brief description of hydrographic surveying at the port of Dublin can give no real indication of the skill and expertise involved, or of Mr Staveley's achievements in this field. His suggestions for improvements in echo sounding apparatus were gladly taken up by the makers Kelvin & Hughes and were internationally recognised. The surveys are also supplied to the pilots and to the Admiralty for inclusion in their charts.

24

Shipbuilding and Ship Repairing

RECORDS of early Dublin shipbuilders and of the ships they built are difficult to trace, although there are references in the city rolls to shipbuilding being carried on in the seventeenth century along the south bank of the Liffey as it was before the building of Sir John Rogerson's Quay. This would be roughly along the line of present-day Townsend Street where the famous *Ouzel Galley* is reputed to have been built; an ouzel (ousel) is a variety of songbird and the term galley was probably merely an addendum to describe the type of vessel. The true story of the *Ouzel* is difficult to distinguish from the legends which grew up to explain her absence from Dublin for five years, following her departure for Mediterranean ports in 1695. The vessel's unexpected arrival back in Dublin in 1700 was no doubt welcomed by the relatives and friends of the crew but it created problems for the commercial interests involved in her outward voyage. Since the vessel had been presumed lost, the underwriters were obliged to pay insurance claims in respect of the ship and her cargo but her belated return posed the problem as to the ownership of the cargo landed since it was not that which was the subject of the original insurance. The controversy was settled when it was submitted to the arbitration of a number of the merchants of the city and the practice of arbitration in commercial disputes became popular as a result, with its attendant advantages of speedy and cheap procedures in contrast to the normal legal processes. A permanent arbitration body was established under the title of the the Ouzel Galley Society which flourished until the early years of the nineteenth century; meanwhile, its importance as a merchants' organisation gave place to a new body known as the Committee of Merchants which was concerned with a much broader range of mercantile issues. This committee in turn was responsible for promoting the idea of a Chamber of Commerce in Dublin in 1783.

Sir William Petty is perhaps best known for his survey of lands confiscated by Cromwell and usually known as the Down survey, carried out in 1655-6. Petty was a man of many parts; he was physician-general to the army and had a high reputation as a mathematician and astronomer. Petty had an abiding interest in ships and the sea and was well versed in the science of navigation. He designed what he claimed to be the first double-hulled vessel in the world, or as he termed it a 'double bottomed machine'. The vessel was described as having been built on the banks of the Liffey 'above the Old Bridge', probably in the vicinity of present-day Ellis Quay or Wolfe Tone Quay. She was launched in 1662 and the mast would probably have been stepped after she was towed seawards of the bridge. Her trials on the river were so successful that early in the following year Petty challenged all boats in the harbour to a sailing 'match' in the bay, possibly the first recorded Dublin Bay sailing race; three challengers appeared but Petty's craft won easily. He arranged for a second similar vessel to be built at Arklow and she out-sailed the mail packet sailing from Holyhead to Howth in July 1663. A third vessel was built for Petty on the Thames; she was named *The Experiment* and made her first voyage to Oporto in April 1665 but was lost with all hands in a storm in the Bay of Biscay on her return voyage. Nothing daunted, Petty returned to Dublin where he had a fourth vessel, fifty feet in length, built at Ringsend but she was so unstable in trials on the river that the crew refused to take her out into the bay. Petty had invested a lot of his own money and that of his friends in his experiments and in his ships and this failure seems to have killed off his interest in ships in general and double hulls in particular.

In 1708 the Ballast Office ordered lighters from shipbuilders James Adair, Nathaniel Dyer and Francis Drake but the location of their yards is unknown. In 1788 a privateer named *Fame* was launched from John King's yard at Ringsend and in 1786 the firm of Cardiff and Kehoe are recorded as operating at City Quay; later the partnership broke up and Cardiff set up at Sir John Rogerson's Quay (see Chapter 6).

In 1801 John Clements of Ringsend built the first of several lifeboats for the port authority and in 1814 the hull of the first steam dredger was built by Anthony Hill at Ringsend. In 1833 George Halpin Senior, in giving evidence to the Commission on Tidal Harbours, stated that there were then only four persons in Dublin engaged in 'building or repairing boats'; their names were given as Clements, Hill, Marshall and Brady.

A revival of shipbuilding at the port was heralded by the setting up of a new shipyard by Thomas Walpole and William Webb in 1862. The shipyard was sited on reclaimed land between the No. 2 graving slip and the graving dock, leased from the port board. The yard's first customer was the board itself which ordered an iron float and the order appears to have been satisfactorily carried out since in the following year three further floats were ordered from the yard whose owners had by then taken in another partner, Thomas Bewley. Contracts for three iron full-rigged ships for English shipowners followed, all of which were delivered before the end of 1865. In the same year the yard's first steamship was launched; this was the *Lady Wodehouse* for the British and Irish Steam Packet Company and thereafter the shipyard concentrated on building steamships, including the steam collier *Dublin* launched in 1866 for the coal merchant Robert Tedcastle.

In 1868, the board considered that the company's successful operations justified their being granted additional land to expand their business. In March 1870 the board ordered three steam screw barges, the first to be delivered early in 1871, but towards the end of 1870 it was clear that the company had overstretched itself and that it would not be able to complete the contract. A Liverpool shipbuilder named Brassey was invited to take over the partly built hull of the first barge and to complete the contract, which was duly carried out.

Walpole dropped out of the firm and Bewley and Webb managed to re-organise their finances sufficiently to continue in the business of repairing vessels; no further ships were built by the company. Their financial problems seem to have stemmed from the fact that there had been no tradition of iron ship construction in Dublin and therefore skilled men had to be recruited ad hoc from Belfast or from cross-channel shipyards. The level of business did not justify retaining a permanent skilled staff and inevitably costs were higher than those in Belfast or cross-channel. The yard slowly declined and by the 1890s, it was practically derelict.

The continued expansion of the port and the growth of its trade had by 1901 brought into focus the lack of ship repairing facilities and the potential advantages to the port and the city if the shipyard could be revived. The Dublin Trades Council instigated a series of meetings at which they, the port board, Dublin Corporation, and the Chamber of Commerce were represented, and considerable publicity attended every move to re-establish the shipyard. Two Scotsmen were interested in the proposal to revive the yard. They were Walter Scott, managing director of a shipyard in Ayr, and John Smellie, chief designer with Denny's shipyard at Dumbarton. Meetings with all the interested parties followed at which it was made clear that the project could be successful only if it could compete with the Scottish yards; this would mean the acceptance by local trade unions of established shipyard practices and wage rates on the Clyde. Agreement was reached on these matters, the port board agreed to grant a lease of the premises, and Scott and Smellie resigned their positions in Scotland to set up under the title of Dublin Dockyard Company.

The sound of rivetting was soon echoing around Alexandra Basin as the new company had suceeded in getting an order for a coasting steamer, the *Gertie*. This ship was launched in November 1902 and she was followed in 1903 by a similar ship, the *Lagan*. A tug for the port board, the *Anna Liffey*, was delivered in 1904 and she was soon followed by vessels for shipowners as far apart as Canada, New Zealand, India, France and Chile, in addition to those for cross-channel owners. Nearer home, we find that a vessel for the Aran Islands service, *Dun Aengus*, was built in the yard; lightships for the Comissioners of Irish Lights, and the fishery cruiser *Helga* which was used to shell Liberty Hall and the GPO in 1916 were also built there. The largest vessel ever built in Dublin was the *Glenstal*, ordered by the Controller of Shipping during the First World War and assigned to Limerick Steamship Company. This ship was 331 feet long and her tonnage was 5,150 gross.

The outbreak of that war in 1914 brought a surge of business to the yard. Ships requisitioned by the Admiralty required to be adapted for carrying the maximum number of troops; in some cases, provision had to be made for carrying horses, wagons and artillery. Steam trawlers were converted for use as armed patrol vessels and minesweepers: and as the war progressed, and British merchant shipping suffered heavy losses, the work of the yard was directed to the repair of damaged vessels, naval and otherwise, and the installation of defensive equipment including guns, submarine detection equipment and mine laying apparatus.

In order to extend the yard from three building berths to five, additional land was leased from the port board and between 1917 and 1919 twelve ships were built for the Controller of Shipping. A high compliment was paid to the yard by the controller when he declared one particular design of the yard to be a standard ship. This was a vessel of 2,450 tons and the yard was ordered to supply other shipbuilders working for the controller with the necessary plans and documentation to enable further vessels of this type to be built.

One large oil tanker, the *Brynton*, presented particular problems to the yard when taken to Dublin for repair since she had suffered damage from a torpedo attack and also from striking a mine; to add to her troubles she had received further damage in a subsequent collision.

Following the retirement of the port engineer, Sir John Purser Griffith, in 1913 he was invited to join the board of the shipyard company. In 1915 he and the other two directors formed an associated company to manufacture shells and a factory was erected for the purpose within the shipyard premises. The building has long since been demolished and the port board's new head office, Port Centre, is located partly on the site.

The yard provided substantial employment in the city for skilled, semi-skilled and unskilled labour, the total number of employees pre-1914 being 700, but this figure doubled during the war.

The port board had undertaken in 1917 to construct a wharf for the shipyard company, running southwards from the east side of the graving dock but although the board's revenues in the period 1914-18 had increased substantially, the increase had been more than offset by increased maintenance and operating costs and no funds were available to provide the promised wharf. Demands from the unions for new wage rates and conditions unrelated to the Clyde conditions punctuated the unsettled political and economic situation in the country generally and in Dublin in particular, in the period 1919-21. The company pointed out that its chances of competing with the Clyde yards in the post-war situation would be destroyed if such claims had to be met. A strike lasting eleven weeks brought no improvement such as had been sought by the unions; on the other hand, the strike had serious effects on the company's commitments which were not assisted by a reduction in pay in 1921 in the cross-channel yards. A second strike followed but it was patched up by a temporary settlement pending discussions with government departments. In 1922 the company found itself unable to continue to pay the higher rates granted under the settlement, and in the following year it went into voluntary liquidation.

Because of its relatively short life, another shipyard which set up in business at Dublin port is hardly known today. As the reclamation of foreshore on each side of Alexandra Road proceeded, the board advertised sites for letting on the reclaimed land from time to time. In 1918 an application for a site for a shipyard was received from the Belfast shipbuilding firm of Workman & Clark but subsequent negotiations with the board were abortive. The proposal had received wide publicity and it was followed in May of the same year by another application, this time from William G. Bailey and Adam H. Gibson who proposed to form a company to build and repair ships at Dublin.

It later became obvious that the skill and expertise of the Workman and Clark yard were involved in the new company. Negotiations with the board were successful and the company was granted a lease of eleven acres to the east of the Alexandra Wharf. In 1919, the new company, entitled Dublin Shipbuilders Limited, announced that it had six ships under construction; these were relatively small coasters of between 500 and 700 tons gross, two of which were regular visitors to the port in subsequent years, the *Moygannon* which regularly carried tar for Irish Tar Distillers Ltd, and the *Lady Anstruther* which brought explosives for Imperial Chemicals Industries Ltd. In 1919 the new company took over the business of the Ringsend Dockyard company which had operated for some years in the Ringsend Docks of the Grand Canal company, using the two small graving docks for the building of small vessels such as the barges used by the Canal company.

The company encountered the same problems as its competitor, the Dublin Dockyard Company, in the matter of labour disputes and for several years its operations were confined to ship repairing. Eventually it was decided to wind up the company voluntarily and the lease was surrendered to the board in 1928. Whether coincidentally or otherwise, the Belfast company of Workman and Clark closed down in the same year. The site of the Dublin Shipbuilders yard was absorbed into the development of the adjacent reclaimed lands and part of it later became the site of the board's warehouse, Stack D, at Alexandra Quay. The Ringsend Dockyard was taken over by other interests and continued in operation until the mid 1960s, its building work being mainly barges for the Canal company while repair work was carried out to vessels on the board's graving slips and in the graving dock.

Notwithstanding the unhappy experience of the older dockyard companies, Bewley & Webb and the Dublin Dockyard Company, there were other shipbuilding concerns convinced of the viability of the original dockyard and in 1923 Vickers of Barrow-in-Furness set up a new company, Vickers (Ireland) Limited, to take over the name and interests of the Dublin Dockyard Company. The first contract secured by the new company was a major overhaul and repair of the dredger *Deepworker*. Between 1923 and 1937 nine vessels were built as follows:

1926	*Kahanui*	Harbour Tug for New Zealand
1927	*Southland*	Harbour Tug for New Zealand
1928	*Maui Pomare*	Cargo ship for New Zealand
1930	*Sligo*	Cargo ship for Sligo Steam Navigation Co.
1931	*Number Eight*	Steam Hopper for Dublin Port and Docks Board
1934	*Glencree*	Collier for ADC Gas Co.
1936	*Number Nine*	Steam Hopper for Dublin Port & Docks Board
1937	*Kilkenny*	Cargo/Livestock ship for B&I

In addition to the above ships, the company built a number of barges for Guinness and the Grand Canal Company, but sixteen years were to pass before another ship was built at Dublin; the problems which had beset the company's predecessors surfaced again. The established policy of adhering to Clyde shipbuilders' wage rates, which were lower than those paid in Dublin to comparable skilled trades, was not acceptable to the trades unions involved and it had become apparent from 1937 onwards that Vickers were considering pulling out of Dublin.

The port board made strenuous efforts to keep the industry alive, even to the extent of pressing the government for a special bill to authorise the board to form a new company for the purpose. In the meantime, the board decided to buy the Dublin Dockyard's interest in the plant, machinery and buildings to save the yard and preserve the possibility of reviving the shipyard business at Dublin. Meetings and preliminary negotiations with government departments and financial institutions were protracted in the years from 1937 to 1940, during which several applications to take over the dockyard were received from interested parties but all proved abortive. Irish shipping interests were very concerned at the loss of the repair facilities in particular which had been available to them since 1902 and in 1940 a group representative of these interests eventually submitted an acceptable proposal to the port board for the formation of a new company to take over and operate the dockyard under the title of Liffey Dockyard Limited. There was no shortage of repair and overhaul work particularly following the establishment of Irish Shipping Limited early in 1941 and its subsequent acquisition of ships, most of which had been marooned in various ports around the world following the outbreak of war in 1939 and all of which were in need of overhaul and repair in varying degrees.

The company was engaged exclusively in ship repair work up to 1952 but in that year it received its first order for building a ship. This was a lightship tender *Isolda* for the Commissioners of Irish Lights to replace the earlier ship of the same name built in the yard in 1928 by the company's predecessors and sunk by German aircraft in December 1940. Post-war conditions and relatively plentiful supplies of steel encouraged, temporarily at least, the resurgence of shipbuilding at Dublin and between 1953 and 1962 nine further vessels were launched from the yard, as follows:

1954	*Irish Fern*	Cargo ship for Irish Shipping Ltd.
1955	*Number Ten*	Steam Hopper for Dublin Port & Docks Board
1956	*Irish Fir*	Cargo ship for Irish Shipping Ltd.
1958	*Naomh Eanna*	Aran Islands ferry for C.I.E.
1958	*Seamrog II*	Sludge vessel for Dublin Corporation
1959	*Curraghour II*	Hopper/dredger for Limerick Harbour Commissioners
1960	*Meath*	Cargo/livestock ship for B&I
1961	*Blarna*	Passenger tender for Cork Harbour Commisioners
1962	*Cill Airne*	Passenger tender for Cork Harbour Commisioners

Over the succeeding five years the business of the dockyard languished and became more and more dependent on Irish shipowners for repair and overhaul work but by 1968 it was evident that the plant and equipment required re-assessment and in many cases renewal, and capital funding was not easy to find. In March 1968 the Liffey Dockyard Company's shares were bought by Mr Archie Kelly, owner of the Ardrossan Dockyard Company. The company continued to operate under its existing name with a new board of which Mr Kelly was chairman.

By 1978 it became clear that the new venture had been no more successful than its predecessors and in March of that year the company sold its interest in the dockyard to Solarship (Ireland) Ltd, a subsidiary of an English group. In granting the new lease the board retained three acres of the dockyard premises for the site of its proposed new head offices. Solarship in turn found it necessary to close in 1981, and the dockyard premises were transferred partly to Arklow Engineering Ltd and partly to Liffey Marine Engineers Ltd, the board retaining the remaining area for its own purposes.

25

Ships and Shipowners

PORTS exist to serve ships and the cavalcade of vessels which has entered Dublin Bay over the centuries has included craft as diverse in type as they have been in purpose. Vessels have been rowed, sailed, or towed or have steamed or motored up the estuary to land explorers, settlers, invaders, traders and cargoes; traditional cargo ships and passenger vessels have given way to container ships, roll-on/roll-off ships and car ferries. It is not easy to establish detailed information on shipping using the port prior to the nineteenth century but in this chapter some of the ships and shipowners associated with the port of Dublin in the nineteenth and twentieth centuries will be reviewed.

In 1803 the largest vessel owned in Dublin was only 300 tons gross; she was the *Columbus* owned by John Furlong. The largest vessel to enter the port that year was the *Copernicus* which at 406 tons was not much larger than the *Columbus* but by 1844 the depths on the bar and in the river channel had been improved sufficiently to enable the *Jane Augusta*, 948 tons gross, to trade regularly to the port.

Increased demand for coal for industrial and domestic purposes was reflected in the number of small sailing colliers owned by Dublin coal merchants, among whom the names of Heiton and Tedcastle will be familiar. Thomas Heiton bought his first two sailing colliers, *Albion* and *Syren*, in 1850. The company continued to operate its own ships up to 1958 and in the 1930s and 1940s the Heiton ships were among the best known in the port, *Saint Mungo, Saint Kenneth, Saint Eunan* and *Saint Fintan*; the last named was sunk off the Welsh coast in March 1941, by German aircraft, while en route to Cardiff to load coal for Dublin. The company acquired another vessel which was also named *Saint Fintan* but after a few trips as a collier she was diverted to cross channel general cargo work.

Robert Tedcastle was operating his own sailing colliers, *Diamond* and *Emerald*, in 1846 and in 1866 his company's first steam collier, *Dublin*, was built by Bewley & Webb in Dublin. The *Dublin* was later converted for carrying passengers and general cargo and, together with a second passenger ship *Magnet,* Tedcastles entered the Dublin-Liverpool passenger trade in 1872. The company had three other ships built for this trade—*Adela* in 1878, *Eblana* in 1892 and *Cumbria* in 1896. In 1875 the company ordered a new paddle tug, the *Toiler,* for public towage at Dublin before the port board took over this work.

Other Dublin coal importers who owned their own ships included S.N. Robinson, P. Donnelly, J.J. Carroll, Michael and William Murphy and John McCormick. In 1897 the last named joined forces with the Tedcastle company to form Tedcastle & McCormick. Among McCormick's ships was one passenger/cargo carrier, *Blackrock,* which joined Tedcastle's Liverpool steamers, charging seven shillings (35p) first-class single fare, and three shillings (15p) for third-class or steerage as it was known; the return fares were ten shillings (50p) and five shillings (25p) respectively. Following the torpedoing of the *Adela* in 1917, the company ordered a new ship, *Killiney,* which was launched in 1918. In her history of the B & I Line, Hazel Smyth states that the area in which the Tedcastle & McCormick vessels berthed (City Quay and Sir John Rogerson's Quay) had a long standing reputation for 'Disaffection with the English'; some members of crews of the company's ships living in the district were involved in gun-running between 1916 and 1922 and it is alleged that when Eamon de Valera escaped from Lincoln gaol in 1919 he was taken to Dublin on the *Cumbria,* returning to Liverpool three days later on the same ship en route to the USA.

When it was first founded, the Dublin Gas Company (Hibernian Gas Company as it was originally known) imported its supplies of coal for production of gas in sailing colliers small enough to negotiate the entrance locks to Ringsend Dock. As the company's requirements increased the coal was delivered to Dublin in larger vessels which, being too large for the Ringsend Dock locks, were berthed at Sir John Rogerson's Quay where they were unloaded by the company's own steam cranes on the quayside, and transferred to the gas works in wagons on a narrow gauge tramway.

In 1919, the company decided to have two steamers built at Lytham, near Preston, with dimensions which would enable them to use the largest of the three entrance locks at Ringsend Dock which was 150 feet long. The first ship was delivered in 1920 and named *Alliance;* she was joined later in the year by the second ship which was named *Glenageary.* In 1921 the *Alliance* was replaced by another new ship from the same yard, the *Glencullen.* The fleet was enlarged to three when the *Glencree* was launched in 1934 at Dublin.

To these three ships, their masters and crews, is due the credit for enabling many Dublin households to use their gas appliances throughout the Emergency of 1939-45, even if on a rationed basis. During those years the three ships suffered attacks by German aircraft; both the

Glencree and the *Glencullen* were bombed and machine-gunned on 21 March 1941 but luckily without casualties while the *Glenageary* was equally fortunate to survive an air attack on 25 October 1941 without any injuries to crew. Both *Glencree* and *Glencullen* were again attacked on 5 November 1941, two of the *Glencree's* crew being wounded on that occasion. In 1946 the company purchased a fourth ship, the *Morion*, a small collier owned by William Robertson of Glasgow, which was renamed *Glenbride* following the change of ownership.

Following the company's decision to change over from coal to oil for the production of its gas, the company's vessels were withdrawn from service in 1968 and the photograph on page 194 taken subsequently by Dr Maurice Craig records one of the few occasions on which the four ships were all in Dublin at the same time.

Another Dublin coal importer which operated its own ships *(Ringwall* and *Broswall)* as late as 1930 was the firm of Wallace Brothers which also used Ringsend Dock for the purpose. Ten years later and in different ownership the *Ringwall* achieved fame when she picked up all 200 passengers and 50 crew of the B&I motor ship *Munster* which was mined in Liverpool Bay in February 1940.

In addition to the Dublin-owned colliers engaged in the import of coal, a number of ships owned by cross-channel and Northern Ireland shipowners and carrying coal to Dublin were such frequent visitors that many of the masters held Dublin Pilotage Certificates, enabling them to navigate into and out of the port without the services of a licensed pilot; indeed the crews were frequently as much at home in Dublin as in their home ports. A comprehensive listing would be impossible for space reasons but among the best known were the 'Rose' boats of Richard Hughes of Liverpool (*Moelfre Rose, Wallace Rose, Dorrien Rose, Wild Rose*), Zillah Shipping and Carrying Company with which was associated the firm of W.A. Savage of Liverpool (*Ashfield, Amy Summerfield, Briarfield, Elmfield, Larchfield, Rowanfield, Silverfield, E. Hayward, Zillah, Sarah Brough*); the 'Gems' of William Robertson of Glasgow (*Gem, Turquoise, Pearl, Beryl, Topaz, Spinel, Pyrope, Prase, Citrine, Cairngorm*) and the John Kelly ships from Belfast (*Cushendall, Cushendun, Annaghmore, Oranmore, Clandeboye, Tamnamore, Glengarriff, Melissa*).

The name of Martin has been associated with the timber trade in Dublin since the 1830s and the partnership of the brothers Thomas and Charles Martin commenced shipping their timber stocks from Canada in their own Canadian-built sailing ships in 1839. Another member of the Martin family, Richard (later Sir Richard Martin, Baronet, Deputy Lieutenant and Justice of the Peace) was, as noted in chapter 17, a member of the port authority for over thirty-six years and chairman in the years 1899, 1900 and 1901. Richard had his own timber business, located at Sir John Rogerson's Quay and the berth used for the landing of his cargoes near Cardiff Lane is still frequently referred to as 'Martin's berth' notwithstanding its official description as Berth No. 5. In 1881 Richard decided to diversify his business and went into shipowning with a small sailing ship, *Lady Cairns,* 265 tons. Between 1883 and 1892 six further vessels were acquired and the Richard Martin fleet thereby became the largest fleet of iron or steel-hulled square rigged ships to be registered in Dublin. These vessels carried cargoes between Europe, North and South America and Australia and the best known of them were the barques *Finglas, Rathdown* and *Howth*—all over 2,000 tons gross, and the smaller *Dunboyne.* The *Rathdown* was the fastest vessel in the fleet but was lost without trace in 1900. Several members of the board's staff in the 1930s and 1940s had served aboard the *Howth* in her Cape Horn days, including Captain William Dowling, master of the *Sandpiper* and Berthing Master William Dalton; the second mate, Thomas Walsh, was uncle to Captain Hubert Walsh, Dublin harbour master from 1967 to 1973. Following the death of Sir Richard Martin in 1901, the company gradually went out of shipowning, the last vessel to be sold being the *Howth* in 1910, and in 1926 the company closed down and its timber trade was taken over by T.&C. Martin.

The largest commercial sailing vessels to trade to Dublin were the grain ships, usually from Australia but sometimes from Canada, and of these the best-known visitors were probably the famous 'P' ships—*Pamir, Passat* and *Pommern.* Other 'tall ships' calling to Dublin were the *Archibald Russell* and *Abraham Rydberg.*

At the other end of the scale the best known of the small sailing vessels have been the Arklow sailing ships which hold a proud place in Irish maritime history. Many of these ships were built in Arklow from the mid nineteenth century onwards at the famous Tyrrell shipyard. Arklow-built vessels, including schooners, ketches, brigs, brigantines and barquentines, traded as far afield as Portugal, Spain and South America; other Arklow owned ships which had been built at cross-channel yards traded as far as the Baltic sea and the Black Sea. Up to the 1950s the Arklow ships were used mainly for carrying coal, china clay, grain, sand, bricks, malt and oats on Irish coastal and cross-channel runs. Ships carrying bricks held their own fascination by reason of the skill of the dockers in unloading the cargo; one man in the hold of the ship would toss four bricks at a time up to another on the deck who in turn would transfer them in the same manner to a third man standing on the quay who would load them usually on a horse-drawn dray, a system which was probably centuries old. The names of the Arklow ships form a tapestry of their own in the history of Irish merchant ships and practically every port, large or small, in Ireland has been host to *Agnes*

Craig, Antelope, Cymric, De Wadden, Gaelic, Happy Harry, Harvest King, Invermore, J.T.&S., James Postlethwaite, Mary B. Mitchell, M.E. Johnson, Venturer and *Windermere*. The *Gaelic* and *Mary B. Mitchell* are believed to have been used as 'Q' ships (decoy ships which appeared to be ordinary sailing vessels but were armed and manned by naval personnel) during the First World War. The *Mary B. Mitchell* and the *Cymric* made voyages to Lisbon during the Second World War and following the withdrawal of British colliers from their ordinary duties in June 1944 to support the invasion of Normandy, all the Arklow vessels except the *Cymric* were pressed into service to maintain coal supplies to the Republic. The *Cymric* was posted missing in February of that year when she was on a voyage to Lisbon.

Gradually, the remaining Arklow ships disappeared from the fleet lists; six were wrecked, five scrapped and two were sold off to foreign owners. By 1961 the last of the Arklow fleet was gone as indeed was the day of the coasting sailing vessel, but the Arklow owners had already turned to motor ships, including the *Halronall* and *Tyrronall*.

The only Irish sailing ship calling to Dublin in the 1980s has been the sail training brigantine *Asgard* which continues the Arklow sailing ship tradition, having been launched from John Tyrrell's yard in 1981.

A proposal in 1886 by the owners of the *Great Eastern*, London Traders Ltd, that the vessel should visit Dublin was not welcomed by the port board although it was greeted by the public at large, many of whom wished to see a ship which was four times larger than any other ship in the world. During her building and protracted launching at Millwall on the Thames, the *Great Eastern* had become a continuous source of colourful copy for newsmen; this was small wonder since her dimensions and design proclaimed that she would be an extraordinary vessel. She was almost 700 feet long, 120 feet beam over the paddle boxes, loaded draft 30 feet and she had two sets of engines—one for the 56-feet diameter paddle wheels and another for the 24-feet diameter propellor which weighed thirty-six tons. In addition to the mechanical propulsion, her crew could set 6,400 square yards of sail on her six masts if need be. Potential passengers were assured of a Grand Salon and general accommodation which would not only be far ahead of the standards of the largest existing passenger liners but would rival those of the most luxurious hotels ashore. No doubt her gross tonnage of 18,000 impressed the public as did the five funnels, twenty anchors and twenty lifeboats.

In the event, the grand design did not quite work out as envisaged by the ship's designer, Isambard Kingdom Brunel; the building costs outran the estimates long before the ship was completed. The project was taken over by another company and considerable cutbacks became necessary in the passenger accommodation, amenities and equipment.

The vessel was dogged by bad luck before she even took the water for the first time. Her great (for those days) length had made it necessary for her to be launched sideways but her enormous weight made the sideways movement so difficult that she was not finally launched until the fourth attempt on 30 January 1858. On the first occasion, two workmen were killed by a runaway windlass. Brunel was too ill to attend the ship's first intended sailing on 7 September 1859; within her first twenty-four hours at sea an explosion in the boiler engine room killed five firemen and blew out a funnel. The ship managed to reach Holyhead where she remained until May of the following year when she was taken back to Southampton for repairs. The master of the *Great Eastern* at this time was Captain William Harrison, a Cunard officer on loan for the purpose of the first voyage. When going ashore at Southampton in the ship's gig, Captain Harrison and two others were drowned when the boat capsized in a squall.

The ship's first transatlantic voyage to New York was eventually made in 1861 without mishap, but on her second trip later in the same year both paddle boxes were smashed in a storm and she had to limp back to Cork. Her third transatlantic crossing in 1862 ended when she struck a rock off Long Island; repairs at New York took a year, to say nothing of a small fortune paid to the shipyard. Two further voyages were financial disasters and in 1865 the *Great Eastern* was sold by auction. She was then employed in cable laying and was used for the laying of the first transatlantic submarine cable from Valentia Island, Co. Kerry to New York; her chief officer for that project was Wicklow-born Robert Halpin who later became master of the ship at the age of thirty-three. Halpin was in command for subsequent cable laying work until she was laid up at Milford Haven in 1874. Eleven years later she was bought and chartered out for use as a veritable travelling advertisement hoarding-cum-showboat.

In view of the vessel's chequered history, it was small wonder that in 1886 the Dublin port board was loth to accept the ship at Dublin, much less to agree to the owners' proposal that she should berth at the new North Wall Extension where the public could visit her. Eventually, the board agreed that she could come to the port but that she should be taken on arrival to the eastern end of the then undeveloped Alexandra Basin where she would have to lie aground at low water. The board's objections to a berth at the North Wall Extension were two-fold; she would be taking up berthage equal to that of three or four ordinary cargo ships, and, because of her size and weight the possibility of her being blown off the berth in a gale and becoming stranded across the river between the North Wall Extension and Ringsend, thus effectively blocking the port for a long period, was a risk that was unacceptable. However, the master of the vessel was not prepared to risk his ship taking the ground at low water in the proposed anchorage at Alexandra Basin; after the pilot boarded her on her arrival in the bay on 14 October 1886 and had taken the ship up the river, he found that he could not with safety take her into Alexandra Basin and the ship was, after all, brought to the North Wall Extension—to the dismay of the board.

As both master and pilot were acting in the interests of the safety of the ship, it was difficult to find a legal objection or grounds for enquiry so far as the pilot was concerned. However, the board was not prepared to acquiesce in the owners' proposals to open the ship to the public and to provide bars and entertainment, and an application by the owners to the court for a 'licence for the sale of intoxicants' was successfully opposed by the board. The proposal to admit the public was more difficult to counteract since at that stage there was no boundary wall to the board's property at East Wall, nor entrance gates guarding the North Wall Extension. There was nothing to be done except to try to control the crowds who thronged to the North Wall Extension; there was less difficulty with those who availed of the company's passenger tender *Cambria,* which had accompanied the ship from Holyhead and on which sightseers could travel downriver from Custom House Quay, board the ship and view her for a small charge.

The board was unable to find legal means to have the vessel removed under the law as it stood and she was still berthed at the North Wall Extension when the new year of 1887 dawned. Even if legal remedies could have been found and enforced there was still danger to the ship herself and to other shipping if she were to be moved to another berth or to the proposed anchorage in Alexandra Basin. News that the ship had been sold to a new owner, who intended taking her to the Clyde, brought great relief to both members and officers of the port board and on 3 April 1887 the *Great Eastern* left Dublin, having enthralled many sightseers, distracted the board and disrupted port operations for almost six months. The ship was eventually sold for scrap in 1889 and broken up at Liverpool.

The early history of the City of Dublin Steam Packet Company and of the British & Irish Steam Packet Company (known nowadays as the B&I Line) has been sketched in Chapter 12. In 1917 a number of shipping companies operating on cross-channel routes, including B&I came together to form the UK based Coast Lines Group. Following the failure of the City of Dublin Company in 1919, the B&I had taken over the assets of that company including four ships which had been used for a twice daily passenger/cargo service between Dublin and Liverpool. These were the *Wicklow, Kerry, Louth* and *Carlow* and in accordance with B&I tradition, they were given the prefix 'Lady' to their names in 1920. These ships were, however, replaced by a new generation of passenger ships specially built for B&I at Ardrossan. These were a new *Lady Louth*, launched in 1923, *Lady Limerick* launched in 1924 and a third similar ship which had been built at the same yard in 1921 for the City of Cork Steam Packet Company, which was also a member of the Coast Lines Group; this was the *Ardmore*, renamed *Lady Longford* by the B&I. In 1929 these three ships were transferred to another company within the group, Burns & Laird Lines, and they were replaced by three ships formerly operated between Belfast & Liverpool by the Belfast Steamship company, yet another group member. The replacement ships were the *Heroic, Patriotic*, and *Graphic*, renamed *Lady Connaught, Lady Leinster* and *Lady Munster* by the B&I. These vessels had all been built in the early years of the century but they were somewhat larger than their younger predecessors.

In 1936 the B&I took over the City of Cork company as a wholly owned subsidiary.

By the mid-1930s it became evident that the Liverpool service could be operated more efficiently and economically with two modern motor ships than by the three old steamships and in 1938 two new motor vessels were launched from the Harland & Wolff yard in Belfast for the B&I. Their gross tonnage was 4,300 tons and their equipment and accomodation were regarded as far superior to that of any other cross-channel ship of the day; the company having decided to drop the prefix 'Lady' from their ship's names, the new ships were named *Leinster* and *Munster* and thereafter all the company's passenger ships were named after provinces, while county or town names were retained for the cargo ships.

On the outbreak of war in 1939 the Liverpool service was suspended and the two ships were withdrawn; it should be remembered that Coast Lines was a UK group. The *Munster* was transferred to Belfast/Liverpool service and, as already noted, she was sunk by a mine in 1940. The *Leinster* survived the war, having served throughout as a hospital ship; in 1945 she was placed on the Belfast/Liverpool service and renamed *Ulster Prince*. In 1946 the B&I ordered two new replacement ships from Harland & Wolff which were slightly longer than their predecessors although the gross tonnage was slightly smaller; otherwise the accomodation and appearance of the new ships was very similar to that of the previous vessels. Maintaining the company's tradition in the matter of names, the new ships were called *Leinster* (4,115 tons gross) and *Munster* (4,142 tons gross) and they took up the Liverpool service in 1948.

In 1965 the Irish government bought out the Coast Lines Group's interest in B&I and appointed a new board which, two years later, decided to replace the conventional passenger ships with ro-ro car ferries of which three were ordered—two for the Dublin/Liverpool service and one for the Cork/Swansea (later Pembroke) service.

The new ferry service from Dublin was opened in May 1968 with the first ship, which was built in Hamburg and named *Munster*; she was joined in 1969 by the second ship *Leinster*, built at the Verolme Dockyard, Cork. By the mid 1970s it appeared that the ships were inadequate for the demands of the service and orders were placed for two new and larger ferries. In 1979 the *Munster* was replaced by a new ferry *Connacht* built at Verolme; with a gross tonnage of 6,812 she was the largest vessel ever built or owned by the B&I. In 1981 the *Connacht* was joined on the service by a new *Leinster*, 6,808 tons gross, a sister ship, which was also built at Verolme.

In 1980 the B&I opened a new daylight passenger service to Liverpool using a jetfoil; as the single journey took just over three hours it was possible to operate two services in each direction in summertime. The jetfoil was not successful for a number of reasons and the service was suspended at the end of the 1981 season.

In 1982 the company opened a service to Holyhead which developed into a double daily service in each direction in 1988 when the Liverpool service was discontinued.

Space does not allow of a detailed account of the B & I cargo ships but they are comprehensively dealt with in Hazel Smyth's book. One ship, however, calls for special notice. This was the *Wicklow*, formerly regarded as one of the City of Dublin crack ships on the Liverpool service between 1895 when she was built and 1919 when she was taken over by B&I and renamed *Lady Wicklow*. With the arrival of the three new passenger ships in the early 1920s, the *Lady Wicklow* was transferred to general cargo and livestock work. In this less glamorous capacity she served the company until she was withdrawn in 1949 (by then having reverted to the name *Wicklow*) having completed fifty-four years service, a record equalled by few of the many ships which have traded regularly to Dublin down the years.

Associated with the B&I within the Coast Lines Group (i.e. before 1965) was the Burns & Laird Line company which operated passenger, cargo and livestock sailings to Glasgow. The best known of their many vessels on this service in the 1930s were the former B&I steamships which had been transferred to Burns & Laird in 1929 and renamed *Lairdshill*, *Lairdsburn* and *Lairdscastle*. This service was taken over in 1953 by a new motor ship the *Irish Coast* which was joined by another new vessel *Scottish Coast* in 1956; both vessels were somewhat similar to the B&I motor ships commissioned in 1948 and built by the same Belfast yard. The Burns & Laird Line closed its Dublin passenger operation in 1968, although the livestock operation continued until 1973.

The long conflict lasting from the mid nineteenth century until 1919

between the City of Dublin Steam Packet Company and the London &
North Western Railway Company was summarised in Chapter 13. In
1921 the LNWR became the London Midland & Scottish Railway
Company and although the passenger ships had been withdrawn from
Dublin in 1908 and transferred to Kingstown, the railway company's
cargo ships continued to operate to Dublin as did those of its
successors-in-title British Transport Commission, British Rail and
Sealink. The best known of these ships were the *South Stack, Slieve
Gallion, Slieve Donard, Slieve More, Slieve Bawn* and *Slieve League*.
Following the change over by Sealink to unit loads in 1970 and the
inauguration of new container terminals at Holyhead and Dublin, two
new container ships were built for the service, *Brian Boroime* and
Rhodri Mawr.

The summer service from Dublin to Douglas, Isle of Man, has always
been popular with Irish holiday-makers. This service has been in
operation since 1842 by the Isle of Man Steam Packet Company, with
the exception of the years 1914-18, and 1939-45 when many of the
company's fleet were taken over for use as troop transports or fleet
auxiliaries. Most of the nineteenth-century fleet were paddle steamers
but from 1905 screw ships were bought in, principally from railway
companies operating cross-channel services; a large fleet was necessary
to maintain the intensive summer sailing schedules from Liverpool,
Fleetwood, Heysham, Ardrossan, Belfast and, of course, Dublin. The
first new ships built for the company for many years were the *Ben-My-
Chree, Lady Of Mann,* and *Mona's Queen* between 1927 and 1934, all
with highly individual profiles and all frequent visitors to Dublin; later
additions to the fleet in 1936 were the *Tynwald* and *Fenella,* somewhat
smaller than the previous three ships but heralding a new standard
design for the fleet. These five ships, together with eight older steam
turbine vessels, made up the company's fleet in 1939. Wartime losses
left the company with only two of the modern ships and eight steamers
of advanced age; a programme of new ships was embarked on and soon
the new ships appeared at Dublin, all bearing names of the older vessels,
names which were very familiar in the port: *Ben-My-Chree, Mona's
Isle, Manxman, Manx Maid, Tynwald, Snaefell,* and *King Orry*.

Although it had always been possible to ship passengers' motor cars
aboard the Isle of Man ships at Liverpool and some of the other UK
ports, the facility was not available at Dublin until the company
replaced its conventional ships with car ferries which were independent
of the normal ro-ro shore installation. This was achieved by a spiral set
of ramps linking with the car deck so that cars can be driven on or off at
the appropriate level irrespective of the state of the tide in the port.
From the commencement of the service in 1846 the IOM ships had
berthed at Sir John Rogerson's Quay but following the withdrawal of

the conventional Liverpool passenger service in 1968 the Douglas service operated from the old Liverpool berth; following the arrival of the car ferries in 1974, they were berthed at the Liverpool berth and later at the former Burns & Laird berth where facilities for passengers awaiting embarkation were minimal. However, since the withdrawal of the jetfoil service in 1981, the IOM car ferries have used the terminal at Custom House Quay formerly used by the jetfoil, which has modern passenger facilities.

A lesser known service between Dublin and Douglas, which extended also to Silloth, was operated by the Dublin, Douglas & Silloth company from 1893 to 1929 with a passenger/cargo/livestock ship named *Yarrow*. Unlike the IOM company's service the *Yarrow* operated throughout the year carrying mainly livestock and a small amount of general cargo; her passenger accomodation was limited and was used mainly by cattle traders. In 1929 the company was taken over by Palgrave Murphy Ltd, the ship being renamed *Assaroe* and she was operated by a subsidiary company of Palgrave Murphy until the service was withdrawn in the 1940s. The *Assaroe's* service life gave her the right to challenge the *Wicklow* for the longest service record on Irish sea trades to Dublin.

In 1975 the P&O Steam Navigation Company formed a subsidiary to operate a new ro-ro freight service between Dublin and Fleetwood in association with the B&I. The new company's name was Pandoro and the service was carried at different times by the *Bison* and *Buffalo*; later the *Ibex* and the *Tipperary* took over the route.

One of the earliest companies to operate paddle steamers from Dublin was the St George Steam Packet Company which opened a service from Dublin to Liverpool in 1822 with their first ship, *St George*. A second ship *St Patrick* commenced trading from Dublin to Bristol in the same year and later both ships operated a Dublin/Bristol/Liverpool service. The company's subsequent history is bound up with that of the War Office Steam Packet Company, which, through various groupings and re-groupings, led in modern times to Bristol Seaway Ltd, the trading link between Dublin and Bristol being maintained throughout until the closure of the latter company's Dublin operation in 1980. The names of the company's ships had classical connotations: *Argo*, *Pluto*, *Cato*, *Melito*, *Juno* and *Capito* amongst others. The War Office company had been established by the British government for the transport between Britain and Ireland of troops and convicts.

Another company with long associations with Dublin was the Clyde Shipping Company which operated a weekly round trip cargo service with limited passenger accommodation from Glasgow to Dublin, calling at Waterford and Cork before returning to Glasgow. The best known ships on this service were *Fastnet, Rathlin, Rockabill, Toward* and *Tuskar,* all named after lighthouses. Before the port board opened a public towage service, the Clyde company had operated a towage service at Dublin for many years. The company closed its cargo service to Dublin in 1960 after over a hundred years trading.

The ships of two closely associated companies were among the best known trading to Dublin. These were the ships owned by Palgrave Murphy and the Ulster Steamship Company, better known as the 'Head' Line because of the company's policy of naming their ships after prominent Irish headlands. The Head Line merged with the Lord Line in 1917, acquiring the *Lord Antrim, Lord Londonderry* and *Lord Downshire* in the process and adding further to the confusion since the names 'Ulster Steam', 'Head Line' and 'Lord Line' were used indiscriminately to refer to the same company. Head Line ships operated usually between Belfast, Dublin, Montreal and Quebec. Among the regular ships on these routes were the *Melmore Head, Kenbane Head, Dunaff Head,* and since 1945, *Ramore Head, Torr Head, Roonagh Head* and *Fanad Head.* The company had smaller ships engaged on continental services, including *Bengore Head, Teelin Head, Orlock Head* and *Fair Head.* In 1934 a subsidiary of Palgrave Murphy was formed, Saorstat and Continental Steamship Company, to take over and operate Head Line ships on these short sea routes, the names of the ships being changed to correspond with the cities served, *City of Limerick, City of Ghent, City of Dublin, City of Waterford, City of Cork* etc. In July 1940 the *City of Limerick* was sunk by German aircraft in the North Atlantic with the loss of two of her crew. The *City of Waterford* survived three attacks before being sunk in 1941 with the loss of five crew. In the post-war years the company expanded its fleet on its continental services and in 1969 it merged with Limerick Steamship Company as part of the Hibernian Transport Group which consisted of six companies. The failure of the group in 1970 had serious repercussions both for the staffs of the component companies and for the group's creditors.

In October 1941 a ship with an unfamiliar name arrived in Dublin from Lisbon with a cargo of grain. She was the *Vassilios Destounis,* the first ship to be bought by the new Irish Shipping company in March of that year. Her voyage to Dublin had been delayed by necessary major repairs and other factors. On arrival she was renamed *Irish Poplar* and she was soon followed by nine more ships acquired by the company and renamed *Irish Elm, Irish Beech, Irish Hazel, Irish Larch, Irish Pine, Irish Oak, Irish Willow* and *Irish Fir.* In 1942 the company acquired four more ships which were renamed *Irish Rose, Irish Alder, Irish Spruce* and *Irish Ash.* Two of the fleet were sunk by torpedo attack, the *Irish Pine* in November 1942 and the *Irish Oak* in May 1943; there were no survivors from the *Irish Pine* but the crew of the *Irish Oak* were picked up by the *Irish Plane*. In 1943 the company chartered its last wartime acquisition, an Italian ship named *Caterina Gerolomich*, 5,430 tons gross, which had been laid up at Dublin since 1940; she was renamed *Irish Cedar* and with the exception of the two vessels sunk in 1942 and 1943, she was the largest of the wartime acquisitions.

Between 1941 and 1945 the vessels of Irish Shipping Ltd brought over one million tons of badly needed commodities to this country, including wheat, coal, timber, phosphate, tobacco, newsprint and general cargo. Several generations of new ships carrying the old names were commissioned by Irish Shipping in between 1945 and 1977 and while most of the intermediate size ships were regular visitors to Dublin, the later and larger ships were built primarily for charter work and seldom came to Dublin.

The ships owned by Limerick Steamship Company and Wexford Steamship Company, small though they were in comparison to Irish Shipping's fleet, were equally valuable to the country during the Second World War and equally vulnerable to attack by aircraft and submarines in the course of voyages to and from Lisbon. Three of the Limerick company's ships were sunk, *Clonlara*, *Kyleclare* and *Luimneach*, with a total loss of twenty-nine crew members and although their *Lanahrone* was attacked she survived and with no casualties. The Wexford ships *Edenvale*, *Kerlogue* and *Menapia* all suffered attacks resulting in six casualties including two of the *Menapia*'s crew and the master of the *Kerlogue*, Captain Desmond Fortune, and three of his crew; all suffered very serious wounds.

It is difficult to understand why a solitary and lowly fishing trawler should be picked out for attack by German aircraft. None the less the Dublin Trawling Company's *Kosmos* was the target for such an attack in September 1940; although the vessel was damaged there were no casualties among the crew. A sister ship, the *Leukos*, was not so fortunate; she was reported missing with all hands in the same year and it is difficult to avoid the conclusion that she had been attacked. The two ships were part of a fleet of trawlers operating out of Dublin for many years, including the *Tom Moore*, *Father O'Flynn*, *Sapphire*, *Mannofield* and *Henry Grattan*, which usually discharged their cargoes of fish at Great Britain Quay.

Although visits to Dublin port by foreign naval vessels have become a regular feature in the port they always attract considerable attention, whether they be American, Canadian, Argentinian, French, German, Norwegian, Swedish, Dutch, Danish, Spanish, Italian or Portuguese— all of whom have been guests of the port over the years. The largest naval vessel to visit Dublin was the US aircraft carrier *Saipan* in 1952, accompanied by two destroyers and a supply ship. The sail training ships of many of these nations are perhaps even more popular with the public, bringing as they do an indication of how the port looked in the days of sail. The best known of the training ships, because of their regular visits, are the Italian *Amerigo Vespucci* and the Spanish *Juan Sebastian de Elcano*. Our own *Asgard* is, of course, frequently seen in the port.

Among the more unusual ships to call at Dublin have been the nuclear powered liner *Savannah* in 1964 and the 39,000 ton Seabee barge-carrier *Tille Lykes* in 1976. The draft of the latter (39 feet) was too great to permit of her berthing at the quays and arrangements were made for her to anchor in the bay where her barges were floated out of the hold of the ship and taken in tow by the board's tugs. The barges were then taken to the 100-ton crane where their 'contents' were lifted off. These were eighteen diesel locomotives consigned to CIE which had been built in Illinois by General Motors, loaded on the barges and taken down the Illinois and Mississippi rivers to New Orleans where they were loaded on the *Tillie Lykes* for transport to Dublin. The Dublin operation depended on a high degree of co-operation and timing for all phases of the project and many tributes were paid subsequently to those of the board's staff concerned for the expeditious manner in which the whole operation was carried out.

An unusual vessel insofar as her appearance is concerned is the modern car carrier, an example of modern shipbuilding technology producing a highly efficient, functional and economic machine for the transport of motor cars in large numbers although somewhat lacking, to say the least, in the graceful lines which characterised the old clipper ships and, indeed, some of the twentieth-century steamships.

Visits by large cruising liners are commonplace nowadays and they create few problems for the harbour master and his staff having regard to the deepwater facilities now available in the port, particularly since usually only one liner at a time requires to be catered for. The situation during the Eucharistic Congress in 1932 was complicated by the fact that seven liners had to be berthed at the quays and the depths of water on the bar, the river channel and the berths were considerably shallower than at present; furthermore the length of deepwater berthage available was relatively limited.

The liners which berthed at the quays in that memorable week were:

Berth	Ship	Line	Gross tonnage
Alexandra Quay	Duchess of Bedford	Canadian Pacific	20,123
	Doric	White Star	16,484
Alexandra Basin	Dresden	North German Lloyd	14,690
	Sierra Cordoba	North German Lloyd	11,469
	De Grasse	French Line (C.G.T.)	17,962
Crossberth	Rio Bravo	Spanish	5,946
Sir John	Marnix Van Sint	Dutch	19,129
Rogerson's Quay	Aldegonde		

In addition the following five ships anchored in Dublin Bay:

Saturnia	Italian Line	23,940
Samaria	Cunard	19,597
Laconia	Cunard	19,695
Antonia	Cunard	13,869
Lapland	Red Star Line	18,866

In the 1960s and 1970s the most frequent caller was the Cunard *Caronia* which regularly anchored in Scotsman's Bay. Ocean Pier has been the berth for more recent visitors including the West German *Europa* (33,819 tons); the French-owned *Mermoz* (13,691); the *Vistafjord* (24,492 tons) which, in spite of her Norwegian name, is owned by Cunard, and the *Royal Viking Sea* (28,400) which, in spite of her English name, is owned in Norway.

Finally we come to a company whose export operations have been part and parcel of the Dublin docks scene for almost 200 years, and whose organisation has been of major significance in the development of the country's export trade and in terms of employment in the city and elsewhere.

The Guinness brewery's earliest record of exports is dated 1796 but Mr Harry Hannon, former distribution director of Guinness Ireland Limited, has stated that there are grounds for believing that the association with the port goes back to the foundation of the company in 1759; the company's earliest foreign exports are believed to have been a shipment to the West Indies in the early 1800s. Up to 1913 the company used regular shipping services or chartered ships but in December of that year it acquired its first ship, the *W.M. Barkley,* which was formerly a steam collier built at Troon in 1898 for the Belfast firm of John Kelly. Direct ownership proving successful, the company bought three more Kelly ships, the *Carrowdore, Clareisland* and *Clarecastle,* the first named in 1914 and the other two in 1915. However all three ships were commandeered by the government for war service and did not return to the company's service until 1919. In the meantime, the career of the *W.M. Barkley* ended when, following a torpedo attack by a German submarine near the Kish lightship in October, 1917, she sank with the loss of her master and four of the crew.

The remaining three ships maintained the company's export trade to the United Kingdom until 1931 when a new ship, the *Guinness,* was launched for the company; she was specially designed to carry 800 tons of stout in the traditional wooden casks on the Dublin/London run. With the arrival of the *Guinness,* the *Clareisland* was sold, and the *Guinness, Carrowdore* and *Clarecastle* maintained the company's trade to London, Liverpool and Manchester until 1938 when following the opening of the company's new brewery at Park Royal, London, all three vessels were engaged on the Liverpool/Manchester trade. The three vessels came through the Second World War relatively unscathed although the *Carrowdore* had a narrow escape when in 1941 she was attacked by a German bomber about fifteen miles off the Irish coast; luckily, the bomb ricochetted off the forecastle into the sea before exploding; the fin of the bomb was caught by deck fittings and is retained in the Dublin brewery as a souvenir.

The *Carrowdore* was replaced in 1952 by a new motor ship *The Lady Grania*, which was specially designed for the transport of stout in transportable circular tanks instead of wooden casks. The tanks were made of stainless steel and aluminium and had a capacity of 500 gallons. In the following year the *Clarecastle* was replaced by another motor ship, also specially designed for the transport of the new tanks; this was *The Lady Gwendolen*. In 1963 the *Guinness* was replaced by another new ship, *The Lady Patricia*, and the three 'ladies' carried the company's trade until 1977 when a new concept in the transport of stout appeared in the form of a new ship, *Miranda Guinness*. This vessel was the first to be specially designed for the transport of stout in bulk and the method of loading and unloading is somewhat similar to that used for oil tankers, by which oil products are pumped aboard or ashore through flexible pipelines. Fifteen stainless steel tanks are permanently installed in the *Miranda*'s hold, with a capacity equal to that of 6,500 barrels, and the stout is pumped aboard from a fleet of road tankers which were also specially designed. The loading and unloading operations and the condition and temperature of the cargo throughout the voyage is continuously monitored on a special console located on the bridge. Following the arrival of the *Miranda*, *The Lady Gwendolen* was sold off in 1977.

For many years, the company used berths at Custom House Quay, directly opposite the Custom House, for their Liverpool trade while the vessels on the London and Manchester routes were berthed at City Quay. The Custom House has provided a dignified background to shipping operations since the early nineteenth century, as illustrated in many contemporary drawings and paintings; in modern times the scene has attracted photographers, both professional and amateur, who were anxious to have two major features of Dublin life in one shot. With the proposal to build a new bridge, the Talbot Memorial bridge, east of the Custom House, all the company's port operations were transferred to City Quay. Stout is exported in containers to other destinations throughout the world via regular shipping services.

Many Dubliners will have memories going back, perhaps, to childhood of watching the Guinness barges steaming downriver with a full cargo of casks of stout to be hoisted aboard the company's ships at Custom House Quay or City Quay, or returning upriver to the brewery wharf at Victoria Quay, near Kingsbridge (now Heuston) station, laden with returned empty casks. The high point of this spectacle was the adroit lowering of the barge's hinged funnel as the vessel approached each bridge over the river, giving rise to speculation among some onlookers as to the consequences should the crewman operating the funnel miss his cue; if personal recollections are anything to go by, the speculation was tinged on occasion with sadistic hopes for the worst. Although there is no record of any such calamity ever having occurred, one of the barges, *Docena*, sank in the river near the Custom House with a full cargo of stout in August 1927. Most of the casks were recovered from the river but some were washed up in various parts of the English and Welsh coasts; one particularly adventurous cask made its way to the Isle of Skye where its subsequent fate is a matter for conjecture.

Equally familiar, if less of a spectacle than the barges, were the drays driven by men in the company's traditional cream-coloured corduroy jackets and trousers with black bowler hats, which in the days before motor transport took over, distributed the stout to the company's customers throughout the city and suburbs. The drays, drawn by the company's famous Clydesdale horses, with gleaming brasswork on their harness, were also a feature at the special competitions in the Royal Dublin Spring and Horse shows.

With the withdrawal of the barges and the drays, the city and the port lost features which, notwithstanding their prosaic functions, endeared themselves to many generations almost as much as did the cargo, and while the squat functional outlines of the company's modern motor ships are essentially dictated by the economies of modern transport, there are some shiplovers who regret the passing of the former Kelly/Guinness steamers with their distinctive profiles and tall cowled funnels.

It has not been possible within the limits of this chapter to refer to the many other ships and shipowners which have traded to the port over the last two centuries but all have found at Dublin a port which was once described by Elizabeth I as 'most commodious and not easily to be overthrown.' The last part of the statement has had a validity that the queen could not have foreseen, having regard to the resilience of the port authority in meeting and overcoming apparently insuperable difficulties in its task of providing and maintaining a port geared to meet the needs of the city and of the nation.

Conclusion

IT might appear impertinent, if not audacious, for a non-historian to attempt to compress several millenia of the history of the Liffey estuary within a few hundred pages. When this book was planned, its justification seemed obvious—the fact that no detailed history of the port of Dublin had ever been written, or at least could be traced if we except the preliminary work of Charles Haliday.

Now that the task has been completed, I believe that the real justification will depend on its success in conveying some idea of the difficulties and achievements of those who, in whatever capacity and whether connected with the port authority or otherwise, contributed to the transformation over the centuries of the banks and channels of the Liffey estuary into the modern port of Dublin. More importantly perhaps, it will be justified if it succeeds in evoking some realisation of the essential rôle which the port of Dublin has played and continues to play in the economic life of the state, and of the port board as a self-supporting public authority, a *rara avis* at any time but more particularly in the 1980s. Since 1786 the port undertaking has been maintained, developed and financially serviced out of the port's own resources with relatively little subsidisation from other sources. In almost every other country, and particularly in the case of member states of the EEC other than the Republic of Ireland, ports are subsidised from central or local government. In addition all EEC ports are entitled to benefit from grants for port improvement works and many ports have benefited therefrom, including ports in Northern Ireland and Britain. Due to the policies of successive governments in this country, Dublin has never been permitted to apply for such grants. The inference to be drawn as to the reason for this anomaly appears to be a belief that since the Dublin port board has always paid its way, it will continue to do so in the future however difficult the circumstances.

In a curious way, no better compliment could be paid to the successive port boards at Dublin, albeit a compliment which most ports would be willing to forego in order to share the benefits enjoyed by other ports within the EEC.

Dublin Port and Docks Board Chairmen 1899–1988

1899/1901
  Sir Richard Martin, D.L., J.P.
1902
  Marcus Goodbody, J.P.
1903
  Michael Murphy
1904
  John Mooney, J.P.
1905
  James D. O'Connor, J.P.
1906
  Laurence Malone
1907
  George MacNie
1908
  Frederick H. Hall
1909
  Ald. William Cotton
1910
  Samuel S. McCormick, J.P.
1911
  William Wallace, J.P.
1912
  William Hewat
1913
  George Byrne
1914
  John Hollwey
1915/16
  William Crowe
1917/18
  Ald. James Moran
1919/20
  John Hollwey
1921
  George Byrne
1922/23
  David Barry
1924
  Sen. James Moran

1925
  Walter Baird
1926/27
  Thomas R. McCullagh
1928/29
  Philip J. Lawrence
1930/32
  Charles E. McGloughlin
1933
  Walter Baird
1934/35
  Thomas F. Laurie, P.C.
1936/38
  Charles M. O'Kelly
1939/40
  Capt. A.S. Gordon
1941/42
  Percy McGrath
1943/45
  Thomas O'Connor
1946 (Jan.–Sept.)
  John McEvoy, P.C.
1946–7/1947–8
  Ald. Martin O'Sullivan T.D., P.C.
1948–9/1949–50
  John Bruton
1950–1/1951–2
  Daniel J. Twohig
1952–3/1953–4
  Patrick J. Munden
1954–5/1955–6
  Stephen MacKenzie
1956–7/1957–8
  Robert W. Sinnott
1958–9/1959–60
  Liam S. Furlong
1960–1/1961–2
  Frank Robbins
1962–3/1963–4
  David D. Frame

Chairmen 1899–1988 continued

1964–5/1965–6
  Edward J. Betson (d. Feb.1966)

1966–7/1967–8
  F. Derek Martin

1968–9
  Sean Moore

1969–70
  Bernard A. Nolan

1970–1/1971–2
  Matthew J. Bruton

1972–3/1973–4
  Thomas D. Watt

1974–5/1975–6
  Edward W. Beck

1976–7/1977–8
  Paul J. Byrne

1978–9/1979–80
  Ray Fay

1980–1/1981–2
  Chris Kirwan

1982–3/1983–4
  John Donovan

1984–5/1985–6
  James A. Lenehan

1986–7/1987–8
  B.W. Lynch

N.B. From 1899 to 1946, the annual election of chairman took place in the month of January; under the Harbours Act 1946 the month was altered to October.

Bibliography

Primary Sources

Extracts from minutes and accounts of the Committee of the Ballast Office, 1708–76: Dublin Corporation Archives.

Journals of the proceedings of the Dublin port authority, 1786–1986.

Journals of the proceedings of the Irish lighthouse authority, 1810–67.

Minute books of the Wide Streets Commissioners covering the period 1758–1801 (Vols. 1–16) Ref. M.R. 16: Dublin Corporation Archives.

Post Office correspondence relating to Holyhead steam packets, 1824.

Correspondence relating to the removal of Post Office packets from Howth to Kingstown, 1834.

Report by Captain Denham on passenger accommodation in steamers between Ireland and Liverpool, 1859.

Correspondence between the government and the City of Dublin Steam Packet Company relating to the plan for the construction of a packet harbour at Holyhead, 1860.

Report of the Commission appointed to inquire into the condition and management of lights, buoys and beacons on the coast of the United Kingdom, 1861.

Reports of House of Commons Debates (Hansard) 1810, 1866, 1867.

Evidence given to Select Committee of the House of Commons on the Dublin Port and Docks Bill, 1867.

Letters to the present writer from Mrs Joan Blundell (great-granddaughter of William Hutchison) dated 14, 16 February 1977, 14, 16 March 1977, 1 April 1977, 14 December 1979, containing family details, photostat of page of family Bible setting out genealogy of William Hutchison and photostat extract from O'Byrne's *Dictionary of Naval Biography*, 1869 edition, relating to William Hutchison's career in the Navy and subsequently.

Bligh, William, and others, *Reports to the Directors of Inland Navigation relative to Dublin Harbour and Bay, 1800–1802*, n.p., in Dublin Port and Docks Board archives.

Newspapers and Periodicals

Freeman's Journal, 1792, 1793, 1922   *Dublin Penny Journal*, 1833
Irish Times, 1866, 1867, 1922   *Irish Builder & Engineer*, 1876–1900
Evening Telegraph, 1887

Articles in *Dublin Historical Record*, **published by the Old Dublin Society.**
Bowen, B.P., 'The North Strand', Vol. 11, No. 2, March/May 1950, Vol. 11, No. 3, June/Aug. 1950.
Clark, Mary, 'Dublin Surveyors and their Maps', Vol. 39, No. 4, Sept. 1986.
Corry, Geoffrey, 'The Dublin Bar—the obstacle to the improvement of the Port of Dublin', Vol. 23, No. 4, July 1970.
Flood, Donal T., 'Dublin Bay in the eighteenth century', Vol. 31, No. 4, Sept. 1975
Flood, Donal T., 'William Petty and the Double Bottom', Vol. 30, No. 3, June 1977
Flood, Donal T., 'The Birth of the Bull Island', Vol. 28, No. 4, Sept. 1975
Hammond, Joseph W., 'George's Quay and Rogerson's Quay in the eighteenth Century', Vol. 5, No. 2, Dec. 1942/Feb. 1943.
Gilligan, H.A., 'Captain William Hutchison and the early Dublin Bay Lifeboats', Vol. 33, No. 2, March 1980.
Goodbody, Olive, 'Old Dun Laoghaire', Vol. 34, No. 2, March 1981
Moore, Desmond F., 'The Port of Dublin', Vol. 16, No. 4, Aug. 1961.
Murphy, Frank, 'Dublin Trams 1872–1950', Vol. 33, No. 1, Dec. 1979.
Murphy, Sean, 'The Corporation of Dublin 1660–1760', Vol. 38, No. 1, Dec. 1984.
Murray, Kevin, 'Old Dunleary Harbour', Vol. 7, No. 4, Sept./Nov. 1945.
O'Flanagan, F.M., 'Glimpses of Old Dalkey', Vol. 4, No. 2. Dec. 1941–Feb. 1942.
O'Rorke, Kevin P., 'Dublin's Mount Herbert', Vol. 30, No. 2, March 1977.
Reeves, William F., 'Dublin Quays and Shipping, 1886–1896', Vol. 11, No. 2, March–May 1950.
Tutty, Michael J., 'Bridges over the Liffey', Vol. 35, No. 1, Dec. 1981.
Tutty, Michael J., 'City of Dublin Steam Packet Company', Vol. 18, No. 3, June 1963.
Tutty, Michael J., 'Clontarf', Vol. 21, No. 1, March/May 1966.

Articles in other Learned Journals
Bagwell, Philip, 'The Post Office Steam Packets, 1821–1836 and the development of shipping on the Irish Sea', in *Maritime History*, Vol. 1, No. 1, London: University College London, April 1971.
McParland, Edward, 'The Wide Streets Commissioners', in *Irish Georgian Society Bulletin*, Vol. XV, No. 1, 1972, 1–32.

Books
Airne, C.W., *The Story of the Isle of Man*, Douglas, Isle of Man: Norris Modern Press Ltd 1964.
Anderson, Ernest D., *Sailing Ships of Ireland*, rev. ed., n.p. 1984.
Beresford, William, ed., *The correspondence of the Right Hon. John Beresford*, London: Woodfall and Kinder 1854.
Boate, Gerard, Molyneux, Thomas and others, *A natural history of Ireland*, Dublin: George and Alex Ewing 1755.
Chappell, Connery, *Island Lifeline*, Prescot, Merseyside: T. Stephenson and Sons Ltd 1980.

Collins, James, *Life in Old Dublin*, Dublin: James Duffy and Co. Ltd 1913

Cullen, L.M., *Merchants, ships and trade, 1660–1830*, Dublin: Gill and Macmillan 1971.

Cullen, L.M., *Princes and Pirates*, Dublin: Dublin Chamber of Commerce 1983.

Craig, Maurice, *Dublin 1660–1860*, Dublin: Allen Figgis 1969.

D'Alton, John, *The History of County Dublin*, Cork: Tower Books 1976.

Dugan, James, *The Great Iron Ship*, London: Hamish Hamilton 1954.

Fitzpatrick, Samuel A. Ossory, *A Historical and Topographical Survey of the City of Dublin*, Cork: Tower Books 1977.

Forde, Frank, *The Long Watch*, Dublin: Gill and Macmillan 1981.

Fox, Christopher, *Skerries Harbour, A Short History*, n.p., 1970.

Geen, G.K., *The Law and administration of Pilotage*, Lloyds of London, 1977.

Gilbert, John T., *A History of the City of Dublin*, Dublin: James McGlashan 1861.

Gilbert, John T. and others (eds.), *Calendar of Ancient Records of Dublin*, Dublin: Joseph Dollard. Vols 1–19, 1889–1944.

Giraldus (Cambrensis), *The Topography of Ireland* in 'The Historical Works of Giraldus Cambrensis', translated by Thomas Forester, and revised by Thomas Wright, London: George Bell & Sons 1881.

Hague, Douglas B., and Christie, Rosemary, *Lighthouses: their architecture, history and archaeology*, Llandysul, Dyfed: Gomer Press Ltd 1975.

Haliday, Charles, *The Scandinavian Kingdom of Dublin*, 2nd edition, Dublin: M. H. Gill and Son 1884.

Jones, Gwyn, *A History of the Vikings*, revised edition, Oxford: Oxford University Press 1984.

Joyce, Weston St John, *The Neighbourhood of Dublin*, Dublin: M. H. Gill and Son Ltd, 1939.

Lewis, Samuel, *A History and Topography of Dublin City and County*, Dublin and Cork: Mercier Press 1980.

Little, George A., *Dublin before the Vikings*, Dublin: M. H. Gill and Son Ltd 1957.

Lloyd's Annual Register of Shipping, London: 1890–1983

Macardle, Dorothy, *The Irish Republic*, 4th edition, Dublin: Irish Press Ltd 1951.

McParland, Edward, 'Strategy in the planning of Dublin 1750–1800', in P. Butel and L.M. Cullen, eds., *Cities and Merchants—French and Irish Perspectives in urban development*, Dublin: Department of Modern History, Trinity College Dublin, 1968, pp. 97–108.

Maxwell, Constantia, *Dublin under the Georges 1714–1830*, revised edition London: Faber and Faber Ltd 1956.

M'Cready C.T., *Dublin Street names, dated and explained*, Blackrock, Co. Dublin: Carraig Books 1975.

McNeill, D.B., *Irish Passenger Steamship Services*, Newton Abbot: David and Charles, vol. 1, 1969; vol. 2, 1971.

Pearson, Peter, *Dunlaoghaire—Kingstown*, Dublin: O'Brien Press 1982.

Peterson, Basil, *Turn of the Tide*, Dublin: Irish Shipping Ltd 1962.

Report of the Dublin Docks Review Group, Dublin: Department of Labour.
1984

Report of the Ports and Harbours Tribunal, Dublin: Stationery Office 1930.

Royal Dublin Golf Club Centenary 1885/1985, Dublin 1985.

Sloane, John S., *Manual for Lightkeepers,* Dublin: J. Goggins 1873.

Smellie, John, *Shipbuilding and Repairing in Dublin, 1901–1923,* Glasgow:
McCorquodale and Co. Ltd 1925.

Somerville-Large, Peter, *Dublin,* St. Alban's: Granada Publishing Ltd 1981.

Spong, H.C., *Irish Shipping Ltd, 1941–1982,* Kendal: World Ship Society
1982.

Thom's Directory 1860–1946

Wallace, Patrick, 'Dublin's waterfront at Wood Quay: 900–1317', in Milne,
Gustav and Hobley, Brian, eds., *Waterfront Archaeology in Britain and
Northern Europe,* based on papers presented to the First International
Conference on Waterfront Archaeology in Northern European Towns held
at the Museum of London 20–22 April 1979, research report No. 41, the
Council for British Archaeology, 1981.

Warburton, J., Whitelaw, J., and Walsh, Robert, *History of the City of
Dublin,* 2 vols, London: T. Cadell and W. Davies 1818.

Watson, Edward, *The Royal Mail to Ireland,* London: Edward Arnold 1917.

Wilson, T.G., *The Irish Lighthouse Service,* Dublin: Allen Figgis 1968

Index

4

To His Grace IAMES
Duke of ORMOND &c.
This is humbly Dedicated & Presented
by Capt G. Collins

P A R T   O F

North

a hard Sand

DUBLIN

Ballibought

Clantarfe

Laringtowne

Clantarf Poole

Larehill

Ringi End

Salmon Poole

Poole Beg

½

Cock Lake

Gullit

South
a hard Sand dry

Bull
at Low water

D

D U B L I N

Merrion

English Miles

0   ½   1   1½   2

Newtowne Castle

C O U N T Y.

Monks towne